NUCLEAR WEAPONS
AND
POWER POLITICS

NUCLEAR WEAPONS AND POWER POLITICS

MANI SHANKAR

COMMONWEALTH

NUCLEAR WEAPONS AND POWER POLITICS

First Published, 2002

ISBN 81-7169-711-9

Published by:
Ajay Verma
***For* Commonwealth Publishers**
4831/24, Prahlad Street,
Ansari Road, Darya Ganj,
New Delhi - 110 002
Ph.: 3272541, 3257835
Fax : 91-011-3257835

Typesetting by:
Sarita Enterprises
Ghaziabad

Printed at:
Efficient Offset Printers
Shahzada Bagh, New Delhi-110035

PREFACE

For about six decades since the end of the Second World War, the world has been living with the horrendous fear of devastation that can be caused by nuclear weapons. It is a dubious good fortune that so far only one country in the world namely Japan has experienced the horrors of nuclear explosions and it is not unrealistic to assume that the damaged caused to the human spirit and psyche by the atomic bombs dropped on Hiroshima and Nagasaki continues to cast a long shadow across the decades to help us and our leaders maintain sanity. The end of the cold war with the collapse of Soviet Union in the early nineties has no doubt lessened the threat of nuclear devastation but it is still an irony of history that brings into being continues to be the basic principle of international political relations. Thus, France and China may continue to test nuclear devices they are less likely to use them in any conflict than say, India and Pakistan. This is one of the ironies of the modern times.

It is in the perspective of international balance of power, preserved precariously by the studious non-use of nuclear weapons that forms the backdrop of the present compilation. The materials presented in the following pages deal with a wide range of issues concerning the power politics of states possessing nuclear weapons. They cover such relevant aspects as, the unceasing efforts of the United Nations Organisation to bring about nuclear weapons free world, through the International Atomic Energy Commission (IAEC); the provision of Comprehensive Test Ban Treaty (CTBT) and India's response to the CTBT; the nuclear weapons falling into the wrong hands specially the 'rogue' states, as we are now preparing to cope with fast changing situation in Afghanistan and therefore South Asia; and the views of various world leaders on the intricacies of what can be described as nuclear politics. The compilation draws from wide range of sources, both India and foreign, and it is hoped that it will be much use and interest to all those interested in the dynamics and politics of nuclear weapon states, besides students and researchers, political analyst and journalist.

Mani Shankar

CONTENTS

Preface v

Chapter *Pages*

1. Document for Disarmament : Comprehensive Nuclear-Test-Ban Treaty 1
2. Nuclear Weapons Debate : An Indian Perspective 21
3. Developing Missile Technology 38
4. Policy of Policing : The United Nations and Nuclear Weapons 68
5. Suitcase Bombs : The Emerging Menace of Nuclear Politics 145
6. India and Nuclear Missile Defence 192
7. S & T Platform : India's Strides in Space 216
8. Nuclear Politics : The NATO Connection 245

Bibliography 264

Index 266

1

DOCUMENT FOR DISARMAMENT : COMPREHENSIVE NUCLEAR-TEST-BAN TREATY

The Comprehensive Nuclear-Test-Ban Treaty is the culmination of 40 years of efforts to ban nuclear test explosions and thereby half the development of new weapons of mass destruction.

The Treaty is "comprehensive" in that it bans nuclear test explosions in all environments. Underground explosions, which were not banned in the Treaty Banning Nuclear Weapon Tests in the Atmosphere, in Outer Space and under Water (Partial Test Ban Treaty) of 1963, are now prohibited. Not only military but also non-military nuclear explosions are banned.

Significance

The Treaty:

- Bans any nuclear-weapon test explosion or any other nuclear explosion anywhere in the world;
- Established a global monitoring system to monitor and verify compliance with the Treaty;
- Has the purpose of attracting the adherence of all States and the objective to contribute effectively to the prevention of the proliferation of nuclear weapons in all its aspects, to the process of nuclear disarmament and therefore to the enhancement of international peace and security.

History

In April 1954, almost 10 years after the first nuclear-weapon test conducted in July 1945 Jawaharlal Nehru the Prime Minister of India proposed that nuclear weapon testing be suspended. His proposal was the first initiative of its kind. Awareness of the harmful effects of atmospheric nuclear tests increasingly contributed to demands for testing to end.

During the cold war, three treaties on nuclear testing were concluded: the multilateral Partial Test Ban Treaty of 1963 and two bilateral treaties on the limitation of yields of nuclear tests for military and peaceful purposes between the former USSR and the United States. None was comprehensive. The latter two treaties, signed in 1974 and 1976, respectively, entered into force in 1990 after intensive negotiation on verification provisions that helped set the stage for progress once the cold war was over.

Over 2,000 nuclear explosions were registered during the 51 years between the conduct of the first nuclear explosive test and the opening for signature of the Comprehensive Nuclear-Test-Ban Treaty in September 1996.

Negotiation, Adoption and Signature

Intensive negotiations on a Comprehensive Nuclear-Test-Ban Treaty began at the Conference on Disarmament of Geneva in January 1994. Two and a half years later, however, the painstakingly elaborated draft treaty could not command consensus at the close of the negotiations in August 1996. A text identical to that discussed at the Conference on Disarmament was then sponsored by 127 States and formally submitted to the General Assembly, where it was adopted as a Treaty by an overwhelming majority on 10 September 1996. The Treaty was opened for signature on 24 September 1996 at United Nations Headquarters in New York. On the first day, 71 States signed the Treaty, including the five nuclear-weapon States and 27 of the other 44 States required by article XIV to ratify it to enable it to enter into force.

Arrangements Until Entry into Force

At a meeting of States signatories on 19 November 1996, convoked by the Secretary-General of the United Nations as Depositary, a Preparatory Commission for the Comprehensive Nuclear-Test-Ban Treaty Organization (CTBTO PrepCom) was established as an international organization, financed by the States signatories, to establish the global verification regime of the Treaty and to prepare for its entry into force. The Preparatory Commission consists of two organs: a plenary body composed of all the States signatories—also known as the Preparatory Commission—and the Provisional Technical Secretariat.

Preparatory Commission

The Preparatory Commission appointed Wolfgang Hoffmann of Germany as its Executive Secretary on 3 March 1997. The Executive Secretary is head of the Provisional Technical Secretariat, which started work at its offices in the Vienna International Centre on 17 March 1997.

The Preparatory Commission has two subsidiary bodies: Working Group A on administrative and budgetary matters and Working Group B on verification issues as well as Advisory Group on financial, budgetary and associated administrative issues. The Working Groups make proposals and recommendations for consideration and adoption by the Preparatory Commission at its plenary sessions.

SUMMERY OF THE TREATY

The Comprehensive Nuclear-Test-Ban Treaty consists of a preamble, 17 articles, an annex containing a list of States grouped by region, and in relation to the entry-into-force provision (article XIV) and a Protocal. The Protocol sets out detailed provisions for verification, on-site inspections and confidence building measures, and contains two annexes. One annex lists the 337 facilities composing the International Monitoring System (IMS) and the other annex describes parameters for standard event screening by the International Data Centre (IDC). The annexes to the Treaty and the Protocol and its annexes form an integral part of the Treaty.

Scope

Under **Article I (Basic obligations):** "1. Each State Party undertakes not to carry out any nuclear weapon test explosion or any other nuclear explosion, and to prohibit and prevent any such nuclear explosion at any place under its jurisdiction or control. 2. Each State Party undertakes, furthermore, to refrain from causing, encouraging, or in any way participating in the carrying out of any nuclear weapon test explosion or any other nuclear explosions."

Implementing Organization

Article II (The Organization) establishes the Comprehensive Nuclear-Test-Ban Treaty Organization to ensure the Treaty's Implementation, including verification of compliance, and to provide a forum for consultation and cooperation. With its seat in Vienna, it will comprise three organs.

The Conference of the States Parties will oversee the Treaty's implementation and the activities of the other two organs, and review compliance.

The Executive Council, with a membership of 51 States Parties, will be the principal decision-making body of the Organization and responsible for supervising the activities of the Technical Secretariat.

The Technical Secretariat, headed by a Director-General will assist States parties to implement the Treaty and carry out verification and other functions. It will supervise and coordinate the operation of the IMS and operate the IDC of Vienna.

Article III (National implementation measures) requires each State party to take any necessary measures to implement it obligations under the Treaty, including the establishment of a National Authority for liaison with the Organization and other States parties.

Verification and Compliance

Article IV (Verification) and the **Protocol** establish the verification regime. Such a regime—consisting of IMS, IDC, consultation and clarification, on-site inspections and confidence-building measures—"shall be capable of meeting the verification requirements of the Treaty" at its entry into force.

Verification activities should be based on objective information, limited to the subject matter of the Treaty, and carried out on the basis of full respect for the sovereignty of States parties and in the least intrusive manner possible consistent with the effective and timely accomplishment of their objectives. Each State party, however, "shall refrain from any abuse of the right of verification."

International Monitoring System. The purpose of IMS is to detect and identify nuclear explosions prohibited under article I. As set out in annex 1 to the Protocol, IMS will comprise 50 primary and 120 auxiliary seismological stations equipped to detect seismic activity and distinguish between natural events—such as earthquakes—and nuclear explosions. It will also include 80 radionuclide stations—40 of them capable of detecting noble gases—designed to identify radioactive particles released during a nuclear explosion. The radionuclide stations will be supported by 16 laboratories. In addition,

60 infrasound and 11 hydroacoustic stations will be designed to pick up the sound of a nuclear explosion in the atmosphere or under water, respectively.

International Data Centre. The monitoring stations will transmit data to the IDC, which is an integral part of the Technical Secretariat of Vienna. As set out in part I of the Protocol, IDC will produce integrated lists of all signals detected by IMS, as well as standard event lists and bulletins, and screened event bulletins that filter out events that appear to be of a non-nuclear nature. Both raw and processed information will be available to all States parties, and "shall be without prejudice to final judgements with regard to the nature of any event, which shall remain the responsibility of States Parties."

Consultation and Clarification. The consultation and clarification component of the verification regime encourages States parties to attempt to resolve, either among themselves or through the Organization, ambiguous events before requesting an on-site inspection. A State party must provide clarification of an ambiguous events within 48 hours of receiving such a request from another State party or the Executive Council.

On-site Inspection. If the matter cannot be resolved through consultation and clarification, each State party can request on on-site inspection. The decision to approve the on-site inspection must be made by at least 30 affirmative votes of the 51 members of the Executive Council. The procedures for on-site inspections, which "shall be carried out in the area where the event that triggered the on-site inspection request occurred", are established in part II of the Protocol.

Confidence-building Measures. To reduce the likelihood that verification data may be misinterpreted, each State party will voluntarily notify the Technical Secretariat of any single chemical explosion using 300 tones or more of TNT-equivalent blasting material on its territory. In order to calibrate the stations of IMS, each

State party may liaise with the Technical Secretariat in carrying out chemical calibration explosions or providing information on chemical explosions planned for other purposes.

Article V (Measures to redress a situation and to ensure compliance, including sanctions) empowers the Conference to revoke a State's rights under the Treaty, to recommend to States parties collective measures in conformity with international law, or, alternatively, if the case is urgent, to bring the issue to the attention of the United Nations.

Disputes

Article VI (Settlement of disputes) describes the mechanisms by which disputes concerning the application or interpretation of the Treaty may be settled. Subject to certain conditions, the International Court of Justice may be requested to give an advisory opinion.

Amendments and Review

Article VII (Amendments) gives each State party the right to propose amendments to the Treaty, the Protocol or the annexes to the Protocol at any time after the Treaty's entry into force. The proposed amendment requires the approval of a majority of States parties at an amendment conference with no party casting a negative vote.

Article VIII (Review of the Treaty) stipulates that a conference to review the operation and effectiveness of the Treaty will be held 10 years after its entry into force, "unless otherwise decided by a majority of the States Parties". Such review would take into account "any new scientific and technological development". Further review conferences may be held with the same objective at intervals of 10 years thereafter, or less, if the conference so decides in the preceding year.

At the request of any State party, the review conference may "consider the possibility of permitting the conduct of underground nuclear explosions for peaceful purposes". If it permits such explosions by consensus, then the review conference "shall commence work without delay, with a view to recommending to States Parties an appropriate amendment to this Treaty that shall preclude any military benefits of such nuclear explosions."

Duration and Withdrawal

Article IX (Duration and withdrawal) states that the Treaty is of unlimited duration.

Other Provisions

The next four articles **(X, XI, XII and XIII)** deal with the status of the Protocol and the annexes; signature; ratification; and accession.

Entry into Force

Under **Article XIV (Entry into force),** the Treaty will enter into force 180 days after the 44 States listed in annex 2 to the Treaty have deposited their instruments of ratification with the Secretary-General of the United Nations, "but in no case earlier than two years after its opening for signature". This list comprises the States that formally participated in the 1996 session of the Conference on Disarmament, and that appear in table 1 of the December 1995 edition of "Nuclear Research Reactors in the World" and table 1 of the April 1996 edition of "Nuclear Power Reactors in the World," both compiled by the International Atomic Energy Agency.

If the Treaty has not entered into force "three years after the date of the anniversary of its opening for signature", the Secretary-General of the United Nations, as Depositary of the Treaty, could, at the request of a majority of States that had ratified it, convence a conference to examine the situation and to "decide by consensus what measures consistent with international law may be undertaken to accelerate the ratification process" in order to facilitate the Treaty's early entry into force.

Reservation

Article XV (Reservations) states that the Treaty's articles and annexes are not subject to reservations. The provisions of the Protocol to the Treaty and the annexes to the Protocol are not subject to reservations incompatible with the object and purpose of the Treaty.

Additional Provisions

Under **Article XVI (Depositary),** the Secretary-General of the United Nations is the Treaty's Depositary.

Under **Article XVII (Authentic texts),** the Treaty texts in Arabic, Chinese, English, French, Russian and Spanish are equally authentic.

Protocol

Part I describes IMS and outlines the functions of IDC.

Part II sets up the procedures for on-site inspections. It specifies the process of designation of inspectors and inspection assistants, their privileges and immunities, points of entry arrangements for use of non-scheduled aircraft, approved inspection equipment, on-site inspection requests, inspection mandate and notification of inspection. Pre-inspection activities and the conduct of inspections are described in detail.

Part III deals with confidence-building measures under article IV (Verification) of the Treaty.

India's Position on CTBT Since 1948

Will a 'political consensus' for signing the Comprehensive Test Ban Treaty (CTBT) lead to India discarding its more than five-decade old 'ethical' stand on nuclear disarmament? A brief rundown on Indian stand on this controversial issue:

- **1948:** India tables a resolution in the United Nations General Assembly (UNGA) stating its support for the Atomic Energy Commission's proposal for controlling atomic energy for peaceful purposes and the elimination from national armaments of atomic weapons.
- **1954:** India among nations leading the call for a CTBT and co-sponsors in subsequent years many of the resolutions that help build the international momentum behind its adoption.
- **1963:** India joins the Partial Test Ban Treaty.
- **1968:** Non-Proliferation Treaty (NPT) signed by leading nuclear weapons states. India calls it 'discriminatory' as it maintains the *status quo*.
- **1971:** War with Pakistan over Bangladesh. The United States navy deploys its Seventh Fleet led by USS Enterprise with nuclear capabilities to threaten India.
- **1974:** India officially "goes nuclear" by carrying out tests in Pokhran.
- **1978:** Nothing that in the 30-year period beginning 1946, nuclear weapon states had threatened deployment of warheads on non-nuclear states as many as 37 times, India proposes at the UNGA a four-point programme of nuclear disarmament which includes the CTBT.
  It calls for formulation of a time-bound programme not exceeding a decade for achieving total elimination of nuclear stockpiles.
- **1982:** India proposes a convention on No First Use or threat of use of nuclear weapons, a freeze on manufacture combined with a cut-off in the production of fissionable material for weapons purposes.
- **1988:** Rajiv Gandhi presents the Action Plan with a time bound framework of 22 years aimed at total elimination of all nuclear weapons.

- **1993:** India enters negotiation on CTBT, which was to be spread over the next three years.
- **1995:** NPT Review and Extension Conference held. India does not participate but points out that recent nuclear tests carried out by some nuclear weapons states constituted a serious setback to the ongoing negotiations for a CTBT. By year-end, India makes its position clear that the CTBT was an unequal treaty, which did not promise much by way of global nuclear security.
- **1996:** India says the CTBT should be "securely anchored in the disarmament context" and proposes several amendments in the treaty, China and the US say 'peaceful nuclear explosions should be excluded from the ambit.' India counters that a CTBT would be useless if development, refinement and production of nuclear weapons continue.

  Chairman of UN Conference on Disarmament proposes a 'clean text' which India finds unacceptable, as the nuclear weapons States made no commitment to eliminate their nuclear weapons in a specific timeframe.

  Also debated by India was the formula adopted to put the CTBT into force. India says it is 'illegal' and aimed at pressurising India to "sign a text which it considered to be against its national interest".

  Indian proposal counters that "the CTBT should enter into force 180 days after the date of the deposit of the Instruments of Ratification by 65 states and no less than two years after its opening for signature." This is rejected.
- **1998:** India carries out underground tests again. Declares moratorium against future tests. Sanctions clamped by EU, most other countries and US. India declares it would seek internal political consensus whether to sign CTBT.

- **2000:** Prime Minister Vajpayee declares 'political consensus' possible by the end of year 2000.

Disarmament Commission Reviews Nuclear Disarmament

The Disarmament Commission concluded its substantive session for 2001 on April 27 with the adoption of its final report and reports of its two working groups, as orally revised.

In her closing remarks, Commission Chairperson Diane Quarless (Jamaica) said that the task of the Commission had set for itself was not an easy one, for the issues' which it currently had under consideration were fundamental and critical to the meaningful advancement of the disarmament agenda, in both the nuclear and conventional fields.

It was fitting, she noted, that the Commission had begun the new millennium with a commitment to explore new ways and means to achieve nuclear disarmament, and to develop practical confidence-building measures in the field of conventional arms. It set the bar high for future action in pursuit of the strengthened regime for the enhancement of international peace and security.

The working paper on ways and means to achieve nuclear disarmament was a good synthesis of the many facets of the issue, she said. It built on the Chairman's compilation of proposals, comments and oral and written submissions from delegations. It attempted to present in a realistic way the achievements and current developments in the field of nuclear disarmament, while acknowledging the work that still remained to be done. In addition, the non-paper on practical confidence-building measures in the field of conventional arms remained a sound basis for deliberation and future negotiation.

Yaw Odei Osei (Ghana), Chairperson of Working Group I on "ways and means to achieve nuclear disarmament", introduced the report of the Group as contained in document A/CN.10/2001/CRP.3/Rev.1. During the 10 meetings the Group held over the past three weeks, it exchanged views and presented oral and written proposals on the papers before it. The text of the Chairman's paper would be the basis for continuing, negotiations next year. The inter-sessional consultations, which would precede the revision of this paper, would be based on the preliminary comments made on the paper during the first reading.

Gabriela Martinic (Argentina), Chairperson of Working Group II, presented the report on practical confidence-building measures in the field of conventional arms (document A/CN.10/2001/CRP.4/Rev.2). She said the Group had held 11 substantive meetings, during which delegations made valuable oral and written proposals on the three working papers were under consideration and discussed preliminary ideas on recommendations for confidence-building measures. The Group benefited by a representative briefing of the Department of Disarmament Affairs on the work being done by the Department and its regional centres in the field. By the next session, the Group should be in a position to make its small but important contribution to practical confidence-building measures in the field of conventional arms.

Closing statements were made by the representatives of Mexico (on behalf of the Latin American and Caribbean States), India, Iraq (on behalf of the League of Arab States), Vietnam (on behalf of the Association of South-East Asian Nations (ASEAN), South Africa (on behalf of the Non-aligned Movement), China and Canada (on behalf of the Group of Western European and Other States).

During this session, the Commission continued to explore ways and means to achieve nuclear disarmament and practical confidence-building measures in the field of nuclear arms. This was the penultimate year of its planned three-year review of those topics. To guide its deliberations, the Commissions's two working groups had before them sets of non-papers, which highlighted delegations' concerns and observations compiled from meetings held in 2000. The current session opened with the election of Diane Quarless, the first woman to chair the Commission, in its near 50-year history.

In her opening remarks, Ms. Quarless said that the year 2000 should be remembered as 8 the year that the door leading to disarmament had been opened. Indeed, significant events, such as the Review Conference of the Treaty on the Non-Proliferation of Nuclear Weapons (NPT) had infused a new spirit into the dialogue on the maintenance of international peace and security, and renewed the collective commitment to both nuclear and conventional non-proliferation and disarmament. But while much remained to be done—ensuring the early entry into force of the Comprehensive Nuclear-Test-Ban Treaty (CTBT) and the opening negotiations on a fissile material cut-off treaty—progress had undoubtedly been achieved.

What was important now, Ms Quarless continued, was to work collectively and diligently to ensure that expressed good intentions could ultimately be transformed into demonstrable action. In those efforts, the Commission's contributions would be invaluable. Indeed, as the only universal body that promoted deliberation, negotiation and consensus-building on disarmament issues, field of international peace and security, where the dividends to be gained through dialogue were immeasurable.

Those sentiments were echoed by Jayantha Dhanapala, Under-Secretary-General for Disarmament Affairs, who praised the Commission's impressive record during the past decade in the slow incremental process of building and maintaining global disarmament norms. In 1999 alone, it had reached consensus on two sets of guidelines concerning the establishment of nuclear-weapon-free zones and on conventional arms control, with particular emphasis on the consideration of peace following armed conflicts. Though not legally binding, those guidelines influenced governments as they established ground rules for national security policies in an increasingly legislative workers, non-governmental groups and the media, a yardstick against which the actions of States could be measured.

Mr. Dhanapala said, however, that reaching global consensus on disarmament would not be easy. And while the 1990s had not been marked by nuclear war, it had been a time of devastating bloodshed involving the use to an ever-expanding variety of conventional arms. The era could also be characterized by the so-called "revolution in military affairs". By some estimates, more than 5 million people had been killed in armed conflicts during the post-cold-war era. At the same time, military budgets had grown to nearly $800 billion a year. The phenomenon of the illicit traffic in small arms had grown from a regional problem to a crisis of global dimensions. He said that those changes—the expenditure, loss of life and disrespect for the rule of law—had eroded human security everywhere.

As the Commission's general debate began, many delegations agreed with the Under-Secretary-General's assessment that escalating production, stockpiling and transfer of weapons made this a critical moment to identify concrete confidence-building measures in the field of conventional arms. Many warned that the build-up of weapons beyond national self-defence levels could only lead to regional and international insecurity and instability, as well as the resumption of a global arms race. Therefore, the representative of Iran said, the interrelationship between building confidence and reliance on conventional arms was an essential element to consider in the process of consolidating peace and containing tensions. The representative of Myanmar, among others, believed that confidence-building measures should be based on the principles of sovereign equality, non-interference in the internal affairs of States and respect for the mutual interest of nations.

The representative of South Africa said one of the underpinning factors to practical confidence-building measures was the overall need for transparency. In that regard, she echoed the sentiments of other delegations that the scope of the Conventional Arms Register was too narrow as it did not include smaller types of arms, which had become the weapons of choice in conflicts destabilizing regions around the globe. An expanded register, or a correlating system, which tracked small arms and light weapons, would enhance confidence among States. Other delegations considered the destruction of surplus and confiscated weapons no longer used by governments as another important confidence-building measure.

The representative of Sweden, speaking on behalf of the European Union, said the Commission's recommendations should be designed to build an environment of cooperative security and emphasize the duty of Member States to refrain from the use of threat of force in their international relations. But cold war mentalities, hegemony and power politics died hard, said China's representative. Therefore, the inclination to acquire absolute security by imposing military advantages remained undiminished. Military superiority never guaranteed security, he added. It was critical then, for countries seeking to ensure their own security to consider ways in which those measures affected the common security of all countries.

Several other delegations said that at the heart of the matter lay actions taken by the United States, which were, in essence, a disguised form of nuclear expansion that had severely shaken the foundation of global nuclear disarmament efforts. They expressed particular concern by that country's attempts to forge ahead with a national missile defence system, including the introduction of weapons into outer space. Indonesia's representative said plans for building a missile defence would inevitably have far-reaching repercussions. Such plans would be incompatible with the limiting provisions of the Treaty on the Limitation of Anti-Ballistic Missile Systems (ABM Treaty)—a critical component of strategic stability and an indispensable element to further reduce strategic armaments.

Mongolia's representative said that the Commission had an increasingly important role to play in the promotion of arms control and disarmament at the regional and global levels. Nuclear disarmament, the most crucial of all disarmament and non-proliferation issues, was a prerequisite for the maintenance and strengthening of international peace and security. In that regard, the representative of India urged the Commission to set down principles and measures that would pave the way to agreed, multilateral, non-discriminatory and irreversible nuclear disarmament. A global "no first use" agreement should be pursued, which should include legally binding assurances of non-use against non-nuclear-weapon States and the recognition of nuclear-weapon-free zones established on the basis of arrangements freely arrived among the States of a region.

Commission Bureau

The Bureau of the Disarmament Commission comprises: Chairman, Diane Quarless (Jamaica); and Vice-Chairpersons, Henrik Salander (Sweden), Niklas Lindquist (Finland) Yurii Onishchenko (Ukraine) Martha Beatriz Lopez de Mitre Shein (Myanmar) was the Commission's Rapporteur.

Stalled Dialogue

Face to face for the first time, President Bush and Russian President Vladimir Putin pledged on June 17 to deepen their nations' bonds and to explore the possibility of compromise on US missile defence plans that Moscow has bitterly opposed. Despite mixed signals from his Russian counterpart, Mr. Bush said, "We have a great moment during our tenures to cast aside the suspicions and doubts that used to plague our nations". Mr. Putin showed surprising "receptivity" to missile defence, particularly the need to conduct research that could violate the 1972 Anti-Ballistic Missile Treaty, Mr. Bush said, "Nothing was rejected out of hand", Mr. Bush said as he closed his first overseas trip and returned to Washington.

Mr. Putin himself hinted at the possibility of a "very constructive development" on the ABM issue, "I think we can work out a common approach," he said. Still, he warned Mr. Bush that any effort to go it alone can only make US-Russian relations "more complicated: Mr. Putin coldly declined to restate Russia's opposition: "The official position of the Russian government is known." Emerging from more than two hours of inaugural talks at Brood Castle, Mr. Bush stressed the positive by announcing that Mr. Putin will visit Mr. Bush's Texas ranch for an autumn summit. Mr. Bush, in turn, will visit Mr. Putin at his home in Russia. Senior officials on both sides were ordered to begin talks, including military-to-military negotiations, designed to bridge differences on issues ranging from missile defence to NATO expansion—both opposed by Moscow. "The differences in approaches do exist, and naturally in one short moment, it's impossible to overcome all of them," Mr. Putin said.

Both sides said no specific breakthroughs were reached, and nor were expected in the short term. The summit brought together two men—one a former KGB agent, the other the son of a former CIA chief—whose sprawling nations stood for years on the brink of nuclear destruction. They, as well as their nations, are adjusting to the shifting dynamics of the post-Cold War world. "Can I trust him?" Mr. Bush said, "I can, And from that basis, we can begin a very fruitful relationship." He called Putin a family man, a patriot. "I was able to get a sense of his soul," Mr. Bush told reporters. Such an unimpeachable endorsement caught Mr. Bush's advisers by surprise and some worried he may regret his words if Mr. Putin strays from democratic reforms. Mr. Bush saluted his Russian counterpart as "an honest, straightforward man who loves his country."

Mr. Bush met Mr. Putin at the elegant 16th-century estate that was a favourite Alpine resort for the late Yugolav dictator Josip Broz Tito. Sweeping green fields and a craggy mountain top formed the backdrop as Bush tried to put his signature charm to work. "I was so impressed that (Putin) was able to simplify his tax code in Russia with a flat tax. I'm not so sure I'll have the same success with Congress," he joked. Mr. Bush hoped to thaw the chill in US-Russian relations over his plan to scrap the 1972 Anti-Ballistic Missile Treaty and pursue missile defence. Mr. Bush argues that the offensive capabilities of "rogue" nations such as Iran and Iraq gravely threaten the US and its allies.

Mr. Putin called the ABM treaty the cornerstone of the modern architecture of international security, and added: "Any unilateral actions can only make more complicated various problems and issues". In the brief interview, Mr. Bush said, "We talked straightforward. Nothing was rejected out of hand". Asked if that included missile defence, Mr. Bush repeated, "Nothing was rejected out of hand, and there was a receptivity that I was most pleased to see.... It became clear to me in our discussion that the Russians feel the same threats we feel".

At the press conference, Mr. Bush said that he did not offer incentives to Mr. Putin to gain Russian acquiescence.

White House aides had said in advance that Mr. Bush hopes to eventually offer Putin inducements such as arms purchase, military aid and joint anti-missile exercises with Russia. But first, advisers must hammer out the details. Mr. Bush asked Secretary of State Colin Powell and Defence Secretary Donald Rumsfeld to work with their Russian counterparts on a "new approach for a new era" in security arrangements. And Treasury Secretary Paul O'Neill and Commerce Secretary Don Evans will lead to Moscow soon to work on economic and commercial ties.

2

NUCLEAR WEAPONS DEBATE : AN INDIAN PERSPECTIVE

A Philosophy of Nuclear Power

Any debate about the future of India and the bomb demands a meeting point between science and religion, ethics and politics, nation-state and civilization. It necessitates thought experiments opening out different questions.

Consider three openings:

- Imagine the scene in the Gita where Arjuna the warrior is reluctant to go into battle. Would Krishna have answered differently if Arjuna's arrows were nuclear missiles?
- Assume you have been invited by a future SAARC meeting to answer a question. How does one inform a future society that sites around the Indo-Pakistan border have enormous radioactive wastes? What semiotic marker does one put to warn a society 10,000 years, hence?
- Consider the Gandhian question. If you were a Japanese citizen and knew that a B-52 with the atomic bomb were flying in, how would you communicate your sense of fearlessness to the pilot?

All these questions raise a set of issues different from those today. Remember the bomb is a social fact. We are no longer waffling. Nehruesque on whether we need the bomb or not. Every child born after Pokhran-II lives with the reality of the bomb. But it is a reality that has not threatened our styles of thought. Vajpayee stands Rajput-like sword in hand, little realizing that his ideal Rana Partap is remote from the nuclear mind of storabel Talbot. We treat the bomb like a large catapult or as odd therapy to exercise our minds of '500 years of Muslim domination' as one rabid IIT student put it. Let us hope she has applied for green card by now.

Our future is caught up in the past of old ideas of scarcity, revenge, masculinity, and territory. If the bomb were to perform one service, it should unleash the imagination, liberate us from the captive texts of the Indian nation-state. Consider a set of thought experiments.

(*i*) Foreign Policy is not the prerogative of the national-state. Civil society of universities, trade unions, also shape foreign policy, India has a responsibility for democracy in Pakistan.

(*ii*) At a time when Islam is being and demonized, India can become a centre for crestive Islam.

(*iii*) We need joint research institute for Himalayan ecology, for river management and not wait for some bureaucrat in EU to suggest it. Let us open the boundary and increase trade and other educational opportunities. Let it go beyond the idea of a joint Indo-Pak cricket team into nuclearadom. If aggression is a part of society let us ritualize it.

(*iv*) Amartya Sen was stating the obvious when he said that the nuclear bomb is ethically and cognitively wrong. It is now up to civil disobedience groups to devise form of civil resistance from non-payment of taxes, to crossing the boundary in groups to spread the message of peace. Both India and Pakistan are indifferent to the brutalization of Sri Lanka. Can't civil society provide forms for discussion whereby peace becomes a possibility in Sri Lanka?

(*v*) Every new paradigm demands new categories of thought. The old ideas of honour and revenge, of the feud will not do Robert Axelord in his Evolution of Cooperation talks remarkable exercise that tried to determine the most successful policy for the prisoners dilemma: The winning policy showed that 'nice guys finished first.' One example is of Sadat who broke the impasse and maximized Egyptian security and even territory. Axelrod makes a profound point. 'For niceness to pay, players must have a future together. The shorter the time-frame of reaction, the more immediate the pay-offs of a zero sum game.'

(*vi*) Only India and China as civilizations can stem the tide of globalization. We have to ask now what Swadhyaya, Sai Baba or Sankaracharya have to offer on the bomb.

Can our religious discourses, our social movements meditate on these disasters as practical problems and bring to it the same pragmatism as a good business.

I am proposing something similar to Robert Jùngk's 'The Everymen project,' Jungk asked Austrain citizens to visualize their own future. The first reactions were passive but after a few tries, the enthusiasm was stunning. Few democracies ask citizens to be futures planners. It is time to make the future a democratic exercise. India through democratic debate might become one of first societies to abandon weapons through open debate-religious, scientific and ethical. A society that invented Gandhi can reinvent satyagraha as a way out of nucleardom. A nuclear future is an oxymoron. But Indian democracy might invent new possibilities from this paradox. Otherwise we have to accept the updating of the old Gandhian wisecrack. The Mahatma was asked sometime after Pokhran-II, what do you think of Indian civilization? He said, 'that would be a good idea.'

Weapons Programme

The Indian nuclear weapons programme goes back to Mrs. Indira Gandhi after her re-election in 1980. She ordered a nuclear test in 1983 and cancelled it, presumably under U.S. pressure. The programme continued under Rajiv Gandhi and was supported by every Prime Minister. Prime Minister Narasimha Rao also ordered nuclear weapon testing December 1995 and again gave in to U.S. pressure. The programme was pushed further under the Prime Ministerships of Deva Gowda and I.K. Gujral. A whole range of weapons are ready for testing when the BJP coalition took office in March 1998. For the third time tests were ordered by Prime Minister Vajpayee. This time care was taken to prevent the U.S. from detecting the tests. Mr. Vajpayee was lucky and the tests went through as planned. The Indian nuclear weapons programme had maximum support from the Congress party, next to that from the United Front and small but significant one from the Janata Dal. Only the credit for conducting the tests successfully in the third attempt goes to the BJP. Why did Indira Gandhi and Rajiv Gandhi who led the struggle for nuclear disarmament at the global level nurture a nuclear weapons programme? Pakistan decided to go nuclear in January 1972 even before India decided on the Pokhran test. It was able to enlist Chinese collaboration for the weapons programme by June, 1976. The U.S.A. imposed sanctions on Pakistan on account of its uranium enrichment programme in April 1979, the sanctions were waived after the Soviet move into Afghanistan. In 1981, during the negotiations to finalise terms of military collaboration to support the proxy war in Afghanistan, Pakistan obtained an assurance from the United States that the Pakistani nuclear programme would not be allowed to become the lynchpin of their relationship. By 1980, Pakistan had formalised its long term nuclear strategy in relation to India and particularly Kashmir. As recorded by Professor Stephen

Cohen in March 1980, the Pakistanis felt that their nuclear capability would neutralise Indian nuclear force and it would provide the umbrella under which Pakistan could reopen the Kashmir issue. As early as June 1983, according to a recently declassified document, the U.S. government was aware of the transfer to Pakistan by China of the design of a nuclear explosive device. Recently Dr. Samar Mubarakmund, the Pakistani nuclear designer, revealed that 1983 was an important milestone in its nuclear programme when the first atomic device was manufactured and tested. The U.S. administration arranged for the Pressler amendment which raised the threshold for U.S. sanctions from 20 per cent uranium enrichment to Pakistan reaching full nuclear explosive capability. This enabled Pakistan to receive full military assistance from the U.S. even as it worked to assemble its nuclear weapon. Then in 1987, the CIA operative in Islamabad Richard Barlow reported to Washington that Pakistan had assembled, a nuclear weapon. Dr. A.Q. Khan openly conveyed the nuclear threat to Mr. Kuldip Nayyar. Yet, successive U.S. Presidents, needing Pakistani support for the Mujahideen war in Afghanistan certified to the U.S. Congress that Pakistan had not reached full nuclear explosive capability. Mr. Agha Shahi, Mr. Abdul Sattar and Air Chief Marshal Zulfikar Ali Khan claim in an article 'Keeping Nuclear Peace' written on October 5, 1999, that Pakistan deterred India through its nuclear capability on three occasions in 1984, 1987 and 1990. In other words, Pakistan conveyed explicit or implicit nuclear threats to India on these occasions. The 1990 threat has been described in U.S. strategic literature. In 1993, China also supplied M-11 missiles to Pakistan. Even after seven years, the U.S. is unwilling to take a determined stand on the issue for fear of its triggering off mandatory sanctions against China. The Chinese help to Pakistan in supplying ring magnets, Khushab plutonium production reactor and setting up of a missile factory are now part of history.

Faced with this Pakistan-China axis connived at by the U.S., the Indian Prime Ministers took the correct decision and initiated and sustained the nuclear weapons and missile programmes.

India tested its "peaceful bomb" in 1974. The next test came fourteen years later. The United States complained loudly both times. Yet the United states tested nuclear weapons may times for many years on end.

The American excuse was first that it anticipated a mortal threat from the Soviet Union and then later actually faced such a threat. America's nonproliferation policy implicitly denies that such reasoning can legitimate other countries' entering the tight circle of nuclear powers. Nevertheless, the reasoning the United States applied to itself was right. If a country requires nuclear weapons for the sake of its security, then it should make them. If national security does not mandate having nuclear weapons a country would be foolish to covert them.

The history of the nuclear era roughly follows this reasoning. America's nuclear weapons called the Soviet Union's into being; the Soviet Union's, China's; China's, India's, India's, Pakistan's. The United States grudgingly accepted the first two steps in this reasoning, but balked at the third and the fourth.

The question raised by India's nuclear tests is not whether they should have been conducted. Rather the question is whether or not India's security can reasonably be said to require its becoming a nuclear power. Some countries need nuclear weapons; some do not.

Brazil and Argentina set themselves on course to become nuclear weapons' states. Both decided to abandon their efforts. Neither posed a threat to the other's vital interests. South Africa became a nuclear weapons' state and then, finding no commensurate threat, wisely reversed its policy.

Whether or not a country decides to "go nuclear" has little to do with its desire for prestige. The decision to enter the nuclear business is a portentous one. No country makes it mainly to puff itself up. So many countries now have the technical ability to become nuclear-weapons' states that more blame than credit accures to the state that decides to do so. A new or a near nuclear state gains attention, not prestige. Think of North Korea.

Pakistan is obviously a state that needs nuclear weapons. Three times since independence it fought and lost wars against its militarily superior neighbour. For Pakistan to compete on conventional military grounds with India is economically impossible. Nuclear weapons, if linked to a sensible strategy, however, are a low-cost way of leveling the playing field.

Can India be seen in a similar light? It needs no nuclear capability, but how about the northern one? Contemplating the question, most American officials give three answers. The first is that the China might threaten India is nonsensical. Yet China and India fought a war as recently as 1962, and they share a long and disputed border. One can hardly think that an Indian worry about a Chinese threat to its security is fanciful, even if one believes that the danger is remote. After all the mighty United States shares a similar and much less warranted worry. The second American answer to the question about the need for, and desirability of, India's having a nuclear capability rests on doubts about the efficacy and affordability of an Indian force. Americans managed somehow to convince themselves that thousands of strategic warheads and multiple means of delivering them were needed in order to deter the Soviet Union. If, however, one thinks politically instead of militarily, it becomes apparent that not much is needed to deter. What political leader would run the risk of losing even a city or two-and-also his own position of power-in military pursuit of problematic gains? To build a nuclear deterrent force is cheap compared with the cost of engaging in a conventional arms race. Poor countries appreciate this more readily than rich countries do. Moreover, new nuclear powers can learn from the foolhardly conduct of the United States and the Soviet Union. Neither of them managed to figure out that once a country has second-strike force, multiplying weapons provides no additional deterrent capability.

The third American worry is that Indian and Pakistani nuclear weapons increase the likelihood of war in South Asia. James Woolsey, former directory of the Central Intelligence Agency, once remarked that he know of no instance in which nuclear weapons contributed to the stability of a region.

Yet certainly they contributed to the stability of American-Soviet relations through the long years of the Cold War. One wonders why nuclear weapons should not have a similarly calming effect on relations between India and Pakistan.

As the late Pakistani general Aslam Beg, once said: In the presence of nuclear weapons, Pakistan and India can no longer fight even a conventional war. Both would fear that the other might begin to use nuclear weapons. And the late Indian General K. Sundarji, concurred.

Nuclear weapons have enhanced the security of their possessors and moderated their behaviour. The mere presence of nuclear weapons induces caution all around and opens at least the possibility of cooperation among countries that have them.

The Nuclear Balance

Anyone who pretends that India's decision to cross the nuclear weapons threshold openly has made no difference to its international standing is either lying or living in fantasy. Of course, the official reaction in the West was one of anger, and disappointment. India with nuclear weapons meant that Pakistan would soon follow. It was a major setback for the American-led effort to sustain the non-proliferation regime, and it appeared to make the world more dangerous especially in the setting of Indo-Pakistan relations.

Perhaps, more troubling for the West than the strategic implications of an Indian bomb, was the public enthusiasm that greeted the news in India. Indeed most commentators tried to reassure the world that Delhi's decision to go nuclear was driven by domestic politics, especially by the BJP's declining popularity. When the Indian defence minister George Fernandes contended that the bomb was intended mainly to improve India's security with respect to nuclear China, the world to the extent that it noticed, laughted off such an explanation as diversionary at best.

After the first year, when talk of sanctions subsided, the sharp edge of India's decision has been dulled even in Washington. Instead, India's nuclear status is being quietly factored into the latest assessments of global security. For instance, in the recent report of the influential Trilateral Commission, entitled 21st Century Strategies of the Trilateral Countries (North America, Europe, Japan), a former high-ranking US state department diplomat, Robert Zoellnik, includes India as "one of the three great challenges of Eurasia" for early in the next century, the other two being China and Russia. Although nuclearism as not explicitly stressed, it would be foolish to suppose its irrelevance. In searching through the literature on geo-strategic threats, I find no mention of India as a challenge before May 1998 and a great deal of attention ever since. It is hardly a coincidence that India was not considered a geo-strategic threat before May 1998.

It is only slowly dawning on informed global opinion that the United States, as the self appointed manager of the nuclear club, cannot credibly claim to occupy the high ground of moral principle. To begin with the US nuclear weapons posture, despite, the end of the cold war, shows no sign of softening. Nuclear weapons continued to be developed and deployed by the thousand, and the US government even now refuses to issue a "no first use" pledge. The United States, along with the other nuclear weapons states have also completely ignored the unanimous view of the World Court in its 1996 Advisory Opinion that states possession nuclear weapons have a solemn legal obligation to engage in good faith negotiations aimed at achieving nuclear disarmament. This American image of irresponsible nuclearism as further reinforced a few months ago when the US Senate refused to ratify the Comprehensive Test Ban Treaty designed to put a global brake on further weapons development. Against such a background, it appears extremely hypocritical to single out India (and Pakistan) as breakers of the international moral code on nuclear weapons.

At worse, India is pursuing a security logic based on the same sort of power politics that have guided the approach of the existing nuclear weapons states. This logic has been reinforced for decades by the fact that the five declared nuclear weapons states were also the five countries given permanent membership in the UN Security Council with the right of veto. How can the rest of the world insist that a democratically-elected Indian government has no right to pursue its security by acquiring nuclear weapons, especially when its decision has been applauded by the overwhelming majority of its citizenry? Is such a move by India More "irresponsible" than Israel's "open secret" that was deliberately ignored by the gatekeepers of the nuclear club? In effect India's crossing of the nuclear threshold was fully consistent with the geopolitical rules of the game of the last century.

India's interest in being finally acknowledged as a great civilisational power is also fully understandable. It is truly sad that it appears to take nuclear weapons to achieve such a result. Being the world's largest democracy is not enough. Having almost one billion people is not enough. But now that India possesses nuclear weapons, is no longer possible to think of the future of Asian security without including India as an indispensable player. In this respect, Mr. Fernandes may have been quite right to insist that India's nuclear weapons had more to do with China than Pakistan, as their main impact has been to close the gap between these two dominant countries in the Asia/ Pacific region. It is no longer plausible to think of China and the rest. Now strategic analysis must consider, at the very least China and India, and the rest.

None of this assessment is meant to be read as a belated note of congratulations to India. Undoubtedly, the region has become more dangerous in the event of crisis and conflict. During the Kargil campaign there were real anxieties and rumours about Pakistan's evident contemplation of a nuclear attack.

Perhaps, more fundamentally, India's decision was a decisive step away from its post-independence identity as a country dedicated to world peace, international morality, and leadership of the Third World. India's geopolitical "normalcy" meant that it could no longer claim such a leadership role or to be an exceptional nation. Arguably, such an undertaking had long since been discarded by Indian politicians as "a mission impossible," yet after the explosions in the Pokhran desert, there was a feeling in the rest of the world that anti-nuclear activists around the world had lost their oldest and most trusted friend.

Post-Cold Wars Polities

The onset of the new millennium sees the two most populous states of the world locked in what appears to be a zero-sum competition in which strategic military and economic rivalry is taking each into a race for superiority.

The signs of this competition are not hard to see: the early dissipation of hopes of co-operation, enunciated in the famous declaration by Chou en-lai of 1954, 'hindi chini bhai bhai', has given way to a broad sense of competition between the two contrasted economic models and, since 1962 to a military rivalry that found its most dramatic expression in the justifications given by India for its nuclear explosion in 1998.

A century ago, it was in East Asia that the most intense, early, signs of inter-state conflict were evident, in the triangular conflict of Russia, China and Japan. Today, as the centre of the world economy shifts, for the first time in half a millennium, from the Atlantic to the Pacific Rim and the Indian ocean, the dangers of inter-state rivalry, construed by some as including not only inter-economic but also inter-cultural rivalry, appear to be growing. There is no room for complacency, or for benign faith in the enlightened character of elites and economic interdependence, as far as the future of this relationship is concerned. But a measure of perspective could serve to cast this process in a different light. This is so in two respects in particular.

First, the challenges facing India and China are far less from each other and far more from a global process, of technological and economic change. The competition is not for a fixed share of a world market, but for a beneficial share of an ever expanding world economy that needs, and can find place for, both states. India and China are not major trading partners with each other, both are seeking to build closer relations with the world economy, by applying methods, and by exporting to developed countries. Moreover, India is, in many ways, better placed than China to meet this global challenge.

By some indices China is certainly doing better than India, China exported $151bn. in manufactured exports in 1996 and India $32bn. By World Bank figures the Chinese

GNP per capita was $860 in 1997, and Indian $390. But on other indices India is doing better. Agricultural value added per hectares of agricultural land in India is $520. China's $184 in 1992. On qualitative indicators India is in far stronger position. India does not have the vast array of state owned, and still heavily subsidised industries that China has. The threats of social disruption, and of regional inequality in India are far less serious than in China. India already has in place many of the social and legal preconditions for successful participation in the world market—the company law, the accountants, the managers needed to do this, China is far behind.

Secondly, India has a political system that is far more adaptable to the outside world than China's. China is living a contradiction which, on most historical criteria, it cannot sustain: rapid economic and social change, fuelled by the influx of capital and new ideas from outside, combined with paralysis of the political system. This affects not only decision-making and the legitimacy of the system, but also allocation of power: corruption, and the retention of a hollow ideology in which few new believe are widespread. The resort of the regime is, inevitably, to fall back on bouts of repression, and on nationalism. The unresolved issue of the division between China and Taiwan provides a pretext for so doing. But sooner or later China will have to confront the implications of this political stagnation, one that grows more battle by the year.

Indian politicians, and much of public opinion, do not, of course, see it this way. It was this sense of lagging behind in a competition with China that underlay the decision to resort to nuclear weapons in 1998. The outside world, including those such as myself who have long compaigned for a halt to nuclear proliferation and a reduction of nuclear arsenals, were not persuaded of India's reasons: China does not, in any direct sense, threaten India, and indeed India figures little on its strategic horizon: Taiwan, Japan, Korea, Russia, ultimately America, are more important. The consequences of the Indian action, in South Asia, the middle east and elsewhere, may in the longer run by ominous. This way an unnecessary, irresponsible, act.

Yet the import of this action will be seen above all in whether India is drawn into a competition with China on China's terms. Here nuclear arsenals, endorsed by shortsighted politicians and by an increasingly nationalistics and unilaterial public opinion, would be the basis of international value and competition. The greatest challenge facing India is not its position relative to China, but that of ridding itself of the myth that its major challenge comes from China at all. India's strengths, political and economic, that fit it for a major role in the world of the next century: it will squander these by re-entering a world of strategic and nationalist competition from which its own history and qualitative strengths have the potential, to free it.

India has a continuing story of the persistence of patterns of the past amidst epochal changes. In the second century before Christ, the sub-continent had about 20 million people; it now has over fifty times that number. But the largest cluster has always lived in the great flood plains of the nidus-Ganga-Brahmaputra. The forests are now much shrunken but they still exist especially in the hill ranges of the peninsula and along the lower reaches of the great Himalayas. The spread of agriculture, especially with modern irrigation, has been one of the most significant transformations of the landscape, producing the food and fibre and sustains millions.

But it is the fate of this mass that comprises a seventh of all humanity that is cause for both celebration and concern. A large, inclusive polity can only be sustained, if not created, through something more than brute force. If India has held together as an entity across the latter half of the 20th century, the vibrancy and flexibility of its democracy has played no small part. In 1952, universal franchise gave the world it's largest ever electorate of over 200 million people. The formation of linguistic states, the greatest ever peaceful recording of political boundaries within a country was accomplished fairly smoothly—Endurance is achievement in itself. India has survived even as the former Soviet Union has crumbled and Pakistan shrunk to half its former size. But much depends on the ability of today's leadership to continue with the blend of flexibility and firmness that defused the stir for linguistic states or the armed movement for an independent Mizoram.

The maturation of democracy requires that many fundamentals are re-examined but India's pluralism-however flawed in practice-remains the bedrock of its existence. This vast experiments in a peaceful mingling of cultures that allows survival for all but primacy for no single voice requires statesman like qualities. These are often wanting in the world of real politic. Exclusionist notion of a part of whole of India constitute the greatest single problem to be surmounted in the second half century of the republic. Even to heal the wounds in the Vale of Kashmir and the North East requires afresh more federally, attempts to play on religiousity to create an Us-versus—Them situation, whether in the dusty plains of the Ganga or elsewhere is tantamount to playing with fire. The very threads of coexistence that bind a society together can come apart as they have in Sri Lanka.

There is no reason for despondency even as there is none for a triumphal optimism. But the deeper challenge that lies ahead is even more difficult. It requires us to realise the ideal of equality in a society long marked by hierarchy. The struggle for equity for all men and women is at least as old as the Buddha. Mahavira went even further to bring all living things in the ambit of harmony. Other cults from Sufism to Bhakti sought to give manual dignity, and women their rightful place in society. The last half century has seen the ripening of a new harvest of the hope of equality among the under-classes. A son of the so-called menial castes was the architect of a republican Constitution, Since then, those who have occupied the highest of power have been drawn from across the spectrum or rather from the underside of the pyramid of society. If democracy is a miracle of modern society, India surely represents it working on a scale and in a manner that is new to the world.

Yet, if much ground has been covered, so much more remains to be done. Reams of statistics can rarely match the eloquence of poetry. Representation in itself is only part of the answer to the call for dignity. Appadoral, the Tamil poet's lament rings true to this day. "Decide mother/Who will go without today/Is it Rama the strongest who may not need it/or Bala the weakest who may not need it much longer/or perhaps it will be Sita who being a girl is expendable/Decide mother/Decide and hate."

The success of India rests on its collective ability as a society and as a legatee of a civilisation to answer the reality behind his verses. The ideal of equality is so often a mirage in the land of multi-layered hierarchy. The great upsurge of these at the margins of society: of advises and Dalits, and women, is still in its early phase. Much will depend on how far their concerns are addressed and their right to dinity given the recognition it deserves and demands.

Even as a young republic, India is heir to the travails and legacies of a long past. The flexible and open-ended idea of India that the republic was founded on had a second, of neglected dimension—the dream of levelling the layers of privilege and status that had burdened our society. The urge for harmony and the striving for equity went together. Neither has remained unaffected by the tumult of the last five-decades.

Each needs to be re-worked to address fresh challenges. It is this task that lies ahead. The polity's successes and failures will be the touchstone for not just our rulers but all those who make up and believe in India not merely as an idea but as an ideal.

3

DEVELOPING MISSILE TECHNOLOGY

On May 11, 1992 the United States imposed sanctions on the Indian Space Research Organisation (ISRO) and Russian space organisation Glavkosmos, banning for two years American licensed exports to these two entities or imports from them and the awarding of US Government contracts to them. The sanctions were imposed since a deal under which ISRO was to import cryogenic rocket engines from Glavkosmos for its geosynchronous launch vehicle (GSLV) programme allegedly constituted a violation of the Missile Technology Control Regime (MTCR). The US action has kicked up a controversy with the Americans justifying it on the grounds that the deal violates MTCR guidelines since the cryogenic engines were intended for use on a launch vehicle that could deliver a 500 kg payload to a range of above 300 km. The proposed GSLV has range of 36,000 kilometres and a payload of 2,500 kg. (See Annexure II for Cryogenic engines).

The Indians and Russians have, however, challenged the application of MTCR deal and have questioned American motives in going through with the action at this particular time. The ISRO Chairman Mr. U.R. Rao said two days after the sanctions were imposed, "The sanctions are purely due to commercial interests and are surprising, unilateral and unjustified. As the Sriharikota range is the second best satellite launching station after Kourou in the French Guyana, owing to its proximity to the Equator and cost effectiveness, the US perceives India as a threat to its business. It believes in free enterprise for itself and no enterprise for others." The Indians are particularly sore since the cryogenic engines in question are for a professed peaceful space programme and can have no possible use in any military missile development programme, since cryogenic engines depend on liquid fuel and propellants, while missiles require solid propellants.

The Indians also claim that the US did not raise any objections when the American firm General Dynamics had offered the same engines to India at an exorbitant cost of Rs. 800 crore, but chose to impose the sanctions when the Indians went in for the Russian engines that cost one-third the General Dynamic offer. The Russians impute the US reaction to pressure from the US space industry which wants to maintain its "monopoly along with France in the international space technology market." Besides, as a Glavkosmos official charged, the United States delayed imposing the sanctions on the Russian space agency and ISRO, while it completed a deal of its own to buy Russian space technology. A working model of the TOPAZ miniature nuclear reactor, one of the most advanced space vehicle engines, was delivered to the US on the weekend of May 9-10, 1992 while the sanctions were imposed only the next day. It is believed that the Americans would take at least two to three years and several billion dollars to develop a similar reactor.

Missile Technology Control Regime

Because of growing concerns of missile proliferation in about 15 third world countries whose value and interests may not be shared in the west, confidential negotiations commenced in 1983 between the United States and six other countries (Canada, France, Germany, Italy, UK and Japan). These countries agreed to make simultaneous national statements in 1987 to abide by guidelines of the

Missile Technology Control Regime (MTCR)). The MTCR partners aim to prevent the spread worldwide of missiles capable of delivering nuclear weapons by controlling exports of missile-related equipment and technology. Although being distinct from the nuclear non-proliferation regime, the MTCR complements international efforts to stem the proliferation of nuclear weapons. In the past five years, the MTCR membership has been extended to another eleven countries namely, Australia, Austria, Belgium, Denmark, Finland, Luxemburg, The Netherlands, New Zealand, Norway, Spain, and Sweden. In June 1990, Soviet Union agreed to adhere by the MTCR guidelines, and had been followed by China, Israel and most recently Hungary.

The MTCR partners have agreed that the regime should be expanded to include all members of NATO, the European Community and the European Space Agency, as well as all European neutral countries. Efforts are also underway to persuade these countries like India to adhere by the MTCR guidelines because its capabilities of exporting missile-related technology. According to a SIPRI report, that Defence Minister, Shri K.C. Pant rejected an invitation in October 1989 for India to become member of the MTCR.

Guidelines

The MTCR is neither an international treaty nor an organisation, but an agreed set of common export policy guidelines applied to a common list of controlled items given in its annex. The MTCR guidelines, including the annex, takes effect only, when each country implements them through their respective national legislation. By voluntarily applying the MTCR guidelines, all of the MTCR partner countries restrict international transfers of large ballistic or cruise missiles as well as transfer of large space launch vehicles capable of delivering a payloads of 500 kilograms or more to a distance of at least 300 kilometres. Consequently, unlike Agni, the Prithvi missile system is lower than the MTCR controlled technology threshold.

The annex of MTCR-controlled equipment and technology is divided into "Category I" and "Category II" items to include equipment and technology, both military and dual-use, that can contribute to missile design, development, production and operation. Category-I systems include complete rocket systems (including ballistic missile systems, space launch vehicles and sounding rockets); unmanned air-vehicle systems such as cruise missiles or target and reconnaissance drones; specially-designed production facilities for these systems; and certain complete subsystems such as rocket engines or stages, re-entry vehicles, guidance sets, thrust-vector controls and warhead safing, arming, fuzing and firing mechanisms. Category II covers a wide range of parts and components and subsystems such as propellants, structural materials, test equipment and facilities, and flight instruments (See Annexure I).

According to the MTCR guidelines, the export of Category I items to a non-MTCR country is subject to a strong presumption of denial. The transfer of Category I production equipment or technology is prohibited. Every MTCR country generally denies licences to its exporters seeking to sell Category I equipment such as complete rocket systems or major rocket subsystems to non-MTCR countries. The cryogenic rocket engines manufactured by the Russian space agency Glavkosmos are said to be Category I items. If the Glavkosmos engines were being exported by a US company, it would not be able to export them to India or any other non-MTCR country. In this context the statement by Chairman, ISRO, Prof U.R. Rao regarding the minutes of his meeting with a General Dynamics official on the US company's intention to sell cryogenic engines to India remains to be examined. If the General Dynamics or the French bid to sell cryogenic engines had approvals from their respective governments then it indicates that the US Government is using legal basis of national security concerns to pursue flexible options of foreign policy or commercial interests in delaying another competitor in launch vehicle services.

Category II items, however, may be exported at the discretion of the MTCR partner country, on a case-by-case basis for acceptable end-uses. In the case of the Indian space programme, the U.S. has in the past granted licences for the export of U.S. origin Category II equipment, such as telementry equipment, electronic components, test instruments and special materials, which was used in projects compatible with MTCR requirements.

The U.S. Government encourages international cooperation in the peaceful use of civilian space technology. Thus, an MTCR partner may, consistent with the MTCR guidelines, approve a licence for the export of Category II equipment to a civilian space programme in a non-MTCR country as long as that equipment does not contribute to the proliferation of large SLV's or missiles whose performance exceeds the MTCR weight/range limits.

National Defence Authorization Act

The U.S. controls exports of missile-related equipment and technology under the Arms Export Control Act for military items, and the Export Administration Act in case of dual-use items. To give teeth to the MTCR regime, the US Congress enacted the National Defence Authorization Act (NDAA) on November 5, 1990. Under this Act, the U.S. may impose sanctions worldwide on U.S. or foreign person, firm or government entity which facilitates trade, in MTCR-controlled equipment and technology with a person, firm or entity in a non-MTCR country.

Foreign firm or organization is liable to U.S. trade sanctions under the NDAA if it knowingly transfers, conspires, attempts and facilitates the export, or otherwise trades in foreign-origin MTCR annex items that contribute to missile development in a country not adhering to the MTCR guidelines such foreign entity would be then subject to U.S. export controls as if the items had originated in the U.S. The US State Department officials are mandated to give advisory opinion if foreign firms are likely to transfer systems contrary to MTCR guidelines.

For a firm or organization involved in a Category I transfer, the sanction is a minimum two-year ban on all U.S. dual-use and munitions export licences and on all U.S. Government procurement from the sanctioned party. For a firm or organization involved in a Category II transfer, the sanction is a two-year ban on U.S. dual-use and munitions export license sin the MTCR controlled list and on U.S. government procurement of such items from the sanctioned party.

NDAA sanctions against a foreign party do not apply to a transfer licenced by an MTCR-adherent country or intended for an end-user in an MTCR country, or if an MTCR government is taking enforcement or judicial action against that party. The U.S. may waive sanctions against a foreign party on national security grounds or to ensure supply of an essential product. This exit opportunity has been probably included in the NDAA to cater for situations like the Japanese company Toshiba's sale of advanced microprocessors to the Soviet Union which went into the development of their submarine propellers.

It is the NDAA which provides the legal basis and not the MTCR, for the U.S. Government to impose U.S. trade sanctions on any party, whether the Russian supplier Glavkosmos for intending to supply cryogenic rocket engines, the export of which the U.S. would control on MTCR grounds as Category I items, as if the engines were of U.S. origin to recipient Indian Space Research Organisation, or anyone else, that is involved in the proposed transfer to India, a country not adhering to the MTCR guidelines. Since the sanctions are preventive and not punitive the two-year ban is the minimum limit in the NDAA. They are imposed before the event of sale in an incremental manner. The sanctions can be prolonged as well as extended to other technologies being imported into India from the US.

US Expectations

The board conceptual approaches adopted by the United States in controlling technologies perceived as competitive or threatening their national security has taken three forms, ever since the Second World War. To check the growth and proliferation of such technologies wherever they can; manage through cooperative structures what the US is unable to block; and finally, confront the states where cooperative frameworks are not established. It is in these contexts that the US approach to India should be examined. The US invitation to India to adhere to or join the MTCR was rejected by the Defence Minister in October 1989 stating that it was as discriminatory as the Nuclear Non Proliferation Treaty (NPT). Somehow, essential differences between the two regimes escaped both the Indian policy makers as well as the media. Where NPT targets indigenous development, MTCR targets international trade of items and systems which can significantly contribute to nuclear capable ballistic missile development. It does not target indigenous missile development as the NPT, but aims at slowing the proliferation of missiles to give time for more effective implementation measures and export controls to be deployed.

It is in this context that NDAA provides the US Secretary of Commerce to negotiate with countries on the threshold of ballistic missile capabilities for establishing their respective national controls for restricting exports of items listed in the MTCR annex. On successful completion of negotiations, the US exports of the MTCR items to that country is treated at par with other MTCR adherent countries. And to get that treatment, it requires an official commitment to the MTCR guidelines; emplacing national legislations for restricting the export of controlled technologies and an annual review to confirm that the adherent country is meeting the requirements. In India's case, export controls in respect of most of these technologies are already in place because of our national concerns on arms trade and missile proliferation. But those technologies which are either being imported or are indigenously developed after importing the processes, will also be required to be placed under government controls. And as technology development is a dynamic as well as globalised process, leading to an element of interdependence, new systems and technologies that are being imported will also have to be brought under export controls.

Intelligence Sharing

MTCR member countries are required to contribute to intelligence sharing on the effectiveness of the MTCR enforcement mechanism. It would give the country an opportunity to voice its concerns about missile proliferation issues in the region. An acceptance of full Indian membership of the MTCR should provide it with a forum to voice its security concerns on transfers of missiles into South Asian region as well as strengthen the Indian position on ensuring restraints on China's transfers of M 11 missiles to Pakistan. It's not, however, clear how far western countries are willing to go as far as intelligence sharing with India's Membership concerned.

A national declaration of adherence to MTCR, and based on country's record of proliferation control measures and its commitment to the MTCR guidelines, full membership is given to a new country only a unanimous consensus to all other members. It is believed that a full membership status to Russia is being opposed by France as the former wants to expand the MTCR membership to include recipients and enforce stricter export guidelines through multilateral transparency.

As licences for transferring missile related technologies are treated on a presumption of denial to countries which are not MTCR adherent, it is difficult to pursue indigenous space oriented programmes because of MTCR restrictions on transferring even a space launch vehicle capability that can be potentially converted into a nuclear weapons launch vehicle. As technology is changing rapidly and getting increasingly globalised, new systems, components and technologies will need to be imported from the most competitive international source. And as the space technology trade is confined to a select group of countries, India can either be part of that structure or go through a prolonged and an expensive process of making every component itself. In case of cryogenic engine technology, India may take up to 20 years to indigenes.

In a similar manner, India's exclusion from the Coordinating Committee of Multilateral Export Controls (COCOM) which controls competitive advanced industrial technologies is only impeding its developmental programmes. Both MTCR and COCOM controls are targeting the high technology trade, and it is in this context these regimes have linkages with national developmental efforts. Unlike the Indian position on NPT which aims at keeping the options open on weaponisation of its nuclear programme, it is essential that any responses in examining MTCR should build negotiating position for obtaining a status of a country with COCOM General licence for trade.

Advantages

As sufficient information is not forthcoming on the advantages accruing to a MTCR member country it is not certain whether on accepting the MTCR guidelines, India will get full benefits as other member countries or get only an adherent status like China and Russia. Under such circumstances, would India be taken off the classified list of countries of concern which is being maintained by the US State Department? Would India be included in the intelligence sharing structure at the State Department's Missile Technology Analysis Group? And if and when significant missile threats are in the process of development, or are being posed to the Indian security, would it trigger similar multilateral responses on controlling missile transfers which threaten Indian security as being done in case of perceptions of threat to the US security?

Indian Responses

Strong reactions have occurred as expected in India on announcement of sanctions for two years against ISRO and Glavkosmos. Sanctions have been imposed for a minimum of two years against all contracts of ISRO to deter the cryogenic deal from going through. The effects of sanctions on the Russian space agency, which has larger relationship emerging with the US has to be studied. It raises the questions, would the sanctions debar trade with the US government agencies or would they be also extended to private US companies who have been looking forward to gaining from the recent commercialisation of the Russian space programmes? Would the US get access to Topaz, the Russian nuclear powered rocket engine, and if Topaz technology has components from Glavkosmos, then what would be the US position?

In India's case, diplomacy has to work towards damage control initiatives to reduce the effects of sanctions. It has to closely monitor the treatment being extended to the two agencies and narrow the effects of sanctions to only the user entity of cryogenic engines, that is Vikram Sarabhai Space Centre at Trivandrum. As ISRO is importing about 40% of electronic components from the US for its satellites, the effects of the extreme end of sanctions need to be examined. All contracts with the US regarding production of aircraft, electronics and space systems could also be put under sanctions, and the period could be extended, besides urging other MTCR partners to follow suit.

The aspect of contesting the legalities of sanctions should be explored on the grounds of extra-territoriality and breaking of international contracts and obligations on the basis of a law which has been legislated *ex post facto* to the bilateral agreements. NDAA, which was to take effect from the US financial year commencing in October 1991, mandates a determination by the US administration that cryogenic engine technology that is proposed to be transferred does "substantially" contribute to development of missiles.

Indian negotiators should explore the channels of contesting such determination through the existing process being employed between the two countries, that is of importers certification of non diversion and despatchers verification of end-use. Although US has rejected the Russian suggestion for independent verification through a team of neutral inspectors, the US cannot or should not disregard or reject such options on the grounds of policy implications as it has an moral obligation not to obstruct the human and social development initiatives in the Third World. But by urging other MTCR member countries to follow their example could lend credibility to the charge that the developed world is trying to perpetuate not only the technology gap but also economic deprivation in developing countries.

Satellites

If the sanctions under the Missile Technology Control Regime (MTCR) would cripple the launch vehicle development capability of the Indian Space Research Organisation (ISRO), the export controls of the kind that US slapped cripple the country's satellite development capability even more.

Though, for various reasons, ISRO's launch vehicle programme has not progressed as well as it could and should have, its satellite fabrication capability has certainly come of age. The indigenous, state-of-the-art polar orbiting remote sensing satellites, IRS-1A & 1B, have been built and flown successfully. The first totally indigenous, multipurpose, geosynchronous satellite, INSAT-2A, is waiting at Kourou, French Guyana, for launch aboard the European Ariane launcher on June 24. But is to be followed up in regular intervals by 2B, 2C, 2D and 2E.

Apart from building satellites, this experience has also given the capability to extend satellite fabrication services—the enormous infrastructure and expertise ISRO is a great asset—to potential buyers. ISRO's bid to enter the contract for building an INMARSAT satellite is indicative of that.

Though the particular contract did not come through, ISRO is well in position to enter the fray soon. Recently, the Chinese, who have adequate launching capabilities, expressed interest in the Indian satellite fabrication expertise, particularly of the IRS kind and the current US embargo will hit ISRO's satellite fabrication area rather adversely.

Just as the US would be wary of Indian competition in launching capabilities it would be more concerned about the more immediate threat of India entering satellite fabrication market. The INSAT-1 series of satellites, from A to D, it would be recalled, were fabricated under ISRO's specifications by Ford Aerospace. INSAT-2, being essentially modelled on INSAT-1, relies heavily on critical components imported substantially from the US. In value terms, 30 to 40 per cent would be import-based, according to sources in the department of space. An INSAT class satellite costs about Rs. 50 crore.

The two-year ban imposed is on US licensed exports to the ISRO, exports to the US from the ISRO and US government contracts with the ISRO. While US exports to ISRO are limited, the other two are issues of concern. Ban on US exports implies ISRO cannot import products under the US department of commerce control list specific to the group of countries that are non-signatory to the NPT, that require validated export licences (VELs) to be obtained by the exporter.

Sabotage

Electronic components required for satellites form a major share of imports for satellites and these will be hard hit. With the devastation of the Semiconductor Complex (SCL), there is virtually no integrated chip manufacturing facility in the country. Some go as far as to suggest that this was an act of sabotage. ISRO had submitted a two-phase project to the SCL for the design and fabrication of 45 types of circuits to the SCL with a four-year time frame for their development. Before it could take shape, the SCL itself was gutted. With the disinvestment in public units in progress in this year's budget the government has not committed any money towards rebuilding the SCL.

The most important electronic component that goes into the satellite is the crucial processor chips on the on-board attitude and orbital control system (AOCS), the heart of the satellite. These are space qualified processors and are speciality components. The chief source of this has been the US in general, the US does remain the main supplier of space qualified and radiation-hardened devices. For example, radiation-hardened solar cells, the main source of power supply for satellites, the detectors for meteorological instrument, VHRR, are imported.

Similarly earth and sun acquisition sensors elements are also imported.

Of the non-electronic components on board a satellite there are many have to be imported today but indigenous capability is emerging in these. In that sense, the problem may not be insurmountable in the distant future, when it comes to INSAT-3 class of satellites, but is definitely a source of worry for the INSAT-2 series after 2B.

The most important of these is the reaction control systems (RCS) that include the high speed (6000 rpm) momentum wheels and reaction wheels. Other items include titanium alloy tanks that hold the fuel as well the helium pressurant tanks, the auxiliary thrusters for satellite's orbit attitude corrections, the beryllium reflector, the meteorological instrument, the C-band antenna etc. Weight being the constraint, these have to be machined with precision and that is where indigenous capability is yet to mature. Similarly, for elements such as space qualified thermal blankets and nickel-cadmium batteries the ISRQ is currently dependent on imports.

Even if some of these are available from the European nations, particularly the non-electronic elements, the US could invoke the 17-nation multilateral COCOM regulations and prevent other nations from exporting.

The launch vehicle programme is, however, not so critically dependent on imports from the US except for cryo-engine technology. The ISRO programme could be redefined to follow the non-cryo route initially and develop cryo-engines indigenously.

Electronic items for launch vehicles, though currently imported from the US, can be obtained from other sources. The one critical element that was banned under the MTCR was mould for rocket nozzle throats. Because of that even the Vikas engine programme for the future PSLVs is already in jeopardy. However, this can be surmounted with some effort.

The other serious threat is that of termination of contracts. This should mean that the US satellite tracking stations will not be available for tracking INSAT-2.

Similarly, the agreement to receive Landsat and NOAA satellite imagery at Hyderabad for remote sensing applications would be terminated. In return, the ISRO could also not honour the commitment of tracking Intelsat satellites from the Master Control Facility at Hassan, but this would only amount to a minor retaliation.

Dr. Pramod Kale, director of the Space Applications Centre (SAC)—a division of the Indian Space Research Organisation (ISRO)—said about the possible strategies for countering the US-inspired technological sanctions on the ISRO, "If we really decide that we have to go on our own, we will find ways of doing things, and I am confident that we can do it." Dr. Kale is leading a eight-member committee, studying the impact of sanctions on the import needs of his centre and arrive at suitable strategies. The main function of the SAC is to fabricate the payload for all satellites.

Currently, the Ahmedabad centre is fabricating payloads for the INSAT-2 series and the Indian Remote Sensing Satellite (IRS) series. The INSAT-2 payload essentially consists of the 18 transponders in the C-band and extended C-band, for communication and TV broadcasting purposes, two S-band transponders, for Broadcasting Satellite Service and the Very High Resolution Radiometer (VHRR) for meteorological imagery.

INSAT-2C onwards, transponders in the Kuband will also be carried. The IRS payload, on the other hand, consists mainly of two advanced charge-coupled device (CCD)-based imaging sensors, called LISS-1 and LISS-2.

"INSAT-2A is already for launch at Kourou, on the European Ariane launcher, on June 24. INSAT-2B is under fabrication, for which components have been procured", Dr. Kale said.

However, Dr. Kale feels, the sanctions could affect the future INSAT-2 satellites (2C, 2D and 2E) and the IRS-1C and 1D (IRS-1A and 1B are in orbit). "The sanctions could necessitate redesigning of the payload systems, but we will try to meet the schedules," Dr. Kale says. "The additional work in terms of redesigning could, of course, cost time. If components are not available we have to make them."

As regards the satellite payloads, semiconductor components are the major concern, even though such materials like high-performance adhesives, graphite fibres, the honeycomb frame for use in satellites are imported. Imported electronic components include even passive such as resistors, capacitors etc.

Dr. Kale says, while these could be easily sourced elsewhere (including indigenously), sourcing of critical active components-like the radio frequency components such as the travelling wave tube (TWTs) used in the satellite operational amplifiers—can be problematic. He also said, these are mostly single source items from the USA. But these can be developed indigenously in a year-and a-half.

The total import of electronic components by the ISRO is less than Rs. 100 crore per year. Dr. Kale feels the integrated circuit fabrication facilities at the Bharat Electronics Ltd., the Indian Telephone Industries Ltd. (ITI), and the Central Electronics Ltd. (CEL) could be easily upgraded to manufacture space-qualified and radiation-hardened devices. In this context, he also mentioned the fire-devastated Semiconductor Complex Ltd (SCL), Chandigarh. The government, though has not provided any funds this year to rebuild this complex, ought to rethink about it now.

According to him, imported components make nearly 20 per cent of a satellite's cost. But the overall impact could be higher since most test equipment, used for satellite fabrication, are imported. In that sense, the dependence could be as high as 40 per cent of the total project cost.

The impact on the launch vehicle programme would be far less because electronics come into play only in launcher avionics and guidance. The other critical technologies, like launch vehicle casing, rocket motors etc., have been developed indigenously. Citing the example of China, Dr. Kale says the Indian space programme should also become totally self-reliant in technologies.

According to him, apart from totally indigenous concepts and designs of satellites (both telecommunication and remote sensing) and launch vehicles, China indigenously makes all components (including semiconductor devices) and sub-systems like batteries and solar cells required for its space programmes.

Significantly, China's semiconductor fabrication units come under the ministry of defence. A similar approach to the space programme can be followed in India as well. And Dr. Kale is confident that the goods can be delivered without depending on foreign technologies.

Commission

Meanwhile, Russia is planning to set up a joint parliamentary commission with the representatives of the Foreign Ministry and "Glavkosmos" for urgent talks with India and United States over the controversial 250 million dollar rocked deal contract, for supply of three cryogenic rocket engines to India.

According to Moscow TV this commission would have three variants in view.

First: Scrap the contract with India, sign the Missile Technology Proliferation Control Regime agreement (MTCR) and demand quota for launching satellites with the help of Russian space launch vehicles.

Second: Try to get an exception in this case and save the 250 million dollar contract.

But for obtaining quota for launching satellites Russia has to get the approval of sovereign Kazakhstan on whose territory the main space launching facilities at Baikonoor are situated.

The Bush administration's action, however, is merely the latest in a series of disagreements that have plagued Indo-US relations in the past few months. A look at the various contentious issues in the Indo-US relations that have come up in the past few months.

There was a major controversy about India's plans to sell an experimental nuclear reactor to Iran. The US administration has itself sold such reactors to many countries. India was forced to scale down its efforts in this direction.

The Bush administration came down heavily upon the Indian plans to export rice to Cuba. It also stymied Indian efforts to import wheat from the US even while the farmers lobby was keen.

After months of Indian efforts to clarify its position on intellectual property rights, the administration imposed retaliatory sanctions under the Special 301 provision withdrawing the GSP (generalised system of preferences) benefits accorded to Indian pharmaceutical products.

The US has claimed that India possesses chemical weapons. Robert Gales, the CIA chief, stated this during the course of a Senate committee hearing.

The latest, of course, are the sanctions against ISRO which threaten to jeopardise the country's geostationary satellite launch vehicle (GSLV) programme.

Soft Line

The Indian government has so far taken a soft line towards the US moves, refusing to take a confrontationist stand. Thus, their only reaction to the latest series of sanctions against ISRO was to term it "an avoidable irritant." The reasons for this circumspect attitude are not hard to understand. With the collapse of the Soviet Union, India has little option but to mend its fences with the US.

Missile Programme

The Indian Integrated Guided Missile Development Programme (IGDMP) initiated in 1983 was based on the missile requirements of the three armed services. It includes development of five missiles—Nag, a third generation anti-tank missile, two surface to air missiles, of which Akash is a medium range missile while Trishul is a short range missile, and two ballistic missiles, Prithvi, which is a short range missile, while Agni is a intermediate range missile.

The decision to develop these missiles was necessitated by a number of factors. One, the prohibitive and escalating costs of importing tactical systems like the anti-tank and air defence missiles. Second, the pace of change of such technologies and refusal by the Soviets, India's principal arms supplier, to provide its state-of-the-art-systems. Third, in case of strategic missile, both short range and intermediate range systems, the foreign arms suppliers would not sell such missiles because of India's nuclear capability which had been demonstrated in 1974. And finally, there was a need to become self reliant in development of this vital family of weapon systems. The integrated approach to concurrently develop multiple projects into one programme was adopted to optimise the available resources in the country and inject an element of competitive dynamism. Besides, the design-production-deployment cycle was drastically shortened from 8 to 10 years.

The IGDMP programme has been initiated not only to develop and manufacture the present generation of missiles, but build a national capacity for national missile development infrastructure. Along with Defence Research and Developmental laboratories, the missile Research

Centre at Imarat and other defence research laboratories constitute an extensive scientific complex for advanced military technology in the country. Although self reliance is one of the objectives of the programme, the dynamic nature of global developments in technology needs to be understood. One can totally indigenise the present generation of missiles as the national skills improve, but for upgradation and developments of subsequent generations of missiles which should have the competitive state-of-the-art technologies, there would be a need to acquire the best available in the global technology market.

Technological independence is not the only requirement expected of the IGDMP, but it needs to become a global player in the missile technologies. It is very difficult to judge the quality of a weapon system other than in battlefield and nor should the value of missiles sold to the national armed forces be used as an indicator of the success of IGDMP, but its potential should be measured in terms of its ongoing ability to compete with other comparable systems internationally.

NAG

A third generation fire and forget antitank guided missile with 4 KM range is being developed to counter contemporary advances in tank armour, that is both the composite and the reactive types. The missile uses in launcher's target acquisition system for initial guidance and on board seekers, (millimeteric wave for act guidance) and infra red imaging for passive model. It act has an ability of top attack where the tank armoured thinnest.

TRISHUL

A short range low level quick reaction surface to-air missile which has been developed for all the services. It uses an automatic command to line of guidance system with high frequency narrow guidance beam. The missile does not have thrust vector conduct facility which does not enable a reduction in its minimum effective range to 500 meters. Its maximum range KM. The import content of the missile is currently 15 per cent of its value and likely to be reduced to about 6 per cent during production.

AKASH

A medium range surface-to-air missile war maximum range of 25 KM. It uses a solid fuel boost motor in the first stage and a ram rocket sustainer move in the second stage. It uses command guidance from ground phased array radar system capable of track multiple targets, and an on board precision home system. It has a pre-fragmented warhead developed from high density alloys which are activated by a proximate fuse. The current import content of the missile is about 10 to 12 per cent of its value and is likely to be reduced to 8 per cent during production.

PRITHVI

A surface-to-surface battlefield support missile which uses a single stage liquid fuel motor. It has a strap down inertial navigation system which reduces its circum error of probability of 250 meters at 250 KMs. Prithvi range is 150 KM with a 1000 Kg warhead. Using either a conventional high explosive or a pre fragment cluster sub-munitions, Prithvi's main targets would be troop concentrations, air bases and static military installations.

Prithvi's Achilles heel well be its highly toxic liquid fuel of Dimethyl Hydrazine with a nitrous oxide based oxidiser. Contemporary missiles like the SCUD uses solid propellent monoblocs which are difficult to fabricate. Solid fuel is more stable, can be stored inside the missile for longer periods and less bulky as opposed to a train of vehicles carrying Prithvi's fuel. It will not only expose Prithvi to satellite and aerial detection, but its relocating ability would be restrained. Although Prithvi range and throw weight combination does not invite technology denial restraints under the Missile technology Control Regime (MTCR), but western observers are circumspective of Prithvi's nuclear warhead capability. The current import content of the missile is about 15 per cent of its value and is likely to be reduced to 5 per cent during production.

AGNI

India's first intermediate range ballistic missile Agni was test fired on May 22, 1989. An intermediate ballistic missile with a 1200 KM range. Agni uses a strap down intertial navigation system for guidance. The first stage is a solid propellent motor and the second stage is twin engined liquid fuel motor. As the government has not decided to mass produce the Agni missile and designated it as a technology demonstrator, no war-heads have been designed for Agni as yet. On May 29, 1992, India's second intermediate range ballistic missile Agni was successfully testfired with a higher one tonne payload, but failed to carry out the final manoeuvres in the re-entry stage, according to the Defence Research and Development Organisation (DRDO). The 2,500 KM range surface-to-surface missile Agni could not achieve its set objectives and "even though the launch phase was normal, later analysis shows that the mission objective of the final manoeuvering could not be fulfilled due to the premature ignition and separation of the second stage," a DRDO release said. According to experts, this could apparently mean that the objective of the defence scientists for pin-point manoeuvring of the missile could not be achieved due to the obvious problems in the re-entry stage. Unless a number of tests are conducted, any assessment of the circular error of probability of this missile would be erroneous. Although significant technologies have been achieved in the Agni test, like the heatshielding, the re-entry systems, the telemetry capabilities and viability of combined solid-liquid propulsion system, but very accurate digital auto pilot and sophisticated terminal guidance systems are still required to be developed to minimize the missile's drift. Particularly for missiles with longer ranges even miniscule errors will result in misses of significant distances. And research into this area is yet to commence. Another significant achievement was of tracking the Agni test by employment of multiple radars and telemetry stations at the launch complex at the Interim Test Range (ITR) at Chandipur. Besides an elaborate networking and tracking system has been developed through INSAT satellite linking the Sriharikota Test Range and telemetry stations on the Car Nicobar Islands as well as the shipborne systems.

Although the Agni missile project had cost Rs. 38 crore till 1990, according to another estimate, Agni's cost in series production would be about Rs. 4 crore. With an import content of about 5 to 6 per cent by value, there is an ongoing criticism of the relative costs of the Agni missile merely as a technology demonstrator. The strategic value of Agni can only be estimated if sufficient number of tests are carried out to reduce the time, effort and resources required for its conversion into an operational missile, should the Indian security environment on demand. Agni has become the focus of western concerns on a belief that it is in step with the Indian aim to develop an ICBM capability. And consequently, the US led initiatives to block or slow down the Indian missile building capacities has led to a greater scrutiny and verification of the end-use certification for the technologies procured for the Indian satellite launch vehicle programmes.

US Perceptions

The American concern over Indian development of Agni and Prithvi ballistic missiles should be viewed at three levels. At the first level, the US concerns with global proliferation of advanced weaponry and ballistic missiles and the effect or concerns it can impose on the US force projection capacities. At second level, more specifically, it looks at the impact of emerging Indian missile potential in the Indian Ocean region and the US interests in the Indian Ocean region in particular. The third level of concerns relate to a perceived future Indian capacity to graduate from an IRBM technology demonstrator to a nuclear capable ICBM. It is assumed that these developments will not only generate responses in China for improving its strategic preponderance *vis-a-vis* India, but in turn, may set off concerns in the Eurasian region with consequent effects cascading onto the existing international security equilibrium.

Options

Conceptually, can the missile race be stabilishing? the answer to this question presumes that it is only a question of time and resources before the other South Asian states will be able to develop missiles with accuracies justifying non-nuclear warheads. Last four decades of development has created sufficient targets of national value to create concerns from an uncontrolled missile trade regime. If targets like dams, chemical and fertilizer plants, refineries, power plants, ports and national communication nodes could become hostage to reciprocal missile strikes, it builds an element of deterrence as well as instability into any security equation with the countries bordering India.

Technology is not only going to improve the ballistic missile accuracies, but capabilities required to build cruise missiles are also reported to be within the reach of a number of Third World countries. With commercialy available GPS receivers costing a few thousand dollars, an entirely new level of potential will be created by using signals transmitted by navigation satellites. This would enable cruise missiles to achieve accuracies of less than

100 metres even at long ranges. By developing inexpensive technologies being used for drones and remotely piloted vehicles, it is possible to graduate to low cost cruise missiles. And when mated with cluster bombs, Fuel Air Explosives (FAE) or sensor fused sub-munitions, it will introduce a different order of destructive accuracies. For the time being, the developed countries plan meeting this challenge by developing techniques for signal degradation of the navigation satellites.

Warheads

Although Fuel Air Explosive (FAE) bombs are reported to produce blast effects approaching those of low yield tactical nuclear weapons, but for a better controlled and localised employment the weaponisation of FAE has been quite erratic. In spite of the fact, that the destructive effect of an FAE bomb is much more than an equivalent sized conventional bomb, is still no substitute for nuclear weapons, as believed by some. Because of the technical difficulties like efficient dispersal of FAE vapour from a high speed delivery vehicle like Agni, for which the re-entry declaration technologies have not yet been developed, the western view is that Agni's weaponisation programme would make it with a nuclear warhead.

FACT SHEET

- On May 11, 1992 the United States imposed sanctions on Indian Space Research Organisation (ISRO) and Russian space agency Glavkosmos for alleged violation of the Missile Technology Control Regime (MTCR) in signing the cryogenic rocket engine deal.
- The sanctions included a two-year ban on US licenced exports to the two entities, a two year ban on export to the US by the two entities and a two-year ban on the two receiving any US Government contract.

- In December, 1990 ISRO and Glavkosmos signed a contract, under which the former would import three cryogenic rocket engines from the latter for Rs. 235 crore.
- Growing concerns about missile proliferation in about 15 Third World countries led to secret negotiations between the US and six other countries agreed to make simultaneous national statements to abide by the guidelines contained in the MTCR.
- In 1989 Indian rejected an offer to join the MTCR on the grounds that like the Nuclear Non-proliferation Treaty, the MTCR too was discriminatory.
- The MTCR is neither an international treaty nor an organisation, but an agreed set of common export policy guidelines applied to the common list of controlled items contained in its annex.
- ISRO Chairman Mr. U.R. Rao said after the US action that the United States had no locus stand in imposing sanctions against his organisation and charged the US with being motivated by commercial interests, since it did not want India to become a major player in the international rocket launching market. Mr. Rao's charge is endorsed by the Russians as well.
- On May 14, 1992, the US increased pressure against the Russians, when the Senate Foreign Relations Committee passed a bill that made American aid for the Commonwealth of Independent States (CIS) conditional on Glavkosmos cancelling its deal with ISRO.
- The US action is expected to come as a serious blow to India's satellite programmes since ISRO depends on imports from the US to a large extent. But it has prompted India to look for alternative sources for components.

Annexure I

MTCR : SUMMARY OF THE EQUIPMENT AND TECHNOLOGY COVERED

Category I Items Include

- Complete rocket systems (including ballistic missile systems, space launch vehicles, and sounding rockets) and unmanned air vehicle systems (including cruise missile systems, target drones, and reconnaissance drones) capable of delivering at least a 500 kg payload to a range of at least 300 km as well as the specially designed production facilities for these systems.
- Complete subsystems usable in the systems in Item 1, as follows, as well as the specially designed production facilities and production equipment therefore :
  - individual vehicles;
  - reentry vehicles;
  - solid or liquid fuel rocket engines;
  - guidance sets;
  - thrust vector controls;
  - warhead safing, arming, fuzing, and firing mechanisms.

Category II Items Include

- Propulsion components;
- Propellants and constituents;
- Propellant production technology and equipment;
- Missile structural composites: production technology and equipment;
- Pyrolytic deposition/densification technology and equipment;
- Structural materials;
- Flight instruments, inertial navigation equipment, software, and production equipment;
- Flight control systems;
- Avionics equipment;
- Launch/ground support equipment and facilities;
- Missile computers;
- Analog-to-digital converters;
- Test facilities and equipment;
- Software and related analog or hybrid computers;
- Reduced observables technology, materials, and devices;
- Nuclear effects protection.

Source: Missile Technology Control Regime: Fact Sheet to Accompany Public Announcement, The White House (16 April 1987), pp. 3-4.

Annexure II

CRYOGENIC ROCKET ENGINES

A Rocket engine is a jet propulsion device that produces thrust by ejecting stored matter, called the propellant. The forward thrust given to the vehicle is in accordance with Newton's Third Law which states that for every action, there will be a reaction of equal magnitude in the opposite direction. Thrust can be increased if the fuel is more efficient. The efficiency of propellant described in terms of its specific impulse, which is expressed in seconds to measure the thrust derived from unit mass of fuel in one second of engine operation. Greater specific impulse means more push from unit mass of propellant. Rocket design should also ensure enormous speed requirement that is, 8 km per second. It is also important to note that the proportion of fuel in a rocket is more than the hardware, unlike in an automobile where the fuel accounts for a small percentage of the total weight.

Propellants

A chemical propellant can either be solid or liquid. The rockets used during the early days were essentially fuelled. A composite solid propellant consisted of an oxidizer in a matrix of organic fuels, ammonium perchlorate as an oxidizer, powdered aluminium as the metallic fuel and a polybutadience based fuel binder. A solid propellant should burn all over the inner surface of the rocket. The chemicals should not explode even though temperatures go upto 3,000°C. The specific impulse when one uses solid propellants varies from 205 to 242 seconds.

Liquid propellants used could be monopropellant that is, liquid containing both fuel and oxidizer like hydrazine. A bipropellant consists of two unmixed or uncombined chemicals (fuel and oxidizer) that are sent separately into a combustion chamber. The conventional liquid propellant consists of unsymmetrical dimethyl hydrazine (UDMH) as fuel and nitrogen tetroxide as oxidizer.

The first Indian sounding rocket launched on November 20, 1967 used solid propellant and the first rocket with a dummy payload using liquid propellant was launched on May 15, 1973. The satellite launch vehicle (called SLV-3) consisted of four stages, all powered by solid propellants. The next generation of SLV-3 was ASLV (Augmented SLV). This vehicle also used solid propellants. The special feature of it being the use of strap-on motors. PSLV (Polar SLV) is designed to put a satellite weighing 1 ton in sunsynchronous (polar) orbit. The most important feature is use of liquid propellant (UDMH as fuel and nitrogen tetroxide as oxidizer) for its second stage. If cryogenic propellants are used as third stage substituting the PSLV third and fourth solid propellant stages, the vehicle would consist of only three stages, and would be capable of launching satellites in geosynchronous orbits.

Cryogenic Engines

Cryogenic propellants are considered for use in the upper stages of spacecraft because they provide the highest performance (specific impulse equal to 391 seconds using hydrogen as fuel and fluorine as oxidizer). Fluorine, although provides very high specific impulse, presents unusual toxicity, reactivity and corrosion difficulties. Hence liquid hydrogen—liquid oxygen propellant is more suitable. Liquid hydrogen is very attractive as a fuel because of its high reactivity and the low molecular weight of its combustion products. Liquid hydrogen is also an excellent regenerative coolant. Liquid oxygen is an excellent oxidizer as it has a decided advantage in cost and it is also non-corrosive and fairly easy to handle by existing methods. A rocket uses five times as much oxidizer as fuel on weight.

Propellants

Cryogenic propellants are selected from considerations of high energy fuel-oxidizer combination and fulfilling the requirements of a low molecular weight. Thus hydrogen is the best choice as a fuel since this has the lowest molecular weight. As far as oxidizer selection is concerned, both oxygen and fluorine are equally good. However, oxygen has an advantage of lower molecular weight whereas fluorine release more energy when burnt with hydrogen.

Clearly a cryogenic liquid cannot conform to the criterion of storeability and it follows that the use of cryogenic propellants is confined to systems in which the time of launch is known in advance of the propellant loading operation. Thus cryogenic propellants are generally unacceptable for most modern military applications, although they are still perfectly viable propellants for satellite launching and space exploration vehicles.

Technological Challenges

The problems associated with a rapid starting sequence become more pronounced in case of cryogenic propellants than if non-cryogenic propellants are employed. Firstly, an adequate precooling of various components is essential if a stable flow is to be achieved within the engine. More serious is the question of the loss of head at the pump inlet on account of pressure drop required to accelerate the flow in the feedline. The existence of such a pressure loss increases still further the tendency for cavitation at the pump inlet during the starting cycle.

As a result of the combined effects of aerodynamic heating on the tank walls, the high vehicle acceleration, and the fact that cryogenic liquids have an-order-of magnitude greater coefficient of thermal expansion than normal liquids, considerable stratification takes place within the tank. Thus a considerable density gradient is set up within the tank. This will cause the pump delivery pressure to fall towards the end of the burning time when the heated liquid reaches the pump. Thus the ratio of oxidizer to fuel gets altered.

An additional complication arises towards the termination of the burning time when the final layers of boiling liquid reach the pump inlet. Thus cavitation becomes a likelihood and in practice shutdown is frequently initiated before this can occur and the penalty of the mass of unburnt propellant has to be accepted.

Cryogenic propellants make accurate gauging difficult since the instruments used must be insensitive to or isolated from any boiling occurring in the liquid.

4

POLICY OF POLICING : THE UNITED NATIONS AND NUCLEAR WEAPONS

Introduction

The Final Document of the 1978 session emphasised the role of the United Nations, working for disarmament and elaborated a world-wide programme of action with specific measures. However, despite the encouraging outcome of the session, the situation continued to deteriorate. Military expenditures by major military Powers reached everhigher levels during the 1980s, resulting in turn in the 1980s being declared the Second United Nations Disarmament Decade setting out the priorities and main areas on which attention should be focused, and in the launching of the World Disarmament Campaign.

Since the beginnings of the United Nations, efforts at disarmament did result in measured successes in some areas. Notable among these were the Treaty Banning Nuclear Weapon Tests in the Atmosphere, in Outer Space and under Water (partial test-ban Treaty) signed in 1963; the 1967 Treaty for the Prohibition of Nuclear Weapons in Latin America; the 1968 Treaty on the Non-Proliferation of Nuclear Weapons; the 1972 Convention on the Prohibition of the Development, Production and Stockpiling of Bacteriological (Biological) and Toxin Weapons and on their Destruction; the 1981 Convention on Prohibitions or Restrictions on the USE of Certain Conventional Weapons Which May be Deemed to Be Excessively Injurious or to

Have Indiscriminate Effects; and the 1985 South Pacific Nuclear-Free Zone Treaty. However, it was only with the end of the cold war that slowing the escalation of deadly weaponry came within reach.

NUCLEAR WEAPONS

First Proposals

Establishment of the Atomic Energy Commission

Mr. Harry S. Truman, President of the United States; Mr. C.R. Attlee, Prime Minister of the United Kingdom; and Mr. W.L. Mackenize King, Prime Minister of Canada, met in Washington, D.C., in November 1945 "to consider the possibility of international action: (*a*) To prevent the use of atomic energy for destructive purposes; and (*b*) to promote the use of recent and future advances in scientific knowledge, particularly in the utilisation of atomic energy, for peaceful and humanitarian ends".

On November 15, 1945, the three heads of Government issued a declaration which stated, among other things, that "in order to attain the most effective means of entirely eliminating the use of atomic energy for destructive purposes and promoting its widest use for industrial and humanitarian purposes, we are of the opinion that at the earliest practicable date a Commission should be set up under the United Nations Organisation to prepare recommendations for submission to the Organisation."

The General Assembly referred the establishment of the proposed commission to its First Committee (Political and Security), which considered the proposed resolution at its second and third meetings on January 21 and 22, 1946.

On January 24 the report and resolution authorising the Commission on Atomic Energy were approved in the

General Assembly with no dissenting votes. According to the resolution, the Commission was to be composed of one representative from each of the States represented on the Security Council, and Canada when that State was not a member of the Security Council.

The Commission was required to inquire with the utmost despatch into all phases of the problems, and to submit its reports and recommendations to the Security Council...

The resolution set forth the terms of reference of the Commission as being to make specific proposals:

(*a*) for extending between all nations the exchange of basic scientific information for peaceful ends;

(*b*) for control of atomic energy to the extent necessary to ensure its use only for peaceful purposes;

(*c*) for the elimination from national armaments of atomic weapons and of all other major weapons adaptable to mass destruction;

(*d*) for effective safeguards by way of inspection and other means to protect complying States against the hazards of violations and evasions.

At the first meeting of the Atomic Energy Commission, the representative of the United States presented a plan for the creation of an International Atomic Development Authority entrusted with all phases of the development and use of atomic energy. Under this plan the Authority would conduct continuous surveys of world supplies of uranium and thorium, and would bring the raw materials under its control. It would possess the exclusive right to conduct research in the field of atomic explosives, and all other research would be open only to nations under licence of the Authority, which would provide them with denatured materials. Dangerous activities of the Authority and its stockpiles would be decentralised and strategically distributed. All nations would grant the freedom of inspection deemed necessary by the Authority. The representative of the United States stressed the importance of immediate punishment for infringements of the rights of the Authority. He urged that "there must be no veto to protect those who violate their solemn agreements not to develop or use atomic energy for destructive purposes".

At the second meeting of the Commission on June 19, 1946, the representative of the USSR suggested that the first measure to be adopted should be the conclusion of an international agreement to prohibit the production and use of atomic energy weapons. Within three months from the entry into force of the agreement, he urged, all atomic weapons should be destroyed. Violation of the agreement should be severely punished under the domestic legislation of the contracting parties. The agreement should be of indefinite duration, coming in force after approval by the Security Council and ratification by the Council's permanent members. All States, whether or not Members of the United Nations, should be obliged to fulfil all provisions of the agreement.

At its sixth meeting on November 13, 1946, the Atomic Energy Commission decided by 10 affirmative votes, with two abstentions, to submit to the Security Council before December 31, 1946, a report on its work, its findings and recommendations...

While this report was being prepared, the second part of the first session of the General Assembly was considering various proposals concerning the regulation and reduction of armaments, including atomic weapons.

Meanwhile, the General Assembly on December 14, 1946, approved unanimously a resolution on the principles governing the general regulation and reduction of armaments, which, among other things, urged the expeditious fulfilment by the Atomic Energy Commission of its terms of reference. It also recommended that the Security Council expedite consideration of the reports made to it by the Atomic Energy Commission, that it facilitate the work of the Commission and that the Security Council expedite consideration of a draft convention or conventions for the creation of an international system of control and inspection, these conventions to include the prohibition of atomic and all other major weapons adaptable now and in the future to mass destruction and the control of atomic energy to the extent necessary to ensure its use only for peaceful purposes.

On December 30 the Commission, with 10 votes in favour and abstentions on the part of the U.S.S.R. and Poland, adopted the draft report of its Working Committee as the report of the Commission and submitted it to the Security Council on December 31, 1946.

On the basis of its findings, the Commission recommended the creation of a strong and comprehensive international system of control and inspection by a treaty or convention in which all Members of the United Nations would participate on fair and equitable terms.

At a meeting of the Security Council on February 18 the representative of the USSR proposed twelve specific amendments and additions to the general findings and recommendations contained in the first report of the Atomic Energy Commission. The USSR proposals included a provision that inspection, supervision and management by an international agency should apply to all existing atomic plants immediately after the entry into force of an appropriate conventions. Another proposal suggested that an effective system of control of atomic energy must be international in scope and established by an enforceable multilateral convention administered within the framework of the Security Council. Further amendments would provide for the destruction of stocks of manufactured and unfinished atomic weapons, and for elimination of the recommendation in the Commission's report that in case of violation there should be no legal right, by veto or otherwise, whereby a wilful violator of the terms of the treaty or convention should be protected from the consequences of violation of its terms.

On March 10, the Security Council adopted unanimously a resolution which, among other things, stated that the Council would transmit the record of its consideration of the first report of the Atomic Energy Commission to urged the Commission to continue its enquiry into all phases of the problem of the international control of atomic energy; and requested the Commission to submit a second report to the Security Council before the next session of the General Assembly.

Shaping the Issue

Consultations among the six powers—Canada, China, France, the USSR, the United Kingdom and the United States—took place on the Atomic Energy Commission's plan for the international control of atomic energy, which would make effective the prohibition of atomic weapons. However, agreement could not be reached on the elimination of atomic weapons under a system of effective international control. In July 1949, the Commission stated that no useful purpose could be served by discussion in the Commission until the six powers reported that a basis for agreement existed. In December 1950, the Assembly, recognising the failure to reach agreement on both the elimination of nuclear weapons and the regulation and reduction of other armaments and armed forces, established a Committee of Twelve (resolution 496 (V) to examine the establishment of a new consolidated disarmament commission by merging the functions of the Atomic Energy Commission with those of the Commission for Conventional Armaments.

Regulation, limitation and balanced reduction of all armed forces and all armaments

The item "Regulation, limitation and balanced

reduction of all armed forces and all armaments" was placed on the agenda of the sixth session of the General Assembly at the joint request of France, the United Kingdom and the United States. The explanatory memorandum accompanying the request referred briefly to the manner in which the problems of the regulation of armaments and the international control of atomic energy had been dealt with in the United Nations in previous years. It also referred to a joint statement issued by the Government of France, the United Kingdom and the United States on 7 November 1951.

This statement, a copy of which was attached to the memorandum, declared the intention of the three Governments to submit proposals to the current Assembly session for proceeding with the regulation, limitation and balanced reduction of all armed forces and all armaments including atomic weapons...

It outlined the main elements of the tripartite proposals, stating; among other things, that the first and indispensable step was disclosure and verification, and stated, it must be on a continuing basis and reveal in successive stages all armed force—including para-military, security and police forces—and all armaments, including atomic. It must also provide for effective international inspection to verify the adequacy and accuracy of the information.

The three governments also believed that a workable programme should include criteria according to which the size of all armed forces would be limited, the portion of national production which could be used for military purposes would be restricted, and mutually agreed national military programmes would be arrived at within the prescribed limits and restrictions. The United Nations plan for the international control of atomic energy and the prohibition of atomic weapons should continue to serve as the basis for the atomic energy aspects of any general programme, unless and until a better and more effective plan could be devised.

At the following plenary meeting of the General Assembly, the representative of the USSR submitted alternative proposals under the title "Measures to combat the threat of a new world war and to strengthen peace and friendship among nations" which would, among other things : (1) condemn participation in the "Atlantic block" and the establishment by certain States, and primarily by the United States, of basis in foreign territories; (2) deem essential the withdrawal of troops from Korea and a cease-fire there; (3) call for a five-Power peace pact to which other States might adhere; and (4) provide for the calling of a world disarmament conference before June 1, 1952.

Report of the Committee of Twelve

On October 23, the Committee of Twelve, established by resolution 486 (V) of December 13, 1950, submitted its report.

The Committee, consisting of the members of the Security Council as of 1 January 1951, together with Canada, had been established to consider and report to the sixth session of the Assembly on ways and means whereby the work of the Atomic Energy Commission and the Commission for Conventional Armaments might be coordinated and on the advisability of their functions being merged and placed under a new and consolidated disarmament commission.

The report recommended that the General Assembly should establish a new commission, to be known as the Commission for the Council of Armaments and Armed Forces, which should be under and report to the Security Council. This Commission should carry forward the tasks currently assigned to the atomic Energy Commission and the Commission for Conventional Armaments which, it proposed, should be dissolved.

Consideration by the First Committee

The General Assembly referred the tripartite proposal, the report of the Committee of Twelve and the USSR proposals to the First Committee.

The Committee considered the tripartite proposal and the report of the Committee of Twelve concurrently at 24 meetings between November 19, and December 19, 1951. The general debate on the items took place from the 447th to 460th meetings from November 19-30.

The discussion in the Committee was based on a joint draft resolution submitted by France, the United Kingdom and the United States, and on USSR amendments to the joint draft.

Appointment and report of Sub-Committee of the four Powers

A draft resolution was submitted jointly by Iraq, Pakistan and Syria calling for the establishment of a sub-committee consisting of the President of the General Assembly as Chairman and the representatives of the France, the USSR, the United Kingdom and the United States, with a view to formulating agreed proposals concerning the control or reduction of armed forces and armaments and the abolition of atomic or other weapons of mass destruction.

Area of agreement and possible agreement

The four powers had agreed to the establishment of a new commission to replace the Atomic Energy Commission and the Commission for Conventional Armaments. They had agreed that it should be called the "Atomic Energy and Conventional Armaments Commission" and that it should be under the Security Council. There was also agreement on its membership and rules of procedure.

There was some agreement on the functions of the new commission—to prepare proposals or measures to be embodied in a draft treaty or treaties (conventions) and intended to achieve "the universal desire for peace, for the regulation, limitation and balanced reduction of all armed forces and all armaments, and for the abolition of atomic another weapons of mass destruction." The USSR, memorandum stated, preferred to define those objectives as the prohibition of atomic weapons, the effective (strict) international control of atomic energy and its use for peaceful (civilian) purposes only, and the limitation and reduction of armaments and armed forces. Grave differences existed as to the principles and methods according to which those tasks should be executed. During the discussions, nevertheless, opinions had been expressed on the possibility of embarking on a common course to solve the problems posed by those questions.

All the four Powers agreed that all armed forces, including para-military, security and police-forces, and all armaments, including atomic, should be included in the commission's terms of reference.

There was an agreement also that there should be full disclosure of information regarding all armaments and all armed forces. While there were some differences regarding the publication of the information disclosed, it was stated that it did not appear that those differences could not be solved, and that they might well be left to the commission. However, the USSR, which favoured the simultaneous disclosure of information on both atomic and non-atomic weapons within one month, was absolutely opposed to the whole concept of "progressive" disclosure by stages. France, the United Kingdom and the United States maintained that disclosure should be both progressive and on a continuing basis.

While all four powers agreed on the necessity of verification and inspection, the USSR objected to inspection on a continuing basis on the ground that the permanent presence at establishments of inspectors or controllers would hinder efficient operation and was incompatible with sovereignty. It held that effective international inspections should be carried out in accordance with decisions of the international control organ, provision being made for control to include also verification of the information submitted. The commission should, further, be entrusted with the task of working out all details and procedures in the draft convention, the USSR representative stated.

All four powers appeared to agree that the control organ should decide the times and places of inspection and that a majority decision by the control organ in that regard would be binding on all, with no right of veto.

Area of disagreement

Serious and fundamental divergence of views was expressed on the specific means for attaining the general objectives of the two proposals and the principles to be established for the guidance of the commission, the memorandum stated. The USSR, for example, was opposed to the three power formulation of balanced reduction to levels adequate for defence but not for aggression, on the ground that the levels envisaged might mean an increase of armaments rather than a reduction, and that was not a concrete proposal for the reduction of armaments.

The three power proposal to achieve effective international control to ensure the prohibition of atomic weapons was opposed by the USSR on the ground that it did not provide for immediate and unconditional prohibition of atomic weapons, that it put control before prohibition, and that unless there was prior prohibition there would be nothing to control.

Other USSR objections concerned : the proposal to use as a basis the United Nations plan for the international control of atomic energy; the system of stages of disclosure proposed by the three Powers; and the directives to be given to the commission.

The United Nations plan for the international control of atomic energy which the three powers wished to retain as a basis for the commission to work on, it was stated, unacceptable to the USSR for the many reasons which it had repeatedly advanced, but chiefly because it would infringe on the sovereignty of nations, would set up a monopolistic trust under the United States, and would indefinitely postpone the prohibition of the atomic weapon.

The USSR proposed that the system of control should be implemented by an international control organ responsible for control of the enforcement of the prohibition of atomic weapons, provision also being made for effective international inspection to be carried out in accordance with the decisions of the control organ.

The USSR was also absolutely opposed to the concept of disclosure of information by stages, as contained in the three power proposal, on the ground that this would only result in the indefinite postponement of disclosure of information on the most destructive and dangerous arms, such as the atomic weapon.

The USSR was also opposed to the directives to be given to the commission, as set out in the tripartite proposal, concerning : (1) the formulation of criteria; (2) proposals for the over-all limits on armed forces and armaments; and (3) the allocation of armaments and armed forces within national military establishments. The three powers maintained that it was necessary to give the commission directives for working out its plans. The USSR stated that it had no objection to the commission's being given directives, but proposed that it should be instructed to prepare and submit to the Security Council within three months practical proposals for implementing the Assembly resolution.

Similarly, the three Powers could not accept the USSR proposals, contained in its amendments to the joint draft resolution, that the General Assembly should immediately and simultaneously declare the unconditional prohibition of the production of atomic weapons and the establishment of strict international control over the enforcement of that prohibition, and should recommend to the Great Powers that they reduce their existing armaments and armed forces by one third within one year.

That was opposed on the ground that, until a system of control was in operation, the prohibition would be unenforceable and illusory, and that the mere declaration of control would have little value unless there were prior agreement on the precise nature of the control and unless the control system was actually put into operation. As regards the one-third reduction of arms, the three Powers stated that the reduction by a fraction arbitrarily fixed, would preserve or possibly even intensify, the present imbalance between them and the USSR. Moreover, they held, the measure of the necessary balanced reduction could be determined only on the basis of verified information as to the existing state of armaments.

The memorandum concluded by stating that, despite the disagreements which existed on a number of matters of major importance in the two proposals, it seemed clear that there was some agreement on a number of aspects. The discussions in the Sub-Committee, it was stated, appeared to have helped to widen the areas of agreement on some points.

Establishment of the Disarmament Commission

Consideration by the General Assembly in plenary session

The report of the First Committee containing the draft resolution adopted by it was placed before the General Assembly at its 358th meeting on January 11, 1952.

The resolution [502(VI)] adopted by the General Assembly at its 358th plenary meeting on January 11, 1952 read:

"*The General Assembly*—

"*Moved* by anxiety at the general lack of confidence plaguing the world and leading to the burden of increasing armaments and the fear of war,

"*Desiring* to lift from the peoples of the world this burden and this fear, and thus to liberate new energies and resources for positive programmes of reconstruction and development,

"*Reaffirming* its desire that the United Nations develop an effective collective security system to maintain the peace and that the armed forces and armaments of the world be progressively reduced in accordance with the Purposes and principles of the Charter,

"*Believing* that a necessary means to this end is the development by the United Nations of comprehensive and co-ordinated plans, under international control, for the regulation, limitation and balanced reduction of all armed forces and all armaments, for the elimination of all major weapons adaptable to mass destruction, and for the effective international control of atomic energy to ensure the prohibition of atomic weapons and the use of atomic energy for peaceful purposes only,

"*Recognising* that a genuine system for disarmament must include all kinds of armed forces and armaments, must be accepted by all nations whose military resources are such that their failure to accept would endanger the system, and must include safeguards that will ensure the compliance of all such nations,

"*Noting* the recommendation of the Committee of Twelve established by resolution 496 (V) that the General Assembly should establish a new commission to carry forward the tasks originally assigned to the Atomic Energy Commission and the Commission for Conventional Armaments,

1. *Establishes* under the Security Council a Disarmament Commission. This Commission shall have the same membership as the Atomic Energy

Commission and the Commission for Conventional Armaments, and shall function under the rules of procedure of the Atomic Energy Commission with such modifications as the Commission shall deem necessary;

2. *Dissolves* the Atomic Energy Commission and recommends to the Security Council that it dissolve the Commission for Conventional Armaments;
3. *Directs* the Disarmament Commission to prepare proposals to be embodied in a draft treaty (or treaties) for the regulation, limitation and balanced reduction of all armed forces and all armaments, for the elimination of all major weapons adaptable to mass destruction, and for effective international control of atomic energy to ensure the prohibition of atomic weapons and the use of atomic energy for peaceful purposes only. The Commission shall be guided by the following principles:

   (*a*) In a system of guaranteed disarmament there must be progressive disclosure and verification on a continuing basis of all armed forces—including paramilitary, security and police forces—and all armaments including atomic;

   (*b*) Such verification must be based on effective international inspection to ensure the adequacy and accuracy of the information disclosed; this inspection to be carried out in accordance with the decisions of the international control organ (or organs) to be established;

   (*c*) The Commission shall be ready to consider any proposals or plans for control that may be put forward involving either conventional armaments or atomic energy. Unless better or no less effective system is devised, the United

Nations plan for the international control of atomic energy and the prohibition of atomic weapons should continue to serve as the basis for the international control of atomic energy to ensure the prohibition of atomic weapons and the use of atomic energy for peaceful purposes only;

(*d*) There must be an adequate system of safeguards to ensure observance of the disarmament programme, so as to provide for the prompt detection of violations while at the same time causing the minimum degree of interference in the internal life of each country;

(*e*) The treaty (or treaties) shall specifically be open to all States for signature and ratification or adherence. The treaty (or treaties) shall provide what States must become parties thereto before the treaty (or treaties) shall enter into force;

4. *Directs* the Commission, when preparing the proposals referred to in the proceeding paragraph, to formulate plans for the establishment, within the framework of the Security Council, of an international control organ (or organs) to ensure the implementation of the treaty (or treaties). The functions and powers of the control organ (or organs) shall be defined in the treaty which establishes it;

5. *Directs* the Commission, in preparing the proposals referred to in paragraph 3 above, to consider from the outset plans for progressive and continuing disclosure and verification, the implementation of which is recognised as a first and indispensable step in carrying out the disarmament programme envisaged in the present resolution;

6. *Directs* the Commission, in working out plans for the regulation, limitation and balanced reduction of all armed forces and all armaments:
   (*a*) To determine how over-all limits and restrictions on all armed forces and all armaments can be calculated and fixed;
   (*b*) To consider methods according to which States can agree by negotiation among themselves, under the auspices of the Commission, concerning the determination of the over-all limits and restrictions referred to in sub-paragraph (*a*) above and the allocation within their respective national military establishments of the permitted national armed forces and armaments;
7. *Directs* the Commission to commence its work not later than thirty days from the adoption of the present resolution and to report periodically, for information, to the Security Council and to the General Assembly, or to the Members of the United Nations when the General Assembly is not in session. The Commission shall submit its first report not later than 1 June 1952.
8. *Declares* that a conference of all States should be convened to consider the proposals for a draft treaty (or treaties) prepared by the Commission as soon as the work of the commission shall have progressed to a point where in the judgment of the Commission any part of its programme is ready for submission to governments;
9. *Requests* the Secretary General to convene such a conference when so advised by the Commission;
10. *Requests* the Secretary General to furnish such experts, staff and facilities as the Commission may consider necessary for the effective accomplishment of the purposes of the present resolution."

Non-proliferation

One of the principal objectives of the international community in the field of disarmament was reaching agreement to prevent the further spread of nuclear weapons. In November 1961, the General Assembly, following a request by Ireland that it discuss the prevention of a wider dissemination of nuclear weapons, called on nuclear weapon States to conclude an international agreement under which they would refrain from relinquishing control of nuclear weapons and from transmitting the information necessary for their manufacture to States not possessing such weapons, and those States would undertake not to manufacture or otherwise acquire control of such weapons [resolution 1665 (XVI)]. In making the request, Ireland said that its proposal was aimed at preventing the danger of a nuclear war from becoming greater—during the period of time it must take to evolve and strengthen a generally accepted system of world security based on international law and law enforcement. In 1965 and 1966, the Assembly called for the early conclusion of a treaty to prevent the proliferation of nuclear weapons and requested the Eighteen-Nation Committee on Disarmament to work towards the achievement of that objective and to report to it in 1968.

Treaty on Non-Proliferation of Nuclear Weapons

Report of the Conference of the Eighteen-Nation Committee on Disarmament on the non-proliferation of nuclear weapons

The Conference of the 18 Nation Committee on Disarmament reconvened in Geneva, Switzerland, from January 18 to March 14, 1968. In view of the urgency of concluding a treaty on the non-proliferation of nuclear weapons, and pursuant to a General Assembly resolution of December 19, 1967, the Conference devoted this period exclusively to the negotiation of the treaty. By the same resolution the General Assembly had also asked the Committee to report on before 15 March 1968 and had decided it would resume its session at an early date after 15 March to consider the report.

Consideration by General Assembly of Treaty on Non-Proliferation of Nuclear Weapons

As decided by the General Assembly on December 19, 1967, an agenda item entitled, "Non-proliferation of nuclear weapons : report of the Conference of the 18 Nation Committee on Disarmament", was maintained on the agenda of the General Assembly's twenty-second session. This session was resumed on April 24, 1968.

The General Assembly had the report of the Conference of the 18 Nation Committee on Disarmament before it, which were annexed the text of a draft treaty on the non-proliferation of nuclear weapons, submitted on March 11, 1968 by the USSR and the United States—Co-Chairmen of the Conference—and other related Conference documents.

The Assembly referred the agenda item to its First Committee which discussed it at meetings held between April 26 and June 10, 1968.

On 31st May, the representatives of the USSR and the United States...agreed to certain revisions of the text of the draft treaty on the non-proliferation of nuclear weapons, which were accepted by the sponsors of the revised draft resolution.

On June 10, 1968, the First Committee approved the 48-power draft resolution...

On June 12, the text was adopted at a plenary meeting of the General Assembly.

The General Assembly,

Recalling its resolutions 2346 A (XXII) of 19 December 1967, 2153 A (XXI) of 17 November 1966, 2149 (XXI) of 4 November 1966, 2028 (XX) of 19 November 1965, and

1965 (XVI) of 4 December 1961.

Convinced of the urgency and great importance of preventing the spread of nuclear weapons and of intensifying international co-operation in the development of peaceful applications of atomic energy.

Having considered the report of the Conference of the 18 Nation Committee of Disarmament, dated 14 March 1968, and appreciative of the work of the Committee on the elaboration of the draft non-proliferation treaty, which is attached to that report.

Convinced that, pursuant to the provisions of the treaty, all signatories have the right to engage in research, production and use of nuclear energy for peaceful purposes and will be able to acquire source and special fissionable materials, as well as equipment for the processing, use and production of nuclear material for peaceful purposes.

Convinced further that an agreement to prevent the further proliferation of nuclear weapons must be followed as soon as possible by effective measures on the cessation of the nuclear arms race and on nuclear disarmament, and that the non-proliferation treaty will contribute to this aim.

Affirming that in the interest of international peace and security both nuclear weapon and non-nuclear weapon States carry the responsibility of acting in accordance with the principles of the Charter of the United Nations that the sovereign equality of all States shall be respected, that the threat or use of force in international relations shall be refrained from and that international disputes shall be settled by peaceful means.

1. *Commends* the Treaty on the Non-Proliferation of Nuclear Weapons, the text of which is annexed to the present resolution;
2. *Requests* the Depositary Governments to open the Treaty for signature and ratification at the earliest possible date;

3. *Expresses the hope* for the widest possible adherence to the Treaty by both nuclear weapon and non-nuclear weapon States;
4. *Requests* the Conference of the 18 Nations Committee on Disarmament and the nuclear weapon States urgently to pursue negotiations on effective measures relating to the cessation of the nuclear arms race at an early date and to nuclear disarmament, and on a treaty on general and complete disarmament under strict and effective international control;
5. *Requests* the Conference of the 18 Nation Committee on Disarmament to report on the progress of its work to the General Assembly at its twenty-third session.

Annex

Treaty on the Non-Proliferation of Nuclear Weapons

The States concluding this Treaty, thereinafter referred to as the "parties to the Treaty".

Considering the devastation that would be visited upon all mankind by a nuclear war and the consequent need to make every effort to avert the danger of such a war and to take measures to safeguard the security of peoples,

Believing that the proliferation of nuclear weapons would seriously enhance the danger of nuclear war,

In conformity with resolutions of the United Nations General Assembly calling for the conclusion of an agreement on the prevention of wider dissemination of nuclear weapons,

Undertaking to co-operate in facilitating the application of International Atomic Energy Agency safeguards on peaceful nuclear activities,

Expressing their support for research, development and other efforts to further the application, within the framework of the International Atomic Energy Agency safeguards system, of the principle of safeguarding effectively the flow of source and special fissionable materials by use of instruments and other techniques at certain strategic points.

Affirming the principle that the benefits of peaceful applications of nuclear technology, including any technological by-products which may be derived by nuclear weapons States from the development of nuclear explosive devices, should be available for peaceful purposes to all parties to the Treaty, whether nuclear weapon or non-nuclear weapon States.

Convinced that, in furtherance of this principle, all Parties to the Treaty are entitled to participate in the fullest possible exchange of scientific information for, and to contribute alone or in co-operation with other States, to the further development of the applications of atomic energy for peaceful purposes.

Declaring their intention to achieve at the earliest possible date the cessation of the nuclear arms race and to undertake effective measures in the direction of nuclear disarmament,

Urging the co-operation of all States in the attainment of this objective,

Recalling the determination expressed by the parties to the 1963 Treaty banning nuclear weapon tests in the atmosphere, in outer space and under water in its preamble to seek to achieve the discontinuance of all test explosions of nuclear weapons for all time and to continue negotiations to this end.

Desiring to further the easing of international tension and the strengthening of trust between States in order to facilitate the cessation of the manufacture of nuclear weapons, the liquidation of all their existing stockpiles, and the elimination from national arsenals of nuclear weapons and the means of their delivery pursuant to a treaty on general and complete disarmament under strict and effective international control,

Recalling that, in accordance with the Charter of the United Nations, States must refrain in their international relations from the threat or use of force against the territorial integrity or political independence of any State, or in any other manner inconsistent with the purposes of the United Nations, and that the establishment and maintenance of international peace and security are to be promoted with the least diversion for armaments of the world's human and economic resources,

Have agreed as follows :

Article I

Each nuclear weapon State Party to the Treaty undertakes not to transfer any recipient whatsoever nuclear weapons or other nuclear explosive devices or control over such weapons or explosive devices directly, or indirectly; and not in any way to assist, encourage, or induce any non-nuclear weapon State to manufacture or otherwise acquire nuclear weapons or other nuclear explosive devices, or control over such weapons or explosive devices.

Article II

Each non-nuclear weapon State Party to the Treaty undertakes not to receive the transfer from any transfer or whatsoever of nuclear weapons or other nuclear explosive devices directly, or indirectly; not to manufacture or otherwise acquire nuclear weapons or other nuclear explosive devices; and not to seek or receive any assistance in the manufacture of nuclear weapons or other nuclear explosive devices.

Article III

1. Each non-nuclear weapon State Party to the Treaty undertakes to accept safeguards, as set forth in an agreement to be negotiated and concluded with the International Atomic Energy Agency in accordance with the Statute of the International Atomic Energy

Agency and the Agency's safeguards system, for the exclusive purpose of verification of the fulfilment of its obligations assumed under this Treaty with a view to preventing diversion of nuclear energy from peaceful uses to nuclear weapons or other nuclear explosive devices. Procedures for the safeguards required by this article shall be followed with respect to source or special fissionable material whether it is being produced, processed or used in any principal nuclear facility or is outside any such facility. The safeguards required by this article shall be applied on all source or special fissionable material in all peaceful nuclear activities within the territory of such State, under its jurisdiction, or carried out under its control anywhere.

2. Act State Party to the Treaty undertakes not to provide: (*a*) source or special fissionable material; or (*b*) equipment or material especially designed or prepared for the processing, use or production of special fissionable material, to any non-nuclear weapon State for peaceful purposes, unless the source or special fissionable material shall be subject to the safeguards required by this article.
3. The safeguards required by this article shall be implemented in a manner designed to comply with article IV of this Treaty, and to avoid hampering the economic or technological development of the Parties or international co-operation in the field of peaceful nuclear activities, including the international change of nuclear material and equipment for the processing, use or production of nuclear material for peaceful purposes in accordance with the provisions of this article and the principle of safeguarding set forth in the Preamble of the Treaty.
4. Non-nuclear weapons States Party to the Treaty

shall conclude agreements with the International Atomic Energy Agency to meet the requirements of this article either individually or together with other States in accordance with the Statute of the International Atomic Energy Agency. Negotiation of such agreements shall commence within 180 days from the original entry into force of this Treaty. For States depositing their instruments of ratification or accession after the 180 days period, negotiation of such agreements shall commence not later than the date of such deposit. Such agreements shall enter into force not later than eighteen months after the date of initiation of negotiations.

Article IV

1. Nothing in this Treaty shall be interpreted as affecting the inalienable right of all the Parties to the Treaty to develop research, production and use of nuclear energy for peaceful purposes without discrimination and in conformity with articles I and II of this Treaty.
2. All the Parties to the Treaty undertake to facilitate, and have the right to participate in the fullest possible exchange of equipment, materials and scientific and technological information for the peaceful uses of nuclear energy. Parties to the Treaty in a position to do so and shall also co-operate in contributing alone or together with other States or international organisations to the further development of the applications of nuclear energy for peaceful purposes, especially in the territories of non-nuclear weapon States Party to the Treaty, with due consideration for the needs of the developing areas of the world.

Article V

Each Party to the Treaty undertakes to take appropriate measures to ensure that, in accordance with this Treaty, under appropriate international observation and through appropriate international procedures, potential benefits from any peaceful applications of nuclear explosions will be made available to non-nuclear weapon States Party to the Treaty on a non-discriminatory basis and that the charge to such Parties for the explosive devices used will be as low as possible and exclude any charge for research and development. Non-nuclear weapon, States Party to the Treaty shall be able to obtain such benefits, pursuant to a special international agreement or agreements, through an appropriate international body with adequate representation of non-nuclear weapon States. Negotiations on this subject shall commence as soon as possible after the Treaty enters into force. Non-nuclear weapon States Party to the Treaty so desiring may also obtain such benefits pursuant to bilateral agreements.

Article VI

Each of the Parties to the Treaty undertakes to pursue negotiations in good faith on effective measures relating to cessation of the nuclear arms race at an early date and to nuclear disarmament and on a treaty on general and complete disarmament under strict and effective international control.

Article VII

Nothing in this Treaty affects the right of any group of States to conclude regional treaties in order to assure the total absence of nuclear weapons in their respective territories.

Article VIII

1. Any Party to the Treaty may propose amendments to this Treaty. The text of any proposed amendment shall be submitted to the Depositary Governments which shall circulate it to all parties to the Treaty. Thereupon, if requested to do so by one third or

more of the Parties to the Treaty, the Depositary Governments shall convene a conference, to which they shall invite all the Parties to the Treaty, to consider such an amendment.

2. Any amendment to this Treaty must be approved by a majority of the votes of all the parties to the Treaty, including the votes of all nuclear weapon States party to the Treaty and all other Parties which, on the data the amendment is circulated, are members of the Board of Governors of the International Atomic Energy Agency. The amendment shall enter into force for each Party that deposits its instrument of ratification of the amendment upon the deposit of such instruments of ratification by a majority of all the Parties, including the instruments of ratification of all nuclear weapon States Party to the Treaty and all other Parties which, on the date the amendment is circulated, are members of the Board of Governors of the International Atomic Energy Agency. Thereafter, it shall enter into force for any other Party upon the deposit of its instrument of ratification of the amendment.
3. Five years after the entry into force of this Treaty, a conference of Parties to the Treaty shall be held in Geneva, Switzerland, in order to review the operation of this Treaty with a view to assuring that the purposes of the Preamble and the provisions of the Treaty are being realised. At intervals of five years thereafter, a majority of the Parties to the Treaty may obtain, by submitting a proposal to this effect to the Depositary Governments, the convening of further conferences with the same objective of reviewing the operation of the Treaty.

Article IX

1. This Treaty shall be open to all States for signature. Any State which does not sign the Treaty before its entry into force in accordance with paragraph 3 of this article may accede to it at any time.
2. This Treaty shall be subject to ratification by signatory States. Instruments of ratification and instruments of accession shall be deposited with the Governments of the United Soviet Socialist Republics, the United Kingdom of Great Britain and Northern Ireland and the United States of America, which are hereby designated the Depositary Governments.
3. This Treaty shall enter into force after its ratification by the States, the Governments of which are designated Depositaries of the Treaty, and 40 other States signatory to this Treaty and the deposit of their instruments of ratification. For the purposes of this Treaty, a nuclear weapon State is one which has manufactured and exploded a nuclear weapons or other nuclear explosive device prior to January 1, 1967.
4. For States whose instruments of ratification or accession are deposited subsequent to the entry into force of this Treaty, it shall enter into force on the date of the deposit of their instruments of ratification or accession.
5. The Depositary Governments shall promptly inform all signatory and acceding States of the date of each signature, the date of deposit of each instrument of ratification or accession, the date of the entry into force of this Treaty, and the date of receipt of any requests for convening a conference or other notices.
6. This Treaty shall be registered by the Depositary Governments pursuant to Article 102 of the Charter of the United Nations.

Article X

1. Each Party shall in exercising its national sovereignty have the right to withdraw from the Treaty if it decides that extraordinary events, related to the subject-matter of this Treaty, have jeopardised the supreme interests of its country. It shall give notice of such withdrawal to all other Parties to the Treaty and to the United Nations Security Council three months in advance. Such notice shall include a statement of the extraordinary events regards as having jeopardised its supreme interests.
2. Twenty-five years after the energy into force of the Treaty, a conference shall be convened to decide whether the Treaty shall continue in force indefinitely, or shall be extended for an additional fixed period or periods. This decision shall be taken by a majority of the Parties to the Treaty.

The nuclear non-proliferating Treaty entered into force on March 5, 1970; as at March 31, 1995, there were 175 parties to it. On the basis of the Treaty, a global nuclear non-proliferation regime has been established, supported by the safeguards system of the International Atomic Energy Agency to prevent the diversion of nuclear material to military activities. Four conferences have been held (1975, 1980, 1985 and 1990) to review the Treaty's operation. The 1995 conference will decide on the Treaty's extension.

Sea-bed Treaty

Another important achievement in preventing the further spread of nuclear weapons was the successful conclusion in 1970 of a Treaty on the Prohibition of the Emplacement of Nuclear Weapons and Other Weapons of Mass Destruction on the Sea-bed and the Ocean Floor and in the Subsoil Thereof. Parties to this Treaty, which was jointly proposed by the United States and the USSR, undertook not to implant nuclear weapons or other weapons of mass destruction, as well as structures, launching installations or other facilities designed for storing, testing or using such weapons, in the sea-bed zone or on the ocean floor. The General Assembly, in commanding the Treaty to Members in December 1970, expressed the conviction that the prevention of a nuclear-arms race on the sea-bed and the ocean floor served the interests of maintaining world peace and reducing international tensions. It also recognised the common interest of mankind in reserving the sea-bed and the ocean floor exclusively for peaceful purposes. The Treaty was signed on February 11, 1971 and entered into force on May 18, 1972.

Nuclear Test-Ban Treaty

The first concrete step in the halting and eventual banning of nuclear testing was the adoption in 1963 of the Treaty banning Nuclear Weapon Tests in the Atmosphere, in Outer Space and under Water (also known as the partial Test-Ban Treaty). Parties to that Treaty expressed the aspiration to achieve the discontinuance of all test explosions of nuclear weapons for all time. This determination was also recalled in the 1968 Treaty on the Non-Proliferation of Nuclear Weapons. However, the goal of a comprehensive ban on nuclear testing could not be realised as the question of the suspension of nuclear and thermo-nuclear tests still remained to be resolved. It was first raised by India in August 1959, and in 1969 the basic differences remained among the members of the Disarmament Commission with regard to extending the test ban of the partial test-ban Treaty to underground tests. The USSR favoured the conclusion of an immediate agreement based on national means of verification, while the United States preferred some form of on-site inspection. In April 1969, Sweden submitted proposals for a possible treaty banning underground tests, except for peaceful purposes, and for the international exchange of seismological data.

Suspension of Nuclear and Thermo-nuclear Tests

The urgent need for suspension of nuclear and thermo-nuclear tests was discussed at the 1971 session of the General Assembly during the disarmament debate in the Assembly's First Committee.

On December 16, 1971, the General Assembly adopted three resolutions concerning the suspension of nuclear and thermo-nuclear testing.

By the first of these—resolution 2828 A (XXVI)—the Assembly reiterated solemnly and most emphatically its condemnation of all nuclear weapon tests and urged the Governments of the nuclear weapon States to half all such tests at the earliest possible date and in any case, not later than August 5, 1973. In taking this decision, the Assembly expressed its conviction that whatever might be the differences on the question of verification, there was no valid reason to delay the conclusion of a comprehensive test ban.

The Assembly also asked the Secretary General to transmit the resolution to the nuclear weapon States and to inform the Assembly at its 1972 session of any measures taken in implementation.

By the second resolution, adopted on December 16, 1971, the General Assembly : (1) appealed to the nuclear powers to desist from carrying out further nuclear tests of any kind; (2) urged all nuclear powers to reach agreement on a cessation of tests without delay; and (3) requested the nuclear powers not to deploy nuclear weapons of mass destruction. By the preamble to this resolution, the Assembly called attention to the health and other hazards arising from nuclear testing.

In its third decision on the question, the Assembly stressed anew the urgency of bringing to a half all nuclear weapon testing in all environments by all States. The Assembly urged all States to adhere without delay to the Treaty Banning Nuclear Weapons Tests in the Atmosphere, in outer space and under water and meanwhile to refrain from testing in the environments covered by that Treaty. It called on all Governments conducting nuclear weapons tests, particularly those of parties to the partial test ban Treaty, immediately to undertake unilateral or negotiated measures of restraint to suspend testing or reduce the size and number of tests, pending the early entry into force of a comprehensive ban.

The Assembly also urged Governments to develop and use more effectively existing capabilities for seismological identification of underground tests in order to facilitate the monitoring of a comprehensive test ban. It asked the Conference of the Committee on Disarmament (CCD) to give highest priority to an underground test ban treaty and asked testing Governments, in particular, to take an active and constructive part in developing in CD specific proposals for such a ban.

Finally, the Assembly expressed the hope that these efforts would enable all States to sign in the near future a treaty banning underground tests.

Comprehensive Test-ban Treaty

Multilateral discussions relating to a comprehensive test ban continued in the Conference on Disarmament. The General Assembly in the latter half of the 1980s called on the parties to the partial test-ban Treaty to hold a conference to convert that Treaty into a total ban. An Amendment Conference was held in New York in January 1991 but could not arrive at a substantive decision on conversion or agree on its suitability as the forum for achieving a comprehensive test ban. However, the president of the Conference, at its request, continued to conduct consultations on the matter. The Assembly (resolution 46/29) requested the Conference on Disarmament to intensify its work on specific and interrelated test-ban issues.

The USSR, on 6 August 1985, unilaterally declared a moratorium on all its nuclear explosive testing for a limited time—eventually 18 months. Between 1988 and 1992, there was a progressive and considerable reduction in the total number of nuclear tests conducted by all the nuclear weapon States. In October 1991, the USSR again unilaterally declared an immediate moratorium. This led, in 1992, to declarations of unilateral moratoriums by France and by the United States; the United Kingdom maintained a *de facto* moratorium. As of March 1995, no further tests have been conducted by France, the Russian Federation, the United Kingdom or the United States.

...the Conference gave the *Ad Hoc* Committee, mandate to negotiate a comprehensive nuclear-test-ban treaty and requested the Chairman to conduct consultations in the inter-sessional period—between 3 September 1993 and 17 January 1994—on the specific mandate, of the organisation. On the basis of that action, the *Ad Hoc* Committee's Chairman initiated consultations on adopting specific wording for a negotiating mandate and on organising the negotiations to begin in January 1994.

The *Ad Hoc* Committee also discussed a draft comprehensive test-ban treaty proposed by Sweden in June, for which verification protocol were yet to be prepared. It devoted considerable attention to questions related to verification, a crucial element of the future treaty... Some of the issues discussed during the session were : (*a*) the substantial role that a global seismic monitoring network would have, especially in underground testing; (*b*) the possible use of additional non-seismic verification technologies to detect nuclear tests in various environments, including in relation to evasion, and the possible use of such techniques to detect pre-testing preparations; (*c*) the costs of a future verification system *vis-a-vis* its capabilities; (*d*) the implementing agency, its powers, functions and costs; (*e*) the close interrelationship between applicable verification techniques and the scope of obligations under the treaty; and (*f*) a possible mix of national and international means of verification, taking into account cost effectiveness.

Moratoriums on Testing

(In 1993), there were developments on moratoriums on testing, pending the achievement of a comprehensive test-ban treaty, which were closely connected with the unilateral moratoriums that had been declared or extended by three nuclear weapon States—France, the Russian Federation and the United States—in 1992.

On 2 July 1993, President William Clinton of the United States announced his decision to extend the 1992 United States moratorium on nuclear testing, at least until the end of September 1994, as long as no other nation tested, and called on the other nuclear Powers to do the same. If those nations were to join the United States in observing the moratorium, the President said, the five nuclear Powers would be in the strongest possible position to negotiate a comprehensive nuclear-test ban and to discourage other nations from developing their own nuclear arsenals. If, however, the moratorium was broken by another nation, approval would be sought from the United States Congress for additional tests.

In a 5 October statement, China informed the Secretary General that it had conducted an underground nuclear test. It stated that it possessed a small number of nuclear weapons entirely for the purpose of self-defence and that it stood for the complete prohibition and thorough destruction of nuclear weapons and for a comprehensive nuclear-test ban. China believed that a comprehensive test-ban treaty would have positive significance and it would take an active part in the negotiating process. After the treaty had been concluded and had come into effect. China would abide by it and carry out no more nuclear tests. Several States, either at the time the text was announced or later in the First Committee, voiced disappointment that China had resumed nuclear testing. On 21st October, the Russian Federation, expressing deep regret over China's action, declared its intention to continue to adhere to the nuclear-testing moratorium, of which it had been the initiator, while retaining the right to reconsider its decision in the event of further unfavourable developments in the nuclear-testing area.

In December 1993, the General Assembly (resolution 48/70) supported the commencement of multilateral negotiations on a comprehensive nuclear-test-ban treaty. Parallel to this effort was that of the parties to the 1963 Treaty Banning Nuclear Weapon Tests in the Atmosphere, in Outer Space and under Water which held an Amendment Conference on 10 August 1993. They agreed to pursue the work on a comprehensive test ban in the Amendment Conference and the Conference on Disarmament.

Chemical and Biological Weapons

In 1925, concerned with the possible use of chemical and bacteriological weapons in war, 42 States signed the Geneva Protocol for the Prohibition of the Use in War of Asphyxiating. Poisonous or other gases, and of Bacteriological Methods of Warfare. Its general objectives were reinforced by the General Assembly in 1947, when it recommended that the Security Council consider proposals for the adoption of measures, *inter alia,* for the early general regulation of all other major weapons adaptable to mass destruction. One issue that impeded progress with respect to chemical and biological weapons was the question of whether these two categories of weapons should be dealt with jointly or separately.

The use of chemical and bacteriological weapons was brought to the attention of the United Nations in March 1952 during consideration of the work programme of the Disarmament Commission, when the USSR asked the Commission to consider, with reference to charges of the use of bacterial weapons in Korea and China, the violation of the prohibition of bacterial warfare so as to prevent its further use and to bring the violators to accounts. The request was not accepted by the Commission but the issue was later considered by the Security Council.

Bacterial Warfare

The following item was included in the provisional agenda of the 577th meeting of the Security Council on 18 June 1952 by the President (representative of the USSR): "Appeal to States to accede to and ratify the Geneva Protocol of 1925 for the prohibition of the use of bacterial warfare". Following a proposal by the representative of the United States, the item was changed to read: "Question of an appeal to States to accede and ratify the Geneva Protocol of 1925 for the prohibition of the use of bacterial warfare"...

The Security Council considered the question at its 577th to 579th and 581st to 583rd meetings between 18 and 26 June, 1952. Before it was a draft resolution by the USSR, under which the Council, having regard to the existence of differences of opinion concerning the admissibility of the use of bacterial weapons, noting that the use of such weapons had been justly condemned by world public opinion, as expressed in the signature by 42 States of the Geneva Protocol on 17 June 1925, would decide to appeal to all States, both Members and non-members, which had not yet acceded or ratified the Protocol, to accede and to ratify it.

Introducing his draft resolution, the President, speaking as the representative of the USSR, stressed the importance of the Geneva Protocol as a factor in restraining the use of bacterial and chemical weapons by the aggressive States which had precipitated the Second World War. He said that 48 States, including all of the Great Powers, had signed or acceded to the Protocol, and only six states, Brazil, El Salvador, Japan, Nicaragua, the United States and Uruguay, had not ratified it. The development of the production of bacterial and chemical weapons, the preparations being made in certain countries for bacterial warfare and the differences of opinion among statesmen and leaders on the use of bacterial weapons created a threat to the peace.

During the debate in the Council, the following points of view emerged. The representatives of Chile, China, Greece, Turkey, the United Kingdom and the United States concurred in the view that the USSR proposals had been timed to coincide with an organised propaganda campaign on the part of the USSR and its supporters that the United Nations Forces in Korea had used germ warfare. The proposals therefore could not be accepted as a genuine effort to secure the prohibition of bacterial weapons. Moreover, these representatives maintained, however praiseworthy and humane the provisions of the Geneva Protocol might have been, they were now obsolete since they contained no safeguards or guarantees and were not accompanied by any system of international control. Mere declarations, they argued, could not secure any real or effective control. What was really needed, they said, was a comprehensive plan of disarmament which would guard against aggression. They, therefore, supported United States motion that the question be referred to the Disarmament Commission.

At the 583rd meeting of the Security Council on June 26, 1952, the USSR draft resolution was rejected. There was one vote in favour (USSR) and 10 abstentions.

The issue of bacterial warfare was further considered during June and July 1952 at four meetings of the Security Council. At that time, there were contentious debates and serious charges and counter-charges between the United States and USSR representatives concerning the use of bacterial weapons in Korea. Various draft resolutions put to the vote were not adopted because of the negative vote of a permanent member of the Council.

At the request of the United States, the General Assembly considered the matter during its March/April 1953 session. The Assembly decided [resolution 706 (VII)] that after the President had received acceptance of the proposal to investigate the issue, a commission, comprising Brazil, Egypt, Pakistan, Sweden and Uruguay, should be established to investigate the charges. Replies were received only from Japan, the Republic of Korea and the United States. The Assembly further considered the matter at its October session and decided [resolution 714 (VIII)] to refer to the Disarmament Commission for consideration a draft resolution proposed by the USSR which would have the Assembly call on all States that had not done so to accede to the 1925 Geneva Protocol prohibiting the use of bacterial weapons.

At the August meeting the Disarmament Commission, the United States had made a statement on bacterial warfare, emphasising that its elimination must be an essential part of a comprehensive disarmament programme. Such a programme should include safeguards for disclosure and verification and provide for the progressive curtailment, dismantling and destruction of stockpiles of bacterial weapons and related appliances. In September, the United States subsequently submitted a working paper setting out its proposals for the elimination of bacterial weapons in connection with the elimination of all major weapons adaptable to mass destruction.

Convention on Bacteriological Weapons

The General Assembly and the negotiating body, the Conference of the Committee on Disarmament, continued to work on all aspects of the problem of the elimination of chemical and bacteriological (biological) weapons. In 1969, two proposals for a draft convention in the prohibition of the development, production and stockpiling and the destruction of such weapons were submitted to the General Assembly for consideration, one by Bulgaria, the Byelorussian SSR, Czechoslovakia, Hungary, Mangolia, Poland, Romania, the Ukrainian SSR and the USSR, and the other by the United Kingdom. The two drafts reflected the differences between the major blocs on the approach to such a convention. The USSR and many other States supported a joint treatment of chemical and bacteriological (biological) weapons in a comprehensive convention, while the United States and the United Kingdom and others preferred a separate convention banning biological weapons as a first step. In 1971, agreement was reached on separating these two categories of weapons. Subsequently, on the basis of draft texts submitted by the USSR and the United States, the Conference of the Committee on Disarmament agreed on a draft convention.

In dealing with the question of chemical and bacteriological (biological) weapons at its 1971 session, the General Assembly's First Committee had before it the report of the Conference of the Committee on Disarmament to which was annexed the text of the draft convention on the prohibition of the development, production and stockpiling of bacteriological (biological) and toxin weapons and on their destruction. In the course of the debate in the First Committee, a majority of States gave general support to the draft convention and welcomed it as the first measure of genuine disarmament, providing for the elimination of one type of weapons of mass destruction. Satisfaction was also widely expressed over the fact that the draft convention was the result of compromise, reflecting the views and suggestions of many States.

At the same time, however, a number of Members expressed disappointment that it had not proved possible to achieve a joint prohibition of chemical and bacteriological (biological) weapons.

On December 16, 1971, the Assembly adopted a resolution by which it commanded the Convention on the Prohibition of the Development. Production and Stockpiling of Bacteriological (Biological) and Toxin Weapons and on their Destruction, and requested the depositary Governments to open it for signature and ratification at the earliest possible date. At the same time, it expressed hope for the widest possible adherence to the Convention.

By the preamble of this resolution, the Assembly, among other things, made the following points. It expressed its conviction of the importance and urgency of eliminating from the arsenals of States such dangerous weapons of mass destruction as those using chemical or bacteriological (biological) agents. The Assembly recognised the important significance of the Protocol for the Prohibition of the Use in War of Asphyxiating, Poisonous or Other Gases, and of Bacteriological Methods of Warfare, signed at Geneva, Switzerland, on June 17, 1925, and expressed its awareness also, of the contribution the Geneva Protocol had already made and continued to make to mitigating the heroes of war.

These Assembly decisions were set forth in resolution 2826 (XXVI), which was adopted by a recorded vote of 110 to 0, with 1 abstention. The text of the resolution was approved by the First Committee by acclamation on 8 December.

The Convention was further strengthened through review conferences held in 1980, 1986 and 1991. At the 1991 Review Conference, the parties to the Convention agreed to expand the confidence-building measures they had agreed to at the Second Review Conference. They also decided on the requirement that parties declare what legislation and other regulations they had enacted to implement the Convention's provisions and to control trade of pathogenic micro-organisms. In addition, the *Ad Hoc* Group of Governmental Experts to Identify and Examine Potential Verification Measures from a scientific and Technical Standpoint, established by the Third Review Conference, in its report, submitted in 1993, concluded that potential verification measures could be useful in enhancing confidence, through transparency, and that States parties were fulfilling their obligation, thereby strengthening the Convention. At the end of 1973 there were 130 parties to the Convention.

In September 1994, a special conference of the States parties was held to consider the experts' report. It decided to establish a further *Ad Hoc* Group to consider appropriate measures, including possible verification, and to draft proposals to strengthen the Convention, to be included, as appropriate, in a legally binding instrument.

Convention on Chemical Weapons

The parties to the 1971 Convention on bacteriological (biological) weapons had undertaken, by the terms of article IX of that Convention, to continue negotiations with a view to reaching early agreement on a comprehensive ban on chemical weapons. This intention was reinforced by the General Assembly in November 1972 [resolution 2933 (XXVII)] Multilateral negotiations on the elaboration of a global convention banning chemical weapons were conducted within the framework of the Conference on Disarmament through its *Ad Hoc* Committee on Chemical Weapons.

After more than a decade of negotiations, the Conference on Disarmament adopted the Convention on the Prohibition of the Development, Production,

Stockpiling and Use of Chemical Weapons and on Their Destruction in 1992. It was the first disarmament agreement negotiated within a multilateral framework. It provided for eliminating an entire category of weapons of mass destruction.

On September 3, 1992, the Conference on Disarmament adopted the report of the *Ad Hoc* Committee and its appendix containing the draft convention and a text on establishing a preparatory commission for the Organisation for the Prohibition of Chemical Weapons. The report also incorporated statements of members on their positions regarding the Convention as a whole and on specific provisions. The Conference agreed by consensus to transmit the draft Convention to the General Assembly.

The Convention on the Prohibition of the Development, Production, Stockpiling and Use of Chemical Weapons and on Their Destruction consisted of a preamble, 24 articles and three annexes. The Convention was to enter into force 180 days after the date of the deposit of the sixty-fifth instrument of ratification, but in no case earlier than two years after its opening for signature in January 1993.

Three annexes—on Chemicals; Implementation and Verification; and Protection of Confidential Information—formed an integral part of the Convention.

On November 30, 1992, the General Assembly welcomed the draft convention and requested the Secretary General to open it for signature in Paris on January 13, 1993. It called on States to sign the convention and to ensure its effective implementation. By the end of 1993. 154 States had signed and 4 States had ratified the Convention.

Conventional Weapons

Reduction of armaments

The question of the reduction of armaments arose in 1946 within the context of the General Assembly's consideration of a USSR proposal that the presence of troops of the United Nations in non-enemy territories be discussed by the Assembly. The USSR suggested that all Member States submit information on their armed forces and air and naval bases located in the Territory of non-enemy States. It had also accepted a United States proposal to include information on Allied troops in former enemy States as well. The USSR, therefore, proposed that the Assembly recommend that the Security Council ask Member States to furnish information on the number of their armed forces present in both categories of territory as well as information on air and naval bases and the size of their garrisons. The United Kingdom amended the proposal to the effect that the submission of information of armed forces was only one aspect of the larger problem of the regulation and reduction of armaments, and that the scope of the information be widened to include all enlisted forces wherever stationed; that it be submitted by January 1, 1947; and that it be subject to a United Nations verification system. On November 28, 1946, the First Committee, after considering further amendments, accepted the United Kingdom proposal as an amendment to the USSR proposal with the exception of the verification provision.

The General Assembly took up the issue on December 10, 1946 and was unable to arrive at a compromise on the various amendments submitted.

... the General Assembly decided to refer the matter to the Sub-Committee of the First Committee on Disarmament.

After long discussing the Sub-Committee concluded that there was no practical possibility of arriving at a balanced text incorporating the amendments submitted by the USSR and the United Kingdom. Moreover, the Sub-Committee found that in dealing with the problem of disarmament it had at the same time dealt with the presence of troops on foreign territory. In the circumstances the Sub-Committee considered to propose it logical that the resolution adopted by the First Committee be dropped and instead the following resolution be adopted :

The General Assembly

Desirous of implementing, as soon as possible, the resolution of December 14, 1946 on the Principles governing the Regulation and Reduction of armaments;

Calls Upon the Security Council to determine, as soon as possible, the information which the States Members should be called upon to furnish, in order to give effect to this resolution.

The General Assembly at its 63rd plenary meeting on December 14, 1946, adopted the substitute resolution as quoted by 36 votes to 6, with 4 abstentions.

Principles Governing the General Regulation and Reduction of Armaments

By a letter of October 29, 1946, the delegation of USSR, submitted a "Proposal Concerning the General Reduction of Armaments", for inclusion in the agenda of the General Assembly. At its 46th plenary meeting on October 31, 1946, the Assembly referred the matter to the First Committee.

On November 26, 1946, the USSR delegation submitted a supplementary proposal concerning the establishment of a system of international control and inspection. The USSR delegation subsequently submitted the following resolution combining the above-mentioned proposals :

1. With a view to strengthening peace and international security in conformity with the aims and principles of the United Nations, the General Assembly recognises the necessity of a general reduction of armaments.
2. The implementing of the decision concerning the reduction of armaments should include as the

primary object the prohibition to produce and use atomic energy for military purposes.

3. To ensure the adoption of measures for the reduction of armaments and prohibiting of the use of atomic energy for military purposes, there shall be established within the framework of the Security Council, which has the primary responsibility for international peace and security, international control operating on the basis of a special provision which should provide for the establishment of special organs of inspection for which purpose there shall be formed :
   (*a*) A Commission for the control of the execution of the decision regarding the reduction of armaments;
   (*b*) A Commission for the control of the execution of the decision regarding the prohibition of the use of atomic energy for military purposes.

The First Committee discussed the question of a general regulation and reduction of armaments at its 30th, 31st, 32nd, 34th, 38th and 44th meetings held on November 28, 29, 30 and December 2, 4 and 13 respectively. Commenting on the USSR delegation's proposal, the Soviet representative stressed the necessity for taking serious measures to put an end to the armament race. Not only armed personnel, but military technique and technical means of war must be considered in the problem of disarmament. The Soviet delegation attached particular importance in this connection to the problem of atomic energy. The conclusion of a convention prohibiting both the production and use of atomic weapons was the first step (the United Nations must take) if a programme of general disarmament was to be successful. The USSR resolution therefore included a specific recommendation to this effect.

Many representatives commented the USSR delegation for taking the initiative in submitting a proposal for the general reduction of armaments, and expressed agreement with the aims of the USSR resolution. A number of representatives, however, felt that the wording of the USSR resolution was too vague and that it was desirable to formulate more precisely the principles which would have to guide a general programme of disarmament.

At the 34th meeting of the First Committee the representative of the United States submitted the following draft resolution :

1. With a view to strengthening international peace and security in conformity with the purposes and principles of the United Nations, the General Assembly recognises the necessity of an early general regulation and reduction of armaments. Accordingly, the General Assembly recommends that the Security Council give prompt consideration to working out the practical measures, according to their priority, which are essential to provide for the general regulation and reduction of armaments pursuant to international treaties and agreements and to assure that such regulation and reduction will be generally observed by all participants and not unilaterally by only some of the participants.
2. The General Assembly recognises that essential to the general regulation and reduction of armaments is the early establishment of international control of atomic energy and other modern technological discoveries to ensure their use only for peaceful purposes. Accordingly, in order to ensure that the general regulation and reduction of armaments are directed towards the major weapons of modern warfare and not merely towards the minor weapons, the General Assembly recommends that the Security Council give five consideration to the report which the Atomic Energy Commission will make to the Security Council before December 31, 1946, and facilitate the progress of the work of that Commission.

3. The General Assembly further recognises that essential to the general regulation and reduction of armaments is the provision of practical and effective safeguards by way of inspection and other means to protect complying States against the hazards of violations and evasions. Accordingly, the General Assembly recommends to the Security Council that it give prompt consideration to the working out of proposals to provide such practical and effective safeguards in connection with the control of atomic energy and other limitations or regulation of armaments.
4. The General Assembly calls upon the Governments of all States to render every possible assistance to the Security Council and the atomic Energy Commission in order to promote the establishment of international peace and collective security with the least diversion for armaments of the world's human and economic resources.

At the 38th meeting of the First Committee the representative of the USSR announced his willingness to accept the United States resolution as a basis of discussion and submitted a number of amendments to that resolution which would render it acceptable to the USSR delegation.

At its 44th meeting on December 13, 1946, the First Committee, after making some further drafting changes, unanimously and by acclamation adopted the resolution recommended by the Sub-Committee. Likewise by unanimous vote, the General Assembly at its 63rd plenary meeting on December 14, 1946, adopted the resolution, which read as follows :

1. In pursuance of Article 11 of the Charter and with a view to strengthening international peace and security in conformity with the Purposes and Principles of the United nations.

1. The General Assembly

Recognises the necessity of an early general regulation and reduction of armaments and armed forces.

2. Accordingly

The General Assembly

Recommends that the Security Council give prompt consideration to formulating the practical measures, according to their priority, which are essential to provide for the general regulation and reduction of armaments and armed forces and to assure that such regulation and reduction of armaments and armed forces will be generally observed by all participants and not unilaterally by only some of the participants. The plans formulated by the Security Council shall be submitted by the Secretary General to the Members of the United Nations for consideration at a special session of the General Assembly. The treaties or conventions approved by the General Assembly shall be submitted to the signatory States for ratification in accordance with article 26 of the Charter.

(3) As an essential step towards the urgent objective of prohibiting and eliminating from national armaments atomic and all other major weapons adaptable now and in the future to mass destruction, and the early establishment of international control of atomic energy and other modern scientific discoveries and technical developments to ensure their use only for peaceful purposes.

3. The General Assembly

Urges the expeditious fulfilment by the Atomic Energy Commission of its terms of reference as set south in Section 5 of the General Assembly resolution of January 24, 1946.

4. In order to ensure that the general prohibition, regulation and reduction of armaments are directed

towards the major weapons of modern warfare and not merely towards the minor weapons.

4. The General Assembly

Recommends that the Security Council expedite consideration of the reports which the Atomic Energy Commission will make to the Security Council and that it facilitate the work of the Commission, and also that the Security Council expedite consideration of a draft convention or conventions for the creation of an international system of control and inspection, these conventions to include the prohibition of atomic and all other major weapons adaptable now and in the future to mass destruction and the control of atomic energy to the extent necessary to ensure its use only for peaceful purposes.

5. The General Assembly,

Further recognises that essential to the general regulation and reduction of armaments and armed forces is the provision of practical and effective safeguards by way of inspection and other means to protect complying States against the hazards of violations and evasions.

Accordingly,

The General Assembly

Recommends to the Security Council that it give prompt consideration to the working out of proposals to provide such practical and effective safeguards in connection with the control of atomic energy and the general regulation and reduction of armaments.

6. To ensure the adoption of measures for the early general regulation and reduction of armaments and armed forces, for the prohibition of the use of atomic energy for military purposes and the elimination from national armaments of atomic and all other major weapons adaptable now or in the future to mass destruction, and

for the control of atomic energy to the extent necessary to ensure its use only for peaceful purposes.

There shall be Established, within the framework of the Security Council, which bears the primary responsibility for the maintenance of international peace and security, an international system, as mentioned in paragraph 4, operating through special organs, which organs shall derive their powers and status from the convention or conventions under which they are established.

7. The General Assembly

Regarding the problem of security as closely connected with that of disarmament, Recommends the Security Council to accelerate as much as possible the placing at its disposal of the armed forces mentioned in Article 43 of the Charter.

Recommends the Members to undertake the progressive and balanced withdrawal, taking account of the needs of occupation, of their armed forces stationed in ex-enemy territories, and the withdrawal without delay of their armed forces stationed in the territories of Members without their consent freely and publicly expressed in treaties or agreements consistent with the Charter and not contradicting international agreements. Further recommends a corresponding reduction of national armed forces, and a general progressive and balanced reduction of national armed forces.

8. Nothing herein contained shall alter or limit the resolution of the General Assembly passed on 24 January 1946, creating the Atomic Energy Commission.

9. The General Assembly

Calls upon all Members of the United Nations to render every possible assistance to the Security Council and the Atomic Energy Commissions in order to promote the establishment and maintenance of international peace and collective security with the least diversion for armaments of the world's human and economic resources.

The general regulation and reduction of armaments and information on armed forces of the United Nations

By a letter dated December 27, 1947, addressed to the Secretary General, the representative of the USSR submitted a proposal regarding the implementation of the resolution adopted by the General Assembly on December 14, 1946, on the "Principles Governing the General Regulation and Reduction of Armaments". The letter advocated the establishment of a commission, to be composed of the representatives of countries members of the Security Council, which should be charged with preparing and submitting to the Council, within a period of not later than three months, proposals for the general regulation and reduction of armaments and armed forces.

At its 88th meeting on December 31, 1946, the Security Council placed the USSR proposal on its agenda, but discussion of the substance of the question was postponed to a later date. The United States representative, however, submitted a draft resolution at the meeting which proposed that the Security Council give first priority to the establishment of international control over atomic energy by considering and acting on the report of the Atomic Energy Commission to the Council.

The issue was further discussed at meetings of the Security Council held on January 9 and February 11, 1947, during which the views of the United States and USSR were reconciled. The final text of the resolution of the Secretary Council concerning the implementation of the resolutions of the General Assembly regarding the principles governing the general regulation and reduction of armaments and information on armed forces of the United Nations was as follows :

The Security Council, having accepted the resolution of the General Assembly of December 14, 1946 and recognising that the general regulation and reduction of armaments and armed forces constitute a most important measure for strengthening international peace and security and that the implementation of the resolution of the General Assembly on the subject is one of the most urgent and important tasks before the Security Council.

Resolves

1. to work out the practical measures for giving effect to the resolutions of the General Assembly on 14 December 1946 concerning, on the one hand, the general regulation and reduction of armaments and armed forces, and the establishment of international control to bring about the reduction of armaments and armed forces, and, on the other hand, information concerning the armed forces of the United Nations;
2. to consider as soon as possible the report submitted by the Atomic Energy Commission and to take suitable decisions in order to facilitate its work;
3. to set up a Commission consisting of representatives of the Members of the Security Council with instructions to prepare and to submit to the Security Council within the space, not more than three months, the proposals :
   (*a*) for the general regulation and reduction of armaments and armed forces; and
   (*b*) for practical and effective safeguards in connection with the general regulation and reduction of armaments which the Commission may be in a position to formulate in order to ensure the implementation of the above-mentioned resolutions of the General Assembly of December 14, 1946, in so far as these

resolutions relate to armaments within the new Commission's jurisdiction.

The Commission shall submit a plan of work to the Council for approval.

Those matters which fall within the competence of the Atomic Energy Commission as determined by the General Assembly Resolution of January 24, 1946 and December 14, 1946 shall be excluded from the jurisdiction of the Commission hereby established.

The title of the Commission shall be the Commission for Conventional Armaments. The Commission shall make such proposals as it may deem advisable concerning the studies which the Military Staff Committee and possibly other organs of the United Nations might be asked to undertake.

The Commission for Conventional Armaments held its first meeting at Lake Success on March 24, 1947. The Commission for Conventional Armaments was subsequently dissolved by the Assembly in 1951 and the Disarmament Commission, established in its place, was requested to consider proposals for the control of conventional weapons within the context of the process of general disarmament.

Convention on Certain Conventional Weapons

The objective of an early general regulation and reduction of armaments and armed forces, enunciated by the General Assembly in 1946, remained elusive. The growth in nuclear arsenals was also accompanied by increased stockpiles of conventional weapons as the arms race continued unabated. In 1978, the general Assembly, in the Final Document of its 10th special session, the first session devoted to disarmament, again called for negotiations on the balanced reduction of armed forces and of conventional weapons as well as on the limitation of international transfer of conventional weapons. It further called for international action to prohibit or restrict for humanitarian reasons the use of specific conventional weapons, including those which might be excessively injurious, cause unnecessary suffering or have indiscriminate effects.

The General Assembly took up the question of incendiary and other conventional weapons which might be subject to prohibition or restriction of use for humanitarian purposes and decided (resolution 32/152) to convene in 1979 a United Nations conference with a view of reaching agreement on banning such weapons. The United Nations Conference on Prohibitions or Restrictions of Use of Certain Conventional Weapons which may be deemed to be excessively injurious or to have indiscriminate effects met at Geneva from 10 to 28 September 1979 to work towards concluding a general treaty. The Conference produced partially agreed texts and adopted a resolution on small-calibre weapons, but was unable to resolve other issues. It decided to reconvene in 1980.

UN Conference on Prohibiting or Restricting use of Certain Conventional Weapons

The United Nations Conference on prohibiting or restricting use of certain excessively injurious or indiscriminate conventional weapons... resumed its work on September 15, 1980 at Geneva.

The Conference itself held four plenary meetings at its resumed session. On 10 October, it approved the reports of the Working Group, of the Committee of the whole and of a Drafting Committee. On the same date, it unanimously adopted its final report to the Assembly to which was annexed the Final Act of the Conference together with the texts of the Convention and its three Protocols. The Conference recommended that the Assembly commend the instruments to States with a view to achieving the widest possible adherence.

The report of the Conference was considered by the First Committee on 20 November 1980, when it approved a draft resolution for consideration by the General Assembly. On December 12, 1980, the Assembly adopted, without vote, resolution 35/153 commenting the Convention and the three Protocols :

The General Assembly

Recalling that, by its resolutions 32/152 and 33/70, it decided to convene in 1979 the United Nations Conference on Prohibitions or Restrictions of Use of Certain Conventional Weapons which may be deemed to be excessively injurious or to have indiscriminate effects and established the mandate of the Conference.

1. *Takes note with appreciation* of the Final Report of the United Nations Conference on Prohibitions and Restrictions of Use of Certain Conventional Weapons Which May be Deemed to Be Excessively Injurious or to Have Indiscriminate Effects, held at Geneva from 10 to 28 September 1979 and from 15 September to 10 October 1980;
2. *Welcomes* the successful conclusion of the Conference, which resulted in the adoption, on 10 October 1980, of the following instruments :
   (*a*) Convention on Prohibitions or Restrictions on the Use of Certain Conventional Weapons Which May Be Deemed to Be Excessively Injurious or to Have Indiscriminate Effects;
   (*b*) Protocol on Non-Detectable Fragmens (Protocol I);
   (*c*) Protocol on Prohibitions or Restrictions on the Use of Mines, Booby Traps and Other Devices (Protocol II);
   (*d*) Protocol on Prohibitions or Restrictions on the Use of Incendiary Weapons (Protocol III);
3. *Takes note* of article 3 of Convention, which stipulates that the Convention shall be open for

signature on 10 April 1981;

4. *Commends* the Convention and the three annexed Protocols to all States, with a view to achieving the widest possible adherence to these instruments;
5. *Notes* that, under article 8 of the Convention, conferences may be convened to consider amendments to the Convention or any of the annexed protocols, to consider additional protocols relating to other categories of conventional weapons not covered by the existing Protocols, or to review the scope and operation of the Convention and the Protocols annexed thereto and to consider any proposal for amendments to the Convention or to the existing Protocols and any proposals for additional protocols relating to other categories of conventional weapons not covered by the existing Protocols.
6. *Requests* the Secretary General, as the Depositary of the Convention and its annexed Protocols, to inform the General Assembly from time to time of the state of adherence to the Convention and its three annexed Protocols.

Convention

The Convention on Prohibitions or Restrictions on the Use of Certain Conventional Weapons Which May Be Deemed to Be Excessively Injurious or to Have Indiscriminate Effects consisted of a preamble and 11 articles.

It was to serve as the legal framework for the application of the three Protocols annexed to it, and it was based on such stated principles as the general principle of the protection of civilian population against the effects of hostilities, the principle of international law that the right to choose methods or means of warfare was not unlimited, and the principle that prohibited the employment of weapons and methods of warfare of a nature to cause superfluous injury, unnecessary suffering, or long-term and severe damage to the natural environment.

Article 1 included in the scope of the convention the situations referred to in the 1949 Geneva Conventions for the protection of war victims, as well as their Additional Protocol I providing protection in conflicts involving national liberation movements. The relationship between the 1949 Conventions and their Protocol and this Convention and its Protocols, and the circumstances in which the various instruments applied to States parties to a conflict in which both parties and non-parties to the relevant instruments were involved, were set forth in article 7.

The review mechanism contained in the Convention (article 8) included arrangements for convening a conference of States parties to consider amendments to the Convention and its Protocols, or for the development of new rules for prohibition or restriction. The convening of such a conference would take place if requested by a majority that was not less than 18 States parties, or by any State party if no conference had been convened for 10 years.

Other provisions prevented the Convention and its Protocols from detracting from obligations under international humanitarian law applicable in armed conflicts (article 2), provided for ratification, acceptance, approval or accession, as well as optional expressions of consent to be bound by any of the Protocols (article 4), contained an undertaking by States parties to disseminate the texts of the instruments to their armed forces (article 6), set forth the terms and means of denunciation of the instruments (article 9), and designated the United Nations Secretary General as Depositary and indicated his functions (article 10), one of which was to receive the six authentic texts—Arabic, Chinese, English, French, Russian and Spanish (article 11). The Convention was to be opened for signature at New York on April 10, 1981 (article 3), and the instruments were to enter into force separately six months after deposit of the twentieth instrument of ratification, acceptance, approval, accession or, in the case of each of the Protocols, notification of consent to be bound by it (article 5).

Protocols

The 26-word Protocol on Non-Detectable Fragments (Protocol I) prohibited the use of non-detectable fragmentation weapons against both civilians and combatants. The weapons in question were those composed of substances such as wood, glass or plastics which in the human body escaped detection by X-rays, making extraction difficult and prolonging suffering and risk of infection.

The Protocol on Prohibitions or Restriction on the Use of Mines, Booby Traps and Other Devices (Protocol II), consisting of nine articles and a technical annex, applied to the devices mentioned in its title, but not to the use of anti-ship mines at sea or in inland waterways (article 1).

Article 2 defined mines and booby traps, as well as the term "other devices", which meant manually emplaced munitions and devices, actuated by remote control or automatically after a lapse of time, and designed to kill, injure or damage.

Article 3 set general restrictions on the use of mines, booby traps and other devices. It prohibited in all circumstances the directing of weapons, either in offence, defence or by way of reprisals, against civilians, or the indiscriminate use meant placement which was not on or directed against a military objective, whose means of delivery could not be directed at a specific military objective, or which might be expected to cause incidental loss of civilian life, injuries or damage to non-military objectives which would be excessive in relation to the anticipated military advantage.

Other provisions restricted the use of mines (other than remotely delivered mines), booby traps and other devices in populated areas (article 4), and of remotely delivered mines (article 5). The locations of the latter type were to be recorded or they were to contain a mechanism for rendering them harmless. Article 6 prohibited the use of booby traps in the form of apparently harmless portable objects or attached to or associated with internationally recognised protective emblems, the wounded or dead, grave sites, medical facilities or supplies, products for children, animals, food or drink, civilian kitchen equipment, religious objects, historic monuments, works of art or places which constituted a cultural or spiritual heritage, or any booby trap designed to cause superfluous injury or unnecessary suffering.

The text contained guidelines for the recording and publication of the location of minefields, mines and booby traps (article 7) and for international co-operation in providing information on and assistance for the removal of such devices (article 9). Guidelines were also laid down for the protection of United Nations forces and missions from the effects of these devices (article 8).

A technical annex attached to Protocol II provided guidelines for recording the location of pre-planned minefields and of large-scale, pre-planned use of booby traps, by maps, diagrams or other records to indicate the extent of the affected area.

The Protocol on Prohibitions or Restrictions on the Use of Incendiary Weapons (Protocol III) was agreed after an attempt to develop rules for the protection of combatants was abandoned in the interest of a consensus. This was on the understanding that consideration of that question would be resumed during the follow-up to the Conference.

The two-article Protocol thus provided for the protection of civilians and civilian objects against incendiary weapons, as defined in the first article. Military objectives located within a concentration of civilians could not be the object of an air-delivered incendiary-weapons attack; such objectives which were clearly separated from civilian concentrations were excluded from these restrictions, provided that all feasible precautions were taken to limit the incendiary effects to the military objective and to avoid or minimise incidental civilian deaths, injury or damage. It prohibited making forests or other plant-cover the object of incendiary-weapons attack except when they concealed combatants or other military objectives or were themselves military objectives.

The Convention and Protocols entered into force in 1983.

Anti-personnel Mines

In 1993, the question had arisen of broadening the scope of the 1980 Convention to include matters related to the prohibition of certain conventional weapons considered to be excessively injurious, especially anti-personnel mines. An enormous quantity of mines had been sown on the territory of many countries causing suffering of civilians, not only in time of war but also after the cessation of hostilities. As a result, three related subjects were discussed : the Convention and its Protocol II (on mines); a moratorium on the export of anti-personnel mines; and assistance in mine clearance. In June, the Secretary General reported that he had instituted a co-ordinated programme for demining. In December, the General Assembly (resolution 48/79) welcomed the request by France to convene a conference to review the 1980 Convention and welcomed (resolution 48/7) the establishment of the Secretariat's mine-clearing programme. It also noted (resolution 48/75 K) the 85 million uncleared mines throughout the world which killed hundreds of persons each week and prohibited the return of refugees and internally displaced persons. The Assembly called on States to agree to a moratorium on the export of anti-personnel land-mines that posed grave dangers to civilian populations.

In 1994, in preparation for the autumn 1995 conference to review the Convention and its Protocols, a group of governmental experts of States parties met three times, focusing on Protocol II.

International Arms Transfers

Recent crises in various parts of the world have brought into sharper focus the necessity to curb illicit arms trade. The Register of Conventional Arms has become an important instrument in that endeavour.

(A study by) the group of experts encouraged States to make all their military activities as open as practicable and to ensure that they had the legal and administrative machinery to regulate and monitor effectively their arms transfers. It recommended establishing, as soon as possible, a universal and non-discriminatory arms transfer register under United Nations auspices and outlined the broad characteristics of such a register. The group further encouraged States to make efforts to achieve regional and sub-regional measures of transparency in relation to arms transfers by means of consultations, arrangements and agreements. The wider sharing of information on defence might be reflected in the provision of information to the United nations in the context of possible regional arrangements or both.

On 9 December 1991, on the recommendation of the First Committee, the General Assembly adopted resolution 46/36 L by recorded vote.

Transparency in armaments

The General Assembly,

7. *Requests* the Secretary General to establish and maintain at United Nations Headquarters in New York a universal and non-discriminatory Register of Conventional Arms, to include data on

international arms transfers as well as information provided by Member States on military holdings, procurement through national production and relevant policies, as set out in paragraph 10 below and in accordance with procedures and input requirements initially comprising those set out in the annex to the present resolution and subsequently incorporating any adjustments to the annex decided upon by the General Assembly at its forty-seventh session in the light of the recommendations of the panel referred to in paragraph 8 below;

8. *Also requests* the Secretary General, with the assistance of a panel of governmental technical experts to be nominated by him on the basis of equitable geographical representation, to elaborate the technical procedures and to make any adjustments to the annex to the present resolution necessary for the effective operation of the Register, and to prepare a report on the modalities for early expansion of the scope of the Register by the addition of further categories of equipment and inclusion of data on military holdings and procurement through national production, and to report to the General Assembly at its forty-seventh session;

9. *Calls upon* all Member States to provide annually for the Register data on imports and exports of arms in accordance with the procedures established by paragraphs 7 and 8 above;

10. *Invites* Member States, pending the expansion of the Register, also to provide to the Secretary General, with their annual report on imports and exports of arms, available background information regarding their military holdings, procurement through national production and relevant policies,

and requests the Secretary General to record this material and to make it available for consultation by Member States at their request.

ANNEX

Register of Conventional Arms

1. The Register of Conventional Arms ("the Register") shall be established, with effect from 1 January 1992, and maintained at the Headquarters of the United Nations in New York.
2. Concerning international arms transfers :
   (*a*) Member States are requested to provide data for the Register, addressed to the Secretary General, on the number of items in the following categories of equipment imported into or exported from their territory;

I. Battle tanks

A tracked or wheeled self-propelled armoured fighting vehicle with high cross-country mobility and a high level of self-protection, at least 16.5 metric tonnes unladen weight, with a high muzzle velocity direct fire main gun of at least 75 millimetres calibre.

II. Armoured combat vehicles

A Tracked or wheeled self-propelled vehicle, with armoured protection and cross-country capability, either : (*a*) designed and equipped to transport a squad of four or more infantrymen, or (*b*) armed with an integral or organic weapon of at least 20 millimetres calibre or an anti-tank missile launcher.

III. Large calibre artillery systems

A gun, howitzer, artillery piece combining the characteristics of a gun and a howitzer, mortar or multiple-launch rocket system, capable of engaging surface targets by delivering primarily indirect fire, with a calibre of 100 millimetres and above.

IV. Combat aircraft

A fixed-wing or variable-geometry wing aircraft armed and equipped to engage targets by employing guided missiles, unaided rockets, bombs, guns, cannons, or other weapons of destruction.

V. Attack helicopters

A rotary-wing aircraft equipped to employ anti-armour, air-to-ground, or air-to-air guided weapons and equipped with an integrated fire control and aiming system for these weapons.

VI. Warships

A vessel or submarine with a standard displacement of 850 metric tonnes or above, armed or equipped for military use.

VII. Missiles or missile systems

A guided rocket, ballistic or cruise missile capable of delivering a payload to a range of at least 25 kilometres, or a vehicle, apparatus or device designed or modified for launching such munitions.

(*b*) Data on imports provided under the present paragraph shall also specify the supplying State; data on exports shall also specify the recipient State and the State of origin if not the exporting State;

(*c*) Each Member State is requested to provide data on an annual basis by 30 April each year in respect of imports into and exports from their territory in the previous calendar year;

(*d*) The first such registration shall take place by 30 April 1993 in respect of the calendar year 1992;

(*e*) The data so provided shall be recorded in respect of each Member State;

(*f*) Arms "exports and imports" represent in the present resolution, including its annex, all forms of arms transfers under terms of grant, credit, barter or cash.

3. Concerning other interrelated information :
   (*a*) Member States are invited also to provide to the Secretary General available background information regarding their military holdings, procurement through national production, and relevant policies;
   (*b*) The information so provided shall be recorded in respect of each Member State.
4. The Register shall be open for consultation by representatives of Member States at any time.
5. In addition, the Secretary General shall provide annually a consolidated report to the General Assembly of the data registered, together with an index of the other interrelated information.

Disarmament Decades

The General Assembly had in 1959 [resolution 1378 (XIV)] proclaimed the goal of general and complete disarmament and in 1961 [resolution 1722 (XVI)] welcomed the agreed principles for disarmament negotiations by the United States and the USSR. Ten years later, in 1969, the goal was far from big achieved. Therefore, in the light of the increased militarisation of States and the ever-present threat of nuclear war, the United Nations declared the 1970, the 1980s and the 1990s as disarmament decades.

First Disarmament Decade

On December 16, 1969, the General Assembly adopted a resolution [2602 E (XXIV)] by which, among other things, it declared the 1970s as a Disarmament Decade and took decisions concerning the work of the Conference of the Committee on Disarmament (CCD)...

By the operative paragraphs of this resolution, the Assembly : (1) declared the 1970s as a Disarmament Decade; (2) called upon Governments to intensify without delay their concerned and concentrated efforts for effective measures relating to the cessation of the nuclear arms race at an early date and to nuclear disarmament and the elimination of other weapons of mass destruction, and for a treaty on general and complete disarmament under strict and effective international control; (3) requested the Conference of the Committee on Disarmament to resume its work as early as possible, bearing in mind that the ultimate goal was general and complete disarmament; (4) further requested CCD, while continuing intensive negotiations with a view to reaching the widest possible agreement on collateral measures, to work out at the same time a comprehensive programme, dealing with all aspects of the problem of the cessation of the arms race and general and complete disarmament under effective international control, which would provide the Conference with a guideline to chart the course of its further work and to report there on to the general Assembly at its twenty-fifth (1970) session; (5) decided to draw the attention of CCD to all pertinent proposals made during the First Committee's debates on disarmament; (6) recommended that consideration be given to channelling a substantial part of the resources freed by measures in the field of disarmament to promote the economic development of developing countries and, in particular, their scientific and technological progress; (7) requested the Secretary General and Governments to publicise the Disarmament Decade; and (8) requested the Secretary General to provide all appropriate facilities to further the implementation of this resolution.

Second Disarmament Decade

... The General Assembly on December 3, 1980 adopted, without vote, the Declaration of the 1980s as the

Second Disarmament Decade. The Declaration, whose elements had been prepared by the Disarmament Commission in May/June, was annexed to Assembly resolution 35/46...

The Declaration consisted of three main sections. A "General" section (section I) enumerated the objectives of the first Disarmament Decade (the 1970s) and briefly outlined the situation at the end of those 10 years, which had ended without the accomplishment of those objectives, although some limited agreements had been reached...

Section II, on "Goals and principles", listed the aims and expectations of the Decade. Consistent with the overall objective of general and complete disarmament under effective international control, the goals of the Decade should include : halting and reversing the arms race, particularly the nuclear arms race; concluding and implementing agreements on disarmament, particularly nuclear disarmament; strengthening international peace and security; and making available a substantial part of the resources released by disarmament measures to attain the objectives of the Third United Nations Development Decade (the 1980s)...

Section III of the Declaration set out in eight sub-sections the priorities and main areas on which attention should be focused. The Decade should witness renewed intensification of efforts to reach agreement and implement disarmament measures leading to discernible progress towards the ultimate goal. Special attention should be focused on certain identifiable elements in the Assembly's 1978 programme of Action. The comprehensive programme of disarmament should be elaborated with a view to its adoption at the 1982 special session.

Third Disarmament Decade

On December 4, 1990, the General Assembly declared the 1990s as the Third Disarmament Decade (resolution

45/62 A) and adopted the text of the following Declaration :

Declaration of the 1990s as the Third Disarmament Decade

1. The present Declaration of the 1990s as the Third Disarmament Decade is addressed to the global community and deals with the hopes and aspirations of people for lasting peace and security.
2. After a period of heightened tensions, the latter part of the decade of the 1980s saw a noticeable improvement in the way many States conducted their relations with one another. Despite this favourable trend, the specific goals of the Second Disarmament Decade were not fully realised.
3. In a world of growing interdependence, it is essential for the international community to stimulate and deepen awareness of the common interests of the global society and of the universal interest in achieving disarmament and strengthening international peace and security. The challenges facing the international community today are enormous. Accordingly, the solution of these difficult and complex issues will require the political will of States in conducting dialogue and negotiations and in promoting international co-operation, including confidence-building measures aimed at reducing tensions and the risk of military confrontation among States, bearing in mind specific conditions prevailing in the region concerned. It will also require acknowledgement of the profound interrelationship of questions relating to disarmament, social and economic development and environmental protection.
4. The international community stands on common ground in determining to make progress in the 1990s by resolutely pursuing disarmament along

with other efforts necessary for attaining genuine peace and security. As members of the international community, we have identified the following common goals. In the nuclear field, we must continue urgently to seek early reductions in, and the eventual elimination of, nuclear weapons and work towards a comprehensive nuclear-test ban. To achieve the objective of non-proliferation in all its aspects, all States are encouraged to make every effort further to strengthen the non-proliferation regime and other measures to halt and prevent the proliferation of nuclear weapons. The aim of the international community should be to promote cooperation in the peaceful use of nuclear energy on a non-discriminatory basis and under agreed and appropriate international safeguards.

The prevention of an arms race in outer space remains an important area to be further addressed. Many States also see the need to address naval confidence-building measures and disarmament issues. In the conventional field, we must seek reductions in arms and armed forces in all areas of the world and, in particular, where levels of concentrations of armaments are highest. In this regard, we urgently seek the successful conclusion of the negotiations on conventional forces in Europe. We aim for continued consideration of arms transfers in all their aspects. In the chemical field, we must work for the earliest conclusion of a convention on the prohibition of the development, production, stockpiling and use of all chemical weapons and on their destruction. The international community also calls for strict compliance with the Protocol for the Prohibition of the Use in War of Asphyxiating, Poisonous or Other Gases, and of Bacteriological Methods of

Warfare, signed at Generva on 17 June 1925. As further steps forward, openness and transparency on all appropriate military matters should be developed, the scope and techniques of verification advanced, the use of science and technology for peaceful purposes promoted and non-military threats to security addressed. All other initiatives to halt and reverse the arms race, in particular the nuclear-arms race, in both its qualitative and quantitative aspects deserve careful consideration. Such initiatives include the establishment of nuclear weapon-free zones on the basis of arrangements freely arrived among States of the region concerned and the creation of zones of peace under appropriate conditions defined and determined freely by the States concerned in the zone. In the pursuity of the foregoing goals, the international community acknowledges the particular responsibility of countries with the largest military arsenals. Resources freed through disarmament could be used for the benefit of a balanced world development. These goals should be included in a comprehensive programme of disarmament, which should be concluded at an appropriate time.

5. The United Nations will continue to foster multilateral co-operation for disarmament, wherein bilateral and regional efforts can be complementary and mutually supportive in attaining the purposes and principles of the United Nations. The international community can further promote disarmament through the United Nations by building upon its achievements in this field, including the Final Document of the Tenth Special Session of the General Assembly, which was adopted by consensus.

6. The international community affirms the positive role that an informed public can play in the process of disarmament by promoting a constructive and realistic dialogue on issues related to disarmament. In this regard, the pursuit of the World Disarmament Campaign and the observance of Disarmament Week will continue to play a useful role. Reflecting a growing understanding and commitment in dealing with the global problems of peace and security, it recognises that non-governmental organisations play an invaluable role. It also supports an enhanced role for women in developing the conditions for enduring peace.
7. As the world move towards the twenty-first century, it is evident that future generations will need increasing knowledge and understanding of the interdependent nature of life on the planet. Education on international peace and security issues will play a fundamental part in allowing every individual to realise his or her role as a responsible member of the world community.

By a 1994 resolution (49/75 B), the General Assembly called for a review and appraisal of the implementation of the Declaration.

World Disarmament Conference

The *Ad Hoc* Committee on the World Disarmament Conference held two sessions in 1980. At the final meeting, on 20 June, it unanimously adopted its report to the General Assembly.

In its report, the *Ad Hoc* committee stated that it had maintained close contact, through its Chairman, with the representatives of the nuclear weapon States, and set out the information gained from those contacts. The USSR continued to stress the need to convene a world disarmament conference, to make it possible to concentrate government attention and world public opinion on the solution of the question of how to halt the arms race and move forward to real disarmament. The four other nuclear Powers maintained their reservations on the practicability or value of such a conference.

The Committee reiterated that the idea of a world disarmament conference had received wide support from United Nations Member States with varying degrees of emphasis and differences. It was also evident that no consensus with respect to the convening of such a conference under current conditions had been reached among the nuclear weapon State, whose participation was generally deemed essential. It suggested the Assembly might wish to decide that, after its 1982 special session, such a conference would take place, as soon as the necessary consensus was reached.

On 12 December, the General Assembly adopted, without vote, resolution 35/151 by which it renewed the mandate of the *Ad Hoc* Committee and requested it to maintain close contact with nuclear weapon and other States.

General Assembly Special Sessions on Disarmament

From 23 May to 1 July 1978, towards the close of the first Disarmament Decade, the General Assembly held its tenth special session, the first to be devoted to disarmament. The holding of a special session devoted to disarmament was originally proposed by the first conference of Heads of State or Government of Non-Aligned Countries in 1961. It laid the foundation of an international disarmament strategy aimed at general and complete disarmament under effective international control.

On June 30, 1978, at the end of the special session, the General Assembly adopted resolution S-10/2 by which it adopted also the Final Document which set out a broad framework for further efforts by the United Nations in the field of disarmament. The Final Document was composed of four sections : an introduction; a Declaration, a Programme of Action; and recommendations concerning new international machinery for disarmament negotiations.

Other special sessions of the Assembly devoted to disarmament were held in 1982 and 1988, but did not result in substantive final documents. In 1994 (resolution 49/75 I), the Assembly decided, in principle, to convene, in 1997 if possible, the fourth special session on disarmament, the date to be determined I 1995.

World Disarmament Campaign

In the Final Document of the Tenth Special Session of the General Assembly, Governments and governmental and non-governmental organisations were urged to develop programmes of education of disarmament to create a greater understanding and awareness of the need for disarmament. In 1982, the Secretary General, in a report to the General Assembly, outlined a programme for a world disarmament campaign which was launched at the twelfth special session of the Assembly, the second devoted to disarmament, held in 1982.

The World Disarmament Campaign, aimed at informing, educating and generating public understanding and support for the disarmament objectives of the United Nations, was launched by the General Assembly on June 7, 1982, at the start of its second special session devoted to disarmament. In December, the Assembly approved the general framework for the Campaign and a 1983 programme of activities. It also invited Member States to co-operate with the United Nations to ensure a better flow of information on disarmament and called on them to encourage their citizens to expressed their views on disarmament questions.

The Secretary General proposed a series of activities for 1983, selected on the basis of their immediate impact, their multiplier effect and their ability to be carried out without extensive preparation. This programme called for the production of United Nations publications and audio-visual materials, interpersonal communication through such means as seminars and training, special events including Disarmament Week activities, publicity for the Campaign, and activities by United Nations information centres and other field offices.

On December 13, 1982, the General Assembly adopted three resolutions dealing with the World Disarmament Campaign (resolutions 37/100 H, 37/100 I and 37/100 J).

By one of these, the Assembly approved the general framework of the Campaign as specified by the Secretary General, including the submission of an annual report to the Assembly, as well as his proposals for a programme of activities for 1983. The Assembly again invited Member States to make voluntary contributions and decided to hold a pledging conference in 1983.

By another resolution, Member States were invited, in implementing activities for the Campaign, to take into account views expressed at the special session, including the proposal on a worldwide collection of signatures in support of disarmament. They were also invited to co-operate with the United Nations to ensure a better flow of disarmament information and to avoid disseminating false and tendentious information.

By the third resolution, adopted without vote, the Assembly called on Member States to facilitate the flow of a broad range of accurate information on disarmament matters, both governmental and non-governmental, to and among their citizens, so as to advance the objectives of the Campaign and of general and complete disarmament under effective international control. Member States were also called upon to encourage their citizens freely and publicly to express their views on disarmament questions and to organise and meet publicly for that purpose. The Secretary General was requested to report to the Assembly annually on implementation of the resolution.

In a 10 December resolution (resolution 37/94 B) United Nations public information activities, based on the recommendations of the Committee on Information, the Assembly requested the Secretary General to ensure that the Campaign gave full consideration to the role of mass media as the most effective way to promote in world public opinion a climate of understanding, confidence and co-operation conducive to peace and disarmament.

In 1992 (resolution 47/53 D), the General Assembly decided that the World Disarmament Campaign would henceforth be known as the United Nations Disarmament Information Programme with the following constituencies: elected representatives, research institutions, educational communities, non-governmental organisations and the media.

Disarmament and Development

In 1977, the General Assembly (resolution 32/88 A) expressed concern over the vast human and material resources being spent on armaments and agreed to initiate a study on the relationship between disarmament and development.

The subject was further considered at the tenth and twelfth special sessions of the Assemble devoted to disarmament which noted the vast increase worldwide in military budgets. In 1984, the Assembly decided to hold an International Conference on the Relationship between Disarmament and Development (resolution 39/160).

Conference on the Relationship between Disarmament and Development

The International Conference on the Relationship between Disarmament and Development, convened in August/September 1987, considered the relationship in all its aspects, the implications of the level and magnitude of continuing military expenditures, and ways and means of releasing additional resources through disarmament measures. It adopted by consensus a Final Document, aimed at fostering an interrelated perspective on disarmament, development and security, and promoting multilateralism and strengthening the central role of the United Nations in that regard.

In November, the General Assembly welcomed the adoption of the Final Document, requested the Secretary General to implement the Document's action programme, and requested the Preparatory Committee for the Assembly's third (1988) special session on disarmament to include a relevant item on that session's agenda (resolution 42/45).

At the third special session devoted to disarmament, in May/June 1988, a proposal was made regarding the relationship between disarmament and development. The Assembly, however, did not take action on any of the proposals submitted and was unable to reach agreement on a concluding document.

Follow-up

In accordance with the recommendation contained in the Final Document of the International Conference, a High-Level Task Force in May 1988 identified areas of specific activities in the area of development and disarmament which included : monitoring trends in military spending; facilitating exchange of experiences in conversion from military to civilian production; and promoting collective knowledge of non-military threats to international security. In 1990, the Task Force felt that the international situation called for a closer look at the economic aspects of disarmament, including its implications for national and global economy. It decided to continue work on the earlier activities as well as on new projects on the impact of arms reductions on the world economy and a publicity and information strategy. A conference was held in Moscow in August 1990 on "Conversion : economic adjustments in an era of arms reduction". The United Nations has established a theoretical framework of indicators for measuring military expenditures as well as to examine the post-cold-war developments for maximising the benefits from arms reduction.

As a result of the end of the cold war, there have been some peace dividends : global military spending has declined by almost a quarter since 1987, reflecting approximately 4 per cent per annum reduction by the United States and former USSR and about 2 per cent a year by the developing countries, giving a saving of some $935 billion.

The 1995 Review and Extension Conference of the Parties to the Treaty on the Non-Proliferation of Nuclear Weapons was held in New York from 17 April to 12 May. The Conference reviewed the implementation of the Treaty, which entered into force in 1970, and decided to extend it indefinitely.

This landmark international treaty has the objective of preventing the spread of nuclear weapons and weapons technology and furthering the goal of general and complete disarmament. It has been ratified by 178 countries at the time of the Conference—more than any other arms limitation and disarmament agreement. Along with other measures in the nuclear non-proliferation regime, it has succeeded in stemming the proliferation of nuclear weapons and in reducing existing arsenals. The outcome of the Conference has significant impact on the non-proliferation regime, military expenditures and thus on international peace and security.

5

"SUITCASE BOMBS" : THE EMERGING MENACE OF NUCLEAR POLITICS

War has become much too expensive to make it an extension of policy, or so analysts claim. Occupation of a country is now a thing of the past, while 'teaching lessons' may have similarly receded into the background, together with a host of other set piece wars that were the norm of yesterday's strategist. Yet media reports are full of reports of unparalleled death and destruction. Afghanistan for instance has seen more than 100,000 casualties, while Algeria total up casualties of 40,000 with 300 killed a week during the worst of the violence. No one can yet total Sri Lankan deaths as explosions rip across the country, while in Bosnia, all are uneasily aware that all it takes is one sniper on a roof to blow apart the Dayton accords.

Fought for differing reasons, and apart from each other by several hundred miles, yet all these conflicts have several factors in common. All were intra state, all saw maximum civilian casualties, and most important all were fought not with aircraft and heavy artillery but with that class of weapons that have been ignored by military experts and arms control buffs alike—the small weapon. Small weapons are usually understood to include everything that is part of an infantry man's kit of lethal weapons—personal defence weapons, (pistols etc) rifles, assault weapons, rifles and grenades, and perhaps for a specialist a few special explosives. As is apparent, the Bosnian fighter or the ever apparent mojahideen is fitted out with these and much more. Afghanistan is littered with some 13 million land mines, while sectarian elements in Karachi are using rocket propelled grenades against security forces. Typically, while NATO can and has dealt with considerable effectiveness against large anti-aircraft batteries and missiles, there is little it can do against the shoulder fired Stingers and SA-7's that are at large in the area. In Chechnya, reports state that more than 30,000 small weapons are at large, while the fear that the LTTE has more shoulder fired weapons in its arsenal continues to affect air operations in the war zone. Clearly there is suddenly not just a quantitative increase but a qualitative jump in weapon availability.

The global nature of the problem has been underlined by various heads of state as major security threats. At the non-aligned meet this year, the Indian Prime Minister identified the spread of small weapons as a threat to international security, while President Clinton called on nations to unite against rogue weaponry ranging from plutonium to land mines. At Russia's urging G-7 leaders have declared international crime and terrorism as major threat toe themselves and emerging democracies, and called for a special task force to deal with the problem.

Clearly the increase in crime, terrorism and the rising 'gun culture' have hit home. It is ironic, however, that the major sources of weapons continue to be governments, and the present spread of weapons in sub-Saharan Africa, Eurasia, Central and Southern Asia are at least in part due to power policies pursued both during the cold war and after. If anything has changed since then, it is that there has occurred a proliferation of weapons (indicating greater manufacturing capability) with lesser powers trying to create a better strategic situation for themselves with the covert/overt supply of weapons increasingly to non-state actors leading to a rising incidence of intra state wars. This paper aims at a limited task of identifying present sources and patterns of weapon diffusion (to be understood as weapon injection into society) and possible controls to handle this dangerous phenomenon.

The largest stocks of weapons supplied to unstable regimes by powerful countries was not only the main source of diffusion, but was all important in converting the conflict between state and society into war. It must be noted that while the quantities of 'aid' that went in to furbish African armories pale besides the cornucopia that flooded into Afghanistan (for instance) nonetheless the wide number of actors involved, and the fact that a very little aid went a long way in cash starved Africa, was enough to incite ethnic differences into ravaging conflicts that created death and destruction, and continues to be a source of instability in present day Africa. The following table gives a fair indication of the various actors involved in Africa. Overall the slide rule that may be used is that 'large' weapons generally went to the governments-in-being while the 'small' weapons typically went to the 'governments-in-waiting.'

Table 1

WAR	Military aid to government	Military aid to Resistance
ANGOLA	Soviet Union, Cuba and other Soviet bloc	South Africa, US and others
CHAD	France, US, Zaire	Libya, possibly Sudan
MOZAMBIQUE	Soviet Union, Zimbabwe, Tanzania, France, Britain	South Africa, private Western groups
RWANDA	France, Belgium, Zaire	Resistance possibly supported by Uganda
SOMALIA	United States, Libya, France, Italy, China	Ethiopia

Covert aid was the norm in Africa. Jonas Savimbi's UNITA is estimated to have received a total weapon aid of $250-300 million with the South Africans providing an equal amount (the latter continuing according to analysts at least till 1994) with 'deniability' achieved initially by routing the weapons through Zaire and possibly Morocco. Somalia, under its new patron received US aid of $296 million dollars in weapons (1981-1989) under the FMS (foreign military sales) and military assistance programme, including a further $2.2 million was strictly commercial sales. Since the ouster of Siad Barrer, Somalia has seen the death of 300-400,000 Somalis mostly by small arms fire (out of a population of 7 million) while more than 50,000 lives were lost in Angola. Weapons milling around in these countries include heavy machine guns, assault weapons, SA-7's, Stingers and thousand of mines. The largesse that Afghanistan received far outstrips anything that Africa received.

Soviet and American weapon aid to Afghanistan has been variously put at between $8-10 billion worth of weapons to all sides. The end effects of this is yet to be seen, since the conflict continues to suck in large quantities of weaponry. These included Chinese, East European, and Soviet type weapons—later including weapons of all kinds and makes. East Europe, as Gen Schwarkopf's testimony notes, continued to be a source of weapons in February 1990. It is important to note that while the aircraft and large weaponry are a prospective source of military adventurism, it is the small weapons that are at present milling around the continent causing instability and endangering peace processes. Today there are an estimated 1.5 million AK-47 unaccounted for in Mozambique alone, while in Angola UNAVEM is already taking casualties. In Namibia a small quantity of maize can be exchanged for a AK-47, while another preferred to turn in a workable gun for a second hand dress. Predictably, weapons are flowing out into the international black and grey markets, even as more weapons flow in from Russia, (clandestine sales) and France (strategic interest) and the US (commercial). Apart from the above, weapons aid in the past, also reached Cambodia, (China, United States funnelling weapons through Thailand), Guatemala (where CIA aid was double that of official weapon aid that was terminated in 1990, Columbia (where guerilla groups are fighting each other, and a month's massacre took more than 100 lives) and Haiti. With many of these conflicts now winding down, the process of conflict resolution has been held back by the sheer numbers of weaponry available, which have filtered into society, and crossed borders into other volatile areas. Before going into the nature of diffusion, another source of weapon diffusion needs to be mentioned.

The CFE Treaty led to a massive drawdown of forces, releasing weapons in their tons. Since passing on weapons to allies at 'no cost' was inevitably cheaper than destroying them, a cascade followed. Though the Treaty attempted to keep a strict verification regime in heavy weapons, it remained entirely silent on the issue of the tons of infantry weapons released as a result of the drastic reduction of manpower levels of armies across Europe. To cite just one instance, the Russian Army was reduced from 5,300,000 (1985) to around two million, while all major East and Central European countries have also reduced their forces. The release of weapons, therefore, amounts to several thousands of tons, and at least a good portion of these are now available to arms dealers worldwide. The scandal surrounding the withdrawing Western Group of Forces has yet to subside, with at least 40 railcars of weapons alleged to have reached all sides in the former Yugoslavia. At least 80,000 tonnes of ammunition is alleged to have disappeared from Russian weapon stocks according to the German government's authorised representative for the withdrawal of the Western Group. These excess weapons rarely made it to the inventory of major states, instead they filtered out to various destination not least the former Yugoslavia.

Where these weapons are now going, forms the crux of the question facing analysts. Patterns suggest that weapons diffuse through society (in small batches) aiding criminal activities, in larger lots to black market dealers, and entire consignments being diverted by arms dealers possibly with the knowledge of governments to other trouble spots in pursuit of strategic aims or sold as commercial transactions to embargoed countries.

Even while the massive weapon shipments to various parts of the 'red' world were going on there is enough evidence to prove that most of its was being skimmed off by various actors, most notably those who were the staging points. Thus Zaire dictator Sese Seko Mobutu skimmed off $ 2.75 million in equipment and material for Zairian use. Mobutu also managed to extract substantial American weapons aid in exchange for his support in much the same way that the military regime of President Zia managed to get aircraft and weapon aid in return for his role in the Afghan crises. The extent of weapons skimmed off 'officially' is obvious from the fact that a Human Rights Arms Watch Report quoted a Pakistani intelligence source who claimed to have three million Kalashnikovs packed and greased in storage. Apart from this, some weapons are thought to have gone to the Pakistan Army.

The weapon caravans (that averaged nearly 60-70 trucks a day) also leaked prodigiously, as apparent from the fact that since this period the arms available in the arms bazaars of the Frontier Province increased in quantity and quality, existing cheek by jowl with drug sellers and currency merchants. Arms sellers were proud to be able to sell anything, anywhere with delivery possible even at home. By late 1986 weapons were in the hands of students, political activists, and most of all in the hands of the drug mafia. Fire exchanges between drug caravans and security forces involve the use of RPG's and heavy machine guns. Since the 1980's the level of violence has increased exponentially with sustained gun battles on the streets of Karachi, and sectarian violence in Punjab. A gun may be hired for the day, and police personnel and their families are increasingly under attack. Secessionist tendencies backed up by more than adequate firepower threatens the very existence of the state. For instance in Malakand, a province well known for its extensive drug cultivation, security forces battled with militants for days, and finally had to give in to their demands for more stringent Islamic laws. Estimates include a 100,000 weapons within Karachi alone, (with more coming in every day) and another three to four million in Afghanistan-Pakistan (outside governmental control) and around half a million in the volatile Frontier Provinces according to Pakistani assessments.

Weapons have inevitably moved into criminal circles—South Africa has a major security problem on the rise in violent crime which according to a study is nearly five times as much as in the United States, this in spite of the fact that the South Africa Police Force stands at a strength of 140,000 (with an additional 44 companies of the Army still deployed with the police). Though political violence has reduced, crime related violence has escalated with at least 400 murdered a month, the rising incidence reflected in public apathy to a slaughter at a prayer meeting which barely made it to an inside page of a daily. KwaZulu, the heart of Zululand has warlords closely allied to organised crime. Private security firms now outnumber the security forces, standing at 180,000 in 2,700 companies.

Crime levels in the former Soviet Union is also directly a result of the availability of light arms, hitting at the state building structure of these newly independent states. There are some 5,500 major criminal gangs in Russia which together control an estimated 40,000 businesses, while security services employ an estimated 80,000 individuals under dubious control. Many in the armed forces are reported as hiring themselves out as hitmen. Weapons stolen from government armouries have appeared in the hands of Yugoslav militia and British drug dealers alike, not to mention the mafia which operates in Germany and Central Europe, and possibly the US. Kazakhstan has also seen a major rise in crime and drug smuggling, with huge numbers in the hands of various disaffected groups. The President of Kazakhstan, reacting to the seizure of 1000 firearms in 1994 condemned it roundly saying: "This is nonsense. There are many more." The rampant crime has led to the promulgation of stricter and harsher laws in an effort to deal with a growing disregard for state authority.

Once the weapon aid was cut off, most warlords turned to various sources of profit. In Pakistan the indefatigable Gulbuddin Hekmatyar, (with his base in Peshawar) was well into the heroin trade by mid 1980s, tying up with international cartels for his processed heroin. Today Pakistan has over three million addicts, starting from virtually a zero base before the Afghan adventure, with a wide acknowledgement of the fact that the infiltration of drug money into the economy, and a spiralling law and order problem (that left over 2000 dead in 1994) is the most serious problem facing the country. In the same period (mid 1980s) with UNITA now required to pay for arms with contraband goods, South Africa became the world's leading entrepot for the trade in poached ivory and rhino horn with officials of military intelligence and secret services all having vested interests. Ivory was sent by air to Taiwan, with Portuguese traders involved in the subcontracting.

A freelance arms dealer told Human Rights Watch in 1994, that a 15-20 per cent kickback was part of any contract which went through UNITA, which also paid high prices to sanctions busters who provided them with weapons. Reminiscent of the Afghan conflict when mojahids often bought weapons from government soldiers, UNITA was accustomed to trade in hard liquor with opposing forces which turned out to be thriving business and a source of funds. In Burma, the rise in drug cultivation and trafficking (after the withdrawal of aid to the Communist Party of Burma) is seriously threatening the neighbouring provinces of China which are now facing a massive problem with both addiction and drug related crime. In all the selected cases related above, drugs (primarily) and other contraband have allowed the increase of conflict/crime and greatly reduced the manouvreability of governments or international agencies involved in conflict resolution.

Most of these activities were carried on with the active help of the intelligence services—the ISI in Pakistan with active CIA help, the South Africans in Angola and Mozambique, and in Burma the powerful Army is alleged to be have encouraged the trade. With their own sources of funds, secret services became even more unaccountable than usual (or so their parent organisations claim). Elsewhere, Thai intelligence agencies are known to have actively channelled weapons to the insurgent groups in Cambodia, in return for valuable gem and mining contracts, (a process which is believed to be still going on) while the veteran druglord Khun Sa of Burma also benefited from the 'Thai connection'. While Thailand is now actively cooperating with the USA in drug interdiction, the continued success of Khmer operations is thought to be due to the availability of weapons from the Thai arms markets.

Once, before this glut of weapons took place, the arms market was largely dominated by arms dealers (the grey market) who operated largely as a conduit for government covert transfers, with perhaps a few lucrative deals to small strategic sideshows. They have an extensive network of informants, corrupt airport and customs staff, shipping and embassy personnel, who all together form the network that channels large consignments to favoured governments/militants/groups in furtherance of government policy or where government tolerates the transfers. Fraudulent and user certificates facilitated this process, allowing manufacturers to feign innocence on their ultimate destination. However, insurgents in areas unimportant to major players, had to depend on the underground arms markets that peddled often unreliable weapons in small lots in exchange for whatever he had to peddle. Pakistani open air arms bazaars sold locally made weapons or old Chinese copies to criminals and warlords.

Today, while the arms dealers continues to operate, new actors have appeared who deal truly in the dark, (the black market) and who may often be one time operators where arms are concerned. Arms sources (often from the military) may deal directly with those who are professional smugglers for anything from gold, drugs, or oil (increasingly an international currency unit as more countries come under embargos) or dealers may approach those weapon units/groups that have excess stocks, and then route it via the shipping companies that fly the flag of convenient countries, often changing both ownership and flags in mid ocean. For instance, the *Nora Heeren* a cargo ship registered in Oldenburg (Germany) but chartered by an Antiguan registered firm docked in Vystock (Russia) and was routed through Plymouth, where it was impounded for carrying $100 million of weapons for Angola. Instances of this type are steadily increasingly, and few may be apprehended considering the number of ships that navigate the world's oceans. Movement of weapons by air is common using the large number of air charter services now available (and the equally large number of unemployed pilots across Europe). While the new strength of the Croatian Armed Forces is possibly result of the 'grey' market, it is assessed that the excess stocks of the Volksarmee (rifles, mortars, grenade launchers etc) went to Croatia. Hungary's post CFE equipment is also reported to have filtered to Zagreb, as also the all important spare parts and ammunition. Arms dealers appear to be cruising the East and Central

European market and finding good buys, if the consistent reports of arms moving from that area is any indication.

Israelis have accused Ukraine of bartering weapons for oil from Iran, while the Armenians have accused them of supplying tanks to the Azeris. Ukrainian aircraft (or flights originating in Ukraine) have been caught several times with lethal cargo. The most publicised was the Maribor scandal (September 1992), when 150 tons of weapons were found at maribor in Slovenia bound for the former Yugoslavia. Oddly enough, the aircraft flew to Sudan, to Hungary and then to Slovenia. Another was detained at the Azores with a cargo of, not medical supplies as claimed, but arms and ammunition for one of the combatants in the dispute between Peru and Ecuador. A flight originating from Belarus similarly was caught with 'seven truckloads of weapons' bound for Sudan while Russian aircraft are reported to be flying arms from Syria to Armenia. Sudan is assessed by Western sources to be a clearing house for all types of weaponry, and representatives from most fundamentalist parties and terrorist groups from all over the world. Sudan is reported to have sent at least two shipments of arms to fighters in Algeria. Egypt, Eritrea, Ethiopia, Kenya and even Uganda have charged Sudan with nurturing trouble makers and supporting them with arms and aid.

Other movements of weapons include the transfer of weapons to 'pariah' states with excess weapon stocks, further leading to diffusion to unstable areas. For instance, Pakistan transferred weapons from the weapon pipeline to Burma, including 150 machine guns, 50,000 rounds of ammunition, and 5000 × 120 mm mortar bombs, assault rifles and ammunition worth US $20 million. Cambodia, when denied weapons from official friends simply turned to the arms market, where it found not only Ukrainian helicopters but reportedly Israeli repair teams.

Given these diverse networks and possibilities for diffusion, the possibility of controls seems incredibly difficult to achieve, and it is, therefore, not without reason that scholars tend to look askance at the numerous proposals put forward by an increasing number of researchers and institutes from various parts of the globe. However, it must be remembered that no arms control treaty was ever conceived or implemented without laying proponents open to the most critical attacks and criticism. The main reason why controls are possible, is at first glance, possibly the worst feature of the problem.

Case studies indicate that the major culprits of weapon proliferation and diffusion are states themselves. Government transfers (covert and overt) are at the basis of most of the conflicts today, a report from a US-based institute reveals. The United States (for instance) continued to supply Somalia with small weapons even after the US-led intervention, while the French have been sharply criticised for arming the Hutu government in Rwanda even while they were housed in camps in south western Rwanda—all this in spite of a UN arms embargo that was in effect since June 1994. However, while it is an inescapable fact that states are not known to act for any other reason other than their own self interest, this interest (especially in matters pertaining to security) are increasingly meshed with a variety of issues and actors, thus increasing the possibilities for the creation of norms and structures.

Secondly, terrorism and militancy are now problems which have spared few countries. National self interest may, therefore, lead countries into evolving controls to a problem for which there is really no defence. The 'boomerang' effect that is readily perceptible in Pakistan, China and South Africa (when weapons flow back into a supplier country) is another reason why states may find it prudent to change their behaviour. Even as analysts continue to work on what is admittedly a thorny problem, the danger inherent to the spread of these weapons continue to increase, as more and more spew out from the world's arsenals and factories, threatening the very basis of the state itself.

Nuclear Disarmament and Western Realpolitik

A panel of 17 American Strategists has come out with a report on "An Evolving US Nuclear Posture" which recommends a four-stage process leading to elimination of nuclear weapons from the arsenals of all countries of the world. The panel was chaired by General Andrew Goodpaster, former Supreme Allied Commander of NATO and included former Defence Secretary Robert McNamara, former Chief Arms Control Negotiator Paul Nitze, General Charles Horner, former Commander of Air Operations in the Gulf War, one Democratic Congressman and a Republican Senator among other familiar names from the US strategic community.

The four phases proposed are to proceed on the following lines. In the first phase, the US and Russia would work to reduce the importance of mutual assured destruction as a stabilising element in their relations and undertake cuts of roughly 2,000 warheads each in their respective nuclear arsenals. During the second phase the stable and cordial relations among he declared nuclear weapon states could further ease the requirements for nuclear deterrence, allowing all five states to reduce their arsenals to hundreds of warheads each. The only military role of nuclear weapons in the first and second phases is to deter nuclear attack. In the third phase all nuclear weapon states would reduce their arsenals to tens of warheads each. To achieve the goals of this phase would require widespread adoption of new principles and mechanisms for national security and further marginalisation of nuclear weapons in inter-state relations. In the last phase all nuclear weapons would be eliminated from all countries. States would need to have established alternatives to the threat of mass violence to maintain their security and advance their interests.

Progress towards the elimination of all weapons of mass destruction would require stringent national and international verification regimes and companion regimes for biological and chemical weapons. Most importantly, the international community would have to possess the requisite political will and the tools to ensure that it can respond rapidly to any aggressor attempting to extract short-term gains from a position of nuclear monopoly.

The authors of the report do not prescribe any time frame for the four phases. The report says "currently it is not clear whether elimination can ever be achieved. Achieving the goal will certainly take decades although reviewing the dramatic changes that have taken place in global politics since World War II makes clear that even such a visionary objective can be reached in one or two generations. Regardless of timing, much can be done in the current environment to reduce global reliance on weapons of mass destruction, while working in the long term to progressively eliminate nuclear dangers".

As a vision and a plan this report trails far behind Rajiv Gandhi's plan of 1988 and, therefore, an Indian is likely to ask what is new in it. The noteworthy aspect of this report is that US establishment strategists, who had contributed significantly to building up the monstrous nuclear arsenals on the basis of spurious threat perceptions, have come round to recognising the need to reduce and eliminate the nuclear weapons. Having been conditioned for nearly half a century by the nuclear theology which some of them did their best to nurture, they are in the process of undergoing a conversion to more humanistic values and rational strategic thinking. This is only a beginning and it would take some time for this thinking to seep though the American strategic establishment. There is bound to be a lot of resistance from the hardline adherents of nuclear theology to this new thinking. The vested interests in the military-industrial-academic-media complex can be expected to come out with their counter-thesis. The proponents of this new posture are cautious and do not totally commit themselves to the elimination of nuclear weapons as a feasible proposition. Nor are they willing to prescribe even tentative time schedules.

Indian strategic thinking has been quite ahead of this new American strategic thinking. In India most of the strategic thinkers have been advocating the third phase of what the US panel recommends. India has always pleaded for reducing the importance of mutual assured destruction and for marginalisation of the role of nuclear weapons as a currency of power in international relations. India has proposed delegitimisation of use and threat of use of nuclear weapons—a proposal consistently opposed by the US till now. A weapon which is deemed legitimate will not get marginalised, reduced or eliminated.

In Western nuclear theology the weapons have tended to be treated as an extrapolation of conventional weapons. Since in the two world wars the Allies gained their victory because of logistical superiority, there has been a strong tendency to rationalise that an arsenal larger than that of the adversary, explicitly declared, is essential for deterrence. Those who argued on these lines never thought of linking up deterrence to the pain one has to suffer in proportion to the stake one had in a particular successful outcome. Most of the Western theorists on deterrence never developed that degree of analytical understanding of strategic doctrines. The French argument in favour of minimum deterrence was more sophisticated. Even in this report which is a significant advance over orthodox nuclear theology, there is insistence on reciprocal reductions in the first two stages. The Indian position has been that for exercise of deterrence it is not necessary to match the weapons in numbers with those of adversaries. It is further argued that the very possibility of the existence of a nuclear retaliatory capability, without explicit demonstration, could constitute adequate deterrence.

The major problem of this new thinking faces is the need to persuade a whole generation of the politico-strategic community that most of the doctrines preached in the last five decades are meaningless and irrational. That is not going to be easy. The Americans ask the Indians in many seminars whether the end of the cold war has changed our thinking. The answer is no doubt in the affirmative. But most of the Americans have not changed their thinking about nuclear weapons and their role as currency of power in international relations. Some of them get upset when asked whether they would not benefit from some Indian strategic thinking inputs on global nuclear issue, instead of their trying all the time to preach to us the virtues of policies they never practise.

The insistence on legitimisation of nuclear weapons through indefinite and unconditional extension of the NPT, the assertion of the Western powers in their submissions to the World Court that they have a right to commit nuclear holocausts, the paranoia exhibited by the US in respect of nuclear weapons as evidenced by their counter-proliferation strategy and theatre ballistic missile defence, their own denigration of the non-proliferation treaty and their utter lack of faith in the non-proliferation commitments of other non-weapon states (which are signatories to the NPT), all together constitute the matrix of proliferation in the world today.

In spite of its shortcomings this report shows the direction in which American thinking is bound to emerge, however belatedly and haltingly. The US, having capped its arsenal, should now be encouraged to reduce and finally eliminate the nuclear arsenal—a formula it repeatedly recommends to India and Pakistan.

We are told about the benefits of the Non-Proliferation Treaty (NPT) Raj and how the possession of nuclear weapons is legitimate for the five most war prone powers but dangerous in the hands of others. During the colonial era the decisions made in the imperial capital were imposed on the entire empire. Now the domestic legislation of one country one nuclear and missile issues is sought to be imposed on the rest of the world. The imperialists called their occupation of the colonies as the white man's burden and a civilising mission. Similarly the five nuclear weapon proliferators assert their right to commit nuclear holocausts and keep the rest of the world under nuclear terror depriving the humanity of their basic human right to live without fear, and thereby claim to preserve international peace and stability. The imperialists used to talk of keeping space in the developing world but it was in Europe that the two world wars started. It was in Europe that the holocaust was committed. It was the involvement of industrial nations in the wars in the developing world, their spread of manportable arms and land mines which have produced another twenty million casualties since the World War II.

The nuclear issue is essentially a human rights issue—whether five countries of the world are to be allowed to terrorise the rest of the world. It is an issue about equality among nations. The nuclear proliferators appear to be the inheritors of the Nazi legacy of master race and the struggle against nuclear weapons, therefore, is a civilisational struggle. When Gandhi launched his civil disobedience movement, India was the only country to do it. He was not worried about being isolated or being mocked at by the Western oriented Indians who collaborated with colonialism. Today Gandhi has once again become relevant in the struggle against nuclear imperialism.

Gandhi discovered non-cooperation as the best answer to colonialism. The same holds true today in the case of struggle against nuclear weapons. Our basic strategy has to be non-cooperation with nuclear imperialism. India, instinctively, adopted non-cooperation as the strategy and has, therefore, refused to accede to the NPT. The NPT disarms the unarmed just as the British Arms Act disarmed the Indians. The Comprehensive Test Ban Treaty (CTBT) in the form in which it is advocated by the five nuclear proliferators is a continuation of the NPT. It does not stop the nuclear proliferators from having their weapons and it does not prevent them from modernising them and designing new weapons. Just as NPT did not subject the nuclear weapon powers to any obligation but laid all restraints on the non-nuclear weapon states, the CTBT as proposed does not require the nuclear weapon powers to close down their weapon research facilities but only ensures that new nations cannot join the nuclear club. Just as imperialists claimed their oppression and domination over the rest of the humanity was for the good of the latter, the nuclear nations assert that their unequal treaties and domination are meant for the good of the victims of nuclear hegemony.

The non-accession to CTBT is a logical extension of India staying out of the NPT, especially when nuclear weapons have been sought to be legitimised through their indefinite and unconditional extension. If nuclear weapons are legitimate, the Nazi holocaust will also become legitimate. What is the difference between collecting people in a concentration camp, gassing them and incinerating their bodies and doing it in one step by dropping a nuclear weapon on a population and killing them through blasts, radiation and high temperature effects. The NPT was hawked as an arms control treaty of the cold war period and hence an interim measure. This is clear from the preamble and Article VI of the Treaty. But to extend it indefinitely and unconditionally makes it a perpetual feature of the international system and removes the possibility of delegitimising and eliminating these instruments of holocausts and terror. The assertion of the nuclear powers of their right to use nuclear weapons before the World Court in the wake of the extension of the NPT should remove any reasonable doubts from the minds of all rational people about the true purpose of the possession of nuclear weapons in the hands of nations which have been most war-prone in this century. A no-first-use agreement like the Geneva Protocol will be the beginning of a process of delegitimisation of nuclear weapons. The nuclear proliferators refuse to commit themselves to it.

We do not have to fear a nuclear war since that is very unlikely. The nuclear weapon nations cannot afford to fight a nuclear war among themselves. The use of a nuclear weapon against a non-nuclear weapon country will completely destroy the present nuclear imperial Raj and unleash worldwide proliferation. It may lead to largescale nuclear terrorism as well. Therefore, nuclear weapons are essentially meant to be used as a currency of power, to dominate and intimidate 'lesser nations.' A nuclear weapon is unusable. Though this is the objective truth one cannot rule out irrationality and racial supremacist behaviour as exhibited by the European nations in the last one century. The city busting raids of the World War II, the mass killings through aerial bombings in the Vietnam War and the Gulf War are acts of genocide committed by the same nations. Therefore, even while shedding the fear of nuclear weapons and excessive concern about nuclear war, one is compelled to operate on the belief systems of such war-prone nations to deter them. Gandhi was a strong advocate of non-violence in attempting to change the *status quo*. But he did not rule out capability for defence when necessary. That was why he approved sending the Indian Army to Kashmir.

Therefore, the country should think of adopting a Gandhian approach of non-cooperation with nuclear imperialism and should not accede to the CTBT. Generation of a sense of deterrence will be in consonance with the tenets of Gandhi but not the first use of nuclear capability. While our example should generate wider non-cooperation with the imposition of nuclear imperial Raj,

India should also avoid any provocative action or behaviour.

Threats to Third World

Recent report from London that Britain has deployed ... nuclear deterrent aimed at the Third World concerns the recent evolution of the nuclear doctrine of the western powers—US, UK and France—who are determined to use their atomic clout to perpetuate their hege... over the South. Since the end of the war in the..... against Saddam Hussein in 1991, the United States, France and Britain have steadily drifted into a strategy ... contemplates the use of their nuclear forces against the emerging powers of the developing world and involves military intervention in defence of Western political and economic interests.

The British newspaper *Guardian* has reported that Britain has deployed submarine missiles with a single warhead that will strike fear into any "Third World dictator tempting to try nuclear blackmail". The British strategic submarines are now being equipped with single warhead, "sub-strategic" missiles that will be employed in regional contingencies. The first British submarine loaded with such missiles, HMS Victorious, sailed out of a British base on New Year's eve. The Royal Navy's move is one of the important results of a long debate in Britain about the role of its nuclear weapons after the demise of the Soviet Union. Britain now believes its nuclear arsenal could play an important role in protecting its vital interests from the alleged danger of nuclear-armed dictators in the developing world.

The British Government first linked its nuclear doctrine to proliferation of nuclear weapons in November 1993. Mr. Malcolm Rifkind, the then Defence Secretary, acknowledged the problems of nuclear use against the Third World. But he warned that, "it would be unwise to ignore completely the potential consequences if, despite our efforts, there is proliferation of nuclear weapons".

Implying the involvement of British nuclear forces around the world, Mr. Rifkind added that "the possibility exists of a proliferator engaging in a conflict in which our interests, or even British forces, are involved". It is with this possibility in mind that Britain has decided to arm Trident missiles with tactical nuclear warheads for a range of military contingencies in the developing world.

France, in fact, has moved even further than Britain, in expanding its nuclear strategy to include so-called threats from the South. Over the last few years, its nuclear orientation has changed from being tied specifically to the European theatre or Soviet threat, to one envisaging new roles in West Asia and the Indian Ocean. According to a recent report of Greenpeace, the French Government and military officials are now frequently linking the French nuclear doctrine to nuclear proliferation concerns and speak openly of using nuclear weapons to deter regional threats. The 1994 White Paper on defence posture declared the broad objective of the French nuclear forces. "The French nuclear concept will continue to be defined by the will and capability to make any aggressor—irrespective of who such aggressors may be or their capabilities—fear unacceptable damage, out of all proportion to the advantage to be gained from conflict, if they seek to attack France's vital interests. In this day and age, nuclear weapons alone have this kind of capability."

A report by the Committee on National Defence and the Armed Services of the French National Assembly in late 1994 even more strongly linked nuclear deterrence to Third World threats : "Even if France has no vital interests to defend in the Middle East, in the Indian Subcontinent, or in the Pacific Zone, France cannot feel uninterested in what is happening in these areas. The prospects of conflicts that exist in the various hot spots force us not to surrender to the advocates of nuclear disarmament but, quite the reverse, to do everything we can to maintain our instrument of deterrence in good operational condition. In a world where crude nuclear weapons will inevitably be more in the hands of irresponsible potentates, the fact that we possess a weapon capable of inducing respect with whatever aggressor, may one day turn out to be indispensable." France has not formally announced the new targets for its nuclear force, but it is reported that they include those countries in the Third World with a capability to build nuclear weapons and missiles.

In the United States, targeting Third World states already appears to have become policy. According to the Greenpeace study, the US has developed a new military doctrine which explicitly sees a role for American nuclear weapons in deterring and countering weapons of mass destruction in regional contingencies around the globe. Unlike in the 1980s, when some Third World nations were on the nuclear hit list as real or potential allies of the Soviet Union, they are now being targeted for their own importance as proliferators of nuclear weapons and missiles.

India's Weapon Option

Largely under warps is an important—one may say crucial—facet of India's nuclear programme and nuclear technology acquisition. It's the linkage between India's nuclear power programme and nuclear weapon capability; that Indian nuclear weapon capability is a spin-off from the nuclear power development programme. To comprehend this novel Indian facet of nuclear technology development, let us take an overall view of the Indian nuclear programme.

Focussed primarily on atomic power generation and other peaceful applications such as in agriculture, industry and the medical domain, India's nuclear programme kept the weapon option open from the beginning. That was the era of the fifties. The horrors of Hiroshima and

Nagasaki were followed by a new vista of atoms for peace, of nuclear power generation, transformations in agriculture and medical diagnostics and therapy using atomic science and technology. But in the backdrop the ultimate horror of nuclear weapons still loomed large, for the big powers, in particular the United States and the Soviet Union, kept up the race for building nuclear weapon arsenals, with the addition of the hydrogen bomb, and later, the neutron bomb.

India under the leadership of Jawaharlal Nehru was dedicated to the peaceful uses of atomic energy but it could not wish away the lurking threat posed by nuclear weapons, and so *per force* Indian option for nuclear weapons was kept one. For both areas—peaceful application and the weapon option—Dr. Homi Bhabha, the architect of India's nuclear programme, had a clear strategic vision and priorities.

A poor country like India cannot afford to give priority to atomic weapons. And uranium enrichment based on the diffusion method, then the prevalent route to weapon making, was ruled out absolutely for the massive input of electricity and other resources that it involved. Bhabha's vision tied Indian weapon option to plutonium technology, the cheapest route and one most suited to Indian needs of a nuclear watch-dog. The Indian weapon option then was to be a by-product of India's nuclear power generation plans.

A landmark in the build up of infrastructure for India's nuclear capability was the construction in 1964-65 of a nuclear spent fuel reprocessing test plant at the Bhabha Atomic Research Centre (BARC) by a team of scientists and engineers headed by Homi Sethna. It is this breakthrough that provided the link between nuclear power production and the weapon option based on the plutonium route. Over the years, as Indian scientists acquired a grip over spent fuel reprocessing technology, the plutonium route to atomic weapons opened up, bypassing the enormously costly uranium enrichment method.

India now has four reprocessing plants—while the pioneering BARC unit has become a full-fledged plant, at Tarapur, a spent fuel reprocessing plant was built and has been operating for a decade and a half, and the most modern and advanced reprocessing plant has come up at Kalpakkam. The fourth unit, a specialist reprocessing plant, has been built at Kalpakkam itself for reprocessing fast breeder spent fuel, to begin with spent fuel of the fast breeder test reactor (FBTR), which contains weapon grade plutonium in far larger percentage than what is obtained from reprocessing spent fuel of other reactors—thermal or research reactors. And a fifth magnum size reprocessing plant is already in the conceptual stage, to be located in north India for reprocessing spent fuel from Narora and possibly Kakrapar and the upcoming reactors in Rajasthan.

The acquisition and rapid development of spent fuel reprocessing technology justifies the Indian scientists' claim that this country's route to nuclear weapon capability is a spin-off from the power programme. The cheapest weapon programme anywhere in the world. Albeit, with the limitation that India's aim is the build up of a credible nuclear deterrent—and no more. It rules out India joining a nuclear arms race of global proportions—on scientific as well as economic considerations.

Another link between the Indian atomic power programme and the weapon option was construction of the high flux research reactor Dhruva, whose indigenous development by a team of leading engineers and scientists headed by Dr. Anil Kakodkar in the eighties, denoted acquisition of nuclear technology of a high order.

Dhruva, an important tool as a research reactor in the atomic power programme, also provided weapon grade plutonium 239, essential in the plutonium route to nuclear weapons. Plutonium obtained from reprocessing spent fuel from power reactors is not weapon grade. Valuable no doubt for the Indian nuclear programme, as reactor grade fuel for fast breeders and the upcoming Advanced PHW Reactor, this reprocessed plutonium's structure has a mixture of Pu239, Pu240 and Pu241, undependable for weapons. A small additional source of Pu239 in India is the Cirus research reactor built with Canadian cooperation in 1962. Now the Kalpakkam plant for reprocessing fast breeder spent fuel will considerably augment India's Pu239 pool. But not till Dhruva spent fuel reprocessed plutonium—was at hand to enable building stockpile—could India have prudently exercised its weapon option.

That flash point in the Indian weapon programme came in 1998 when on May 11 and 13 five tests of varied strength, which included testing of a thermonuclear device, were conducted with great success at Pokhran. In this run up, the 1974 Pokhran test served as a dress rehearsal. Between Pokhran I and Pokhran II, a vast scientific and nuclear technology acquisition by Indian scientific institutions is revealed, a striking advance on all sectors of nuclear capability.

But glamorous as the Pokhran II tests appear to be, far more fascinating and absorbing is the uphill road taken by India for building atomic power generation capacity as mapped out by Bhabha, overcoming the constraints of denial by the West of advanced reactor technology. To overcome uranium enrichment problems for reactor fuel—later encountered for operation of the Tarapur reactors build with American turn-key collaboration—India took to pressurised heavy water reactor (PHWR) design of the Canadian type, and has built a chain of PHWRs in different locations of the country, upgrading the design and operational features, particularly the safety aspects, in the process. These are 220 MW reactors, fuelled by natural uranium, obviating the need for enriched uranium fuel.

The last commissioned being the state-of-the-art reactors at Kaiga and Rawatbatta. The next line of 500 MW PHWR construction has now commenced. The second generation reactors now under construction are the fast breeders and the PHWR.

Here is the integral link between the nuclear power programme and weapon capability development; and part of the route for the weapon option and the power programme are common, symbolised by Dhruva and spent fuel reprocessing plants. Without these technology achievements the power programme would be lame duck and the weapon option unrealisable.

Reaching this stage of capability, India's nuclear establishment had to cover a long and uphill road—of mastering different facets of nuclear science and technology, building nuclear infrastructure and related industrial capacity even while overcoming the constraints of a severe nuclear blockade imposed on India by the Western powers after the first Indian atomic detonation at Pokhran in 1974. Traversing these stages of India's nuclear journey is among the glorious chapters in Indian nuclear technology acquisition.

On way to implementation of the Bhabha strategy of constructing pressurised heavy water reactors in the first phase, followed by fast breeders, the second and third generation reactors, activating India's vast thorium reserves in the process, a strong base has been laid for Indian nuclear capability overall by creating a comprehensive research and development network all over the country. This R and D network serves both the nuclear power programme and nuclear weapon capability build-up.

In laying this R and D base for nuclear capability, India is ahead of China and Japan, next only to the nuclear big four—United States, France, Russia and Britain. The country can proudly proclaim this. A glimpse of some of these centres is inspiring : from the Tata Institute of Fundamental Research (TIFR) to BARC to IGCAR at Kalpakkam, the Centre of Advanced Technology (CAT) at Indore, Variable Energy Cyclotron at Calcutta, the Institute of Plasma Research at Ahmedabad. Here is a chain of advanced research centres which provide backup for India's nuclear operations, overwhelmingly in peaceful nuclear applications—power generation, medical domain, agriculture and industry—but also in the exercise of the weapon option.

Today, under the purview of the Atomic Energy Commission and the Department of Atomic Energy (DAE), along with the atomic power programme and other nuclear applications, the chain of research institutions have generated a number of high technologies, which include lasers for use in surgery and industry, accelerators for nuclear research, Giant Metrewave Radio Telescope (GMRT) at Pune, the biggest in the world outclassing the largest radio telescope presently in the United States, supercomputer systems using parallel processing techniques, advanced remote handling and robotic devices and servo-manipulators for application in industry, scientigraphic techniques used in organ imging in medical diagnosis, and sophisticated facilities for analysis and characterisation of ultra-pure materials—non-destructive material testing. These technologies provide a reliable common base for atomic capability development, both in peaceful applications and for an effective nuclear weapon deterrent.

India was able to chart this route to acquisition of nuclear technology thanks to Dr. Bhabha's vision and foresight. Bhabha minced no bones that India's priority had to be nuclear technology for developing power generation capacity. But he also had the scientific knowledge that the route to power development and the weapon option could be inter-related.

Dr. Bhabha ruled out the setting up of an uranium enrichment plant based on the diffusion method by India, if for no other reason than its economic implications. He however favoured India's acquisition of centrifuge technology for uranium enrichment, still in the process of development in the sixties. Alongside, the Indian nuclear establishment guided by Bhabha's foresight, focussed on the advanced technology of reprocessing nuclear spent fuel which enabled extraction of the valuable man-made fissile element, plutonium.

Reactor grade plutonium obtained by reprocessing nuclear spent fuel is a valuable requisite in the Bhabha-deviced long-term strategy for building India's capacity for power generation based on fast breeders. Simultaneously, weapon grade plutonium, obtained by reprocessing spent fuel from research reactors, opened the weapon option for India. Indian weapon capability was thus a spin off from peaceful applications—the novel Indian route linking nuclear power capacity build-up with weapon capability. This unique Indian route to weapon capability was also the cheapest weapon route anywhere in the world. It imposed no harsh burdens on the Indian economy.

On both these considerations, the Indian nuclear establishment under Bhabha's guidance laid great stress on developing scientific and engineering capabilities for a breakthrough in the advanced technology of reprocessing nuclear spent fuel. And that was in the early years of this country's nuclear programme. The Indian nuclear establishment knew that reprocessing technology was a closely guarded secret which only the nuclear big four—USA, Soviet Union, France and Britain—possessed. India was the fifth nation to acquire this technology. The Indian break-through in this advanced technology came as early as in 1964-65.

Unfortunately, this important milestone in India's developing nuclear capability received no recognition from the nuclear powers. Nor did the Indian political leadership proclaim this great feat of India's nuclear scientists with a sense of pride. Rather, the Indian leadership, suffering from obsession that it might be bracketed along with powers opting for nuclear weapons, kept this major nuclear technological breakthrough more or less under wraps. For this sin, India suffered—and continues to suffer. Its status downgraded, it was lumped with the non-weapon untouchables under the NPT. For its PNE in 1974, India was barricaded with a 'Chakravieu' thrown round it, from which it has still not been able to break out completely.

The issue picked up and during the Partial Test Ban Treaty Amendment Conference, held at New York between 7 January and 18 January 1991, non-aligned states proposed such amendment. The idea, however, met stiff opposition by the United States and Britain. It was only later, in April 1993, at the Vancouver Summit that the US President Bill Clinton and Russian President Boris Yeltsin agreed to negotiate a test ban. The negotiations resumed on January 25, 1994 at the Geneva Conference on Disarmament. During the talks, none of the five nuclear powers questioned the wisdom of a test ban. But they had basic disagreement on the issue of scope. These disagreements varied from exempting low yield nuclear testing up to the protecting peaceful nuclear explosions from the treaty. The pace of negotiations was initially slow. However, after the NPT was permanently extended, the nuclear powers compromised on a treaty text, which was neither "comprehensive" nor did it contribute to the process of disarmament. As is known the treaty exempts sub-critical testing and also permits laboratory tests and other computer simulated tests necessary to maintain a nuclear arsenal. India was opposed to such a draft and hence vetoed it. However in a procedural camouflage, the treaty was adopted at the General Assembly Session on September 24, 1996. The treaty is yet to enter into force following its rejection by the United States Senate.

From the discussion, it is clear, that the search for disarmament contains both a paradox and a dilemma. The paradox is states' search for security by acquiring nuclear weapons. The dilemma then for each state will be how to be sure that each stage in the process of disarmament no nation violates its pledge or at least does not benefit for the purpose of dominating other nations. The United Nation's efforts to promote partial disarmament measures then may not be effective. The world can get rid of the nuclear threat only by achieving its goal of complete nuclear disarmament.

This commitment was earlier reiterated by Mr. Vajpayee at the UN Millennium Summit in September 2000. The Indian Prime Minister recalled the Indian commitment of global disarmament and the disturbing trend wherein nuclear arsenals continue to be nurtured and remain virtually untouched. He cautioned : "It would seem that we are still far away from achieving a goal that can assure the survival of humanity in the new millennium... We (India) continue to press for universal, verifiable nuclear disarmament with undiminished commitment, even while safeguarding our strategic space and autonomy in decision-making". It is relevant here that India after May 1998 unilaterally adopted a no-first-use (NFU) doctrine and embedded in this is an enormous risk that India has undertaken. It flows from the commitment to pacifism and a determination to nudge the world towards elimination of nuclear weapons.

Even if India had not intended it, there is a certain irony in recalling the disarmament developments post May 1998. Soon after the Indian nuclear tests, eight of the medium powers of the world formed a New Agenda Coalition and applied pressure on the five declared nuclear powers to fulfil their commitment to disarmament as stipulated in Article VI of the NPT. This momentum was strengthened in the May 200 NPT Review Conference but the sad truth is that the five weapon powers—also the permanent members of the UN Security Council only agreed to an unequivocal undertaking in terms of their commitment to disarmament. No other legal binding resolutions could be added to what emerged from the May 2000 conference.

Almost a year later Delhi has once again stirred the consciousness of the world and reminded it of both India's impeccable credentials in adhering to nuclear nonproliferation norms, the spirit of disarmament and the need for the others to follow suit. Total disarmament is the ultimated Holy Grail. Theologically the Holy Grail is an elusive and arduously difficult goal to reach. But in striving towards it, humanity will be refining its innate sensibilities towards a higher moral plateau. One hopes that Mr. Vajpayee's exhortations will not fall on deaf ears.

Ban Nuclear Weapons : WPC

World Peace Conference held recently at Athens, in its appeal has asked for total ban and elimination of nuclear weapons.

There still exist around 30,000 nuclear warheads in the world. It is a first priority towards a 21st century for the world peace movement to realise a world without nuclear weapons. The 1st resolution of the United Nations General Assembly (UNGA), 1946 demanded a total destruction and prohibition of atomic weapons. This original demand of post-war politics has to be urgently realised.

The 53rd UNGA adopted, by a overwhelming majority, a resolution initiated by "New Agenda Coalition" demanding an unequivocal commitment of nuclear weapon states to nuclear disarmament on an early date as well as one submitted by non-alined countries calling for nuclear abolition within a time-bound framework. In the Review Conference of Non-Proliferation Treaty (NPT) (April-May 2000), a strong voice was expressed calling upon nuclear weapon states to implement their obligation for nuclear disarmament. The proposal of UN General Secretary was made for the Millennium Assembly, "to convening a major international conference that would help to identify ways of eliminating nuclear danger". The contradiction between forces clinging to nuclear deterrence policy and international public opinion against nuclear weapons is further deepening.

Among others, global criticism is growing against the arrogant attitude of the US administration which makes its nuclear superiority untouchable by stifling other states' development program and rejecting the ratification of Comprehensive Test Ban Treaty (CTBT). At the same time, the voice calling for strict observation of the Anti-Ballistic Missiles (ABM) Treaty and implementation of START II is also strengthening. World concerns are expressed to the danger of new nuclear arms race in South Africa as well as Israeli nuclear capability which would provoke proliferation of weapons of mass destruction in the region.

We demand an unequivocal commitment by all nuclear weapon states to the elimination of nuclear weapons, and commencement of negotiations for the conclusion of a treaty to totally ban nuclear weapons.

We call for concrete measures for disarmament: (*a*) establishment and enlargement of Nuclear Weapon Free Zones (NWFZ); (*b*) a total ban on all forms of nuclear weapons tests; (c) abandonment of a policy of preemptive and first use of nuclear weapons; (*d*) de-alerting and separating war-heads from their delivering system.

Let us develop, beyond differences in thoughts, political creeds, and religions, worldwide opinion and movements to pressure pro-nuclear forces to realise above task. Further, promoting national activities such as signature campaigns, we propose international day of actions for nuclear abolition : days of Hiroshima and

Nagasaki (6 and 9 August) and the Disarmament Week (starting from October 24).

Radical cuts in military expenditure have become important for better people's lives and welfare, economic and social development as well as for world peace and security. Western countries are increasing military budgets responding to a new strategy of interference. Increasing arms trade is serious burden to the Third World people as well as the rest.

We call for a campaign for the reduction of military expenses in solidarity with social and labour movement for a better life and welfare, and development. In Africa, the arms trade is accelerated by regional conflicts. Those who generate tensions are selling arms and profiting it. We demand the restruction and ban on arms trade and the control of light weapons. We reject the militarisation of the EU and the installation of its intervention force. Chechenya crisis have to be solved peacefully.

For a New World Order

The Charter of the United Nations, based on the lessons of World War-II, states that its purpose is "to develop friendly relations among nations based on respect for the principle of equal rights and self-determination of people", and that conflicts and problems are to be solved "by peaceful means, and in conformity with the principles of justice and international law" as well as of non-interference into internal affairs. It is the central task of world peace movement towards 21st century to defend a world order of peace based on these principles. UNO should function on the bases of their principles.

The war of NATO against Yugoslavia which was designated a "humanitarian intervention" was an open military intervention that violated the UN Charter and the sovereignty of Yugoslavia. It was the implementation of NATO's new strategic doctrine that overthrows basic principles of International Law. The ministerial meeting of non-aligned countries in 1999 firmly rejected interference into internal affairs of a country under the name of "humanitarian intervention". However, the US administration and NATO leadership declared in public that they will carry out pre-emptive attacks against nations in case of "humanitarian" necessity.

The "New Strategic Concept" of NATO is to establish a policy of pre-emptive attack beyond its border in cooperation with this US policy. With this new strategy, NATO overthrew officially every sense of International Law, such as the principles of non-interference into internal affairs of a state and of refraining from the threat of force. Thus, the UN Charter is brutally violated by NATO (US and its allies) which consists nowadays a great threat and is enemy to peace and security in Asia and the pacific. A new guidelines on US-Japan military cooperation and its related regulation were established enabling Japan to join a war generated by the US. Korean reunification should be achieved independently and peacefully. US policy of intervention is also revealed in Latin American region.

Such a global strategy of pre-emptive attack contradicts a world order of peace envisaged in the UN Charter and constitutes the most serious threat to world peace. We call upon peace movements of the world to struggle together, and press their own government and international institutions, against that threat and for the defence of a peaceful world order and its realisation.

US and other military bases situated in other countries create various problems and negative influences. The extra-territoriality of its military activities infringe upon the life and human rights of residents as well as the sovereignty and security of host countries by vital accidents, crimes, noise pollution, and other environmental problems.

We support people's movement against a privileged status for foreign US troops, for restruction of military activities of foreign bases, compensation for damages to people's live and their elimination, environmental protection, reduction of bases and their removal. We call for international cooperation and exchange with broad forest putting aside different opinions on the issues of military alliance and blocks.

Military alliances and blocks are aimed at mobilising allied nations to US world strategy, while minimizing their sovereignty. We urge efforts to develop public opinion calling for their abrogation. We also support the idea of a non-aligned movement and to strengthen our solidarity with it.

Socio Economic Development

The importance for tackling a task for "Disarmament for Development" was stressed in the 53rd UNGA. It is essential for peace and security to eradicate hunger and poverty and to realise sustainable development. They are the very meaning of the peace movement.

Under the name of "Globalisation" an international order only beneficial for transnational companies, is being forced onto peoples of the world, and it is seriously damaging socio economic development of Third World countries, people's lives, agriculture, resources, and natural environment. Thus, it is seriously affecting national sovereignty. Annual Report of the UN Development Program (1999) emphasising the harmful effects of "globalisation" stating that the international gap in income and living standards has become "grotesque."

However "globalisation" is facing a worldwide upsurge of public movement. Demonstrations in Seattle in December 1999 and Washington DC in April 2000 have inspired peace forces. They marched against the policies of the World Bank, World Trade Organization, International Monetary Fund that are aimed at the lives of all people, both in the developed and under-developing world. Serving the exploitation by multinational companies, these policies are producing unprecedented poverty, hunger and unemployment.

Fighting under-development, in particular through disarmament, we call for promotion of worldwide cooperation in solidarity with people fighting against the negative effects of economic, financial and commercial globalisation.

"The weight of the debt is a destructive weapon against development" (UN General Secretary). We are in solidarity with "Jubilee 2000" for canceling the debt of developing countries without any political and economic condition.

In violation of International Law, embargo and blockades are utilised as a method to enforce serious damage on people. We demand the lifting of the illegal usage against Cuba with the Helms-Burton Law by the US. There is also growing public opinion opposing sanctions imposing too much suffering on people in particular and on children and women as in the case of Iraq and Yugoslavia.

The independent state of Palestine, its recognition and admittance as a full member state of the UN, should have been realised prior to the Millennium Summit in September 2000. We appeal to peace movement to support that proclamation.

Culture of Peace

The history of 20th century shows that racism, racial discrimination, xenophobia, fascism, neofascism, and neo-colonialism had been serious causes of war and human rights violation. It is an important task of peace movement to fight against all forms of these tendencies.

Let us support the "International Year of Culture of Peace" and "International Decade for Culture of Peace and Non-violence for the Children of the World" proclaimed by the UN. It is necessary to intensify activities of education for peace, disarmament, development, environmental protection, role of information, and for human rights.

The danger of terrorism either by certain groups, sects or states, is a threat to peace and security, national sovereignty, and integrity. To eliminate terrorism is an important task of peace movement.

We support the struggle of indigenous people for their rights to the land, identity, and self-determination.

We call upon all peace movements to cooperate and work together for the above mentioned tasks and demands, towards a 21st century, peace and security, instead of the present world order of war and intervention.

The New Balance of Power

Major turning points in history come but once in a few decades, or even a century. The disintegration of the Soviet empire and the end of the cold war is one such landmark. It is not quite the "end of history." For, it has not resulted in a total victory of liberal democracy as Francis Fukuyama had predicted. Rather, it is a return of history in a diversity of new and emerging developments. Even the nature of its coming as new. It has come not as the consequence of a global confrontation of arms and a subsequent peace conference. Instead it came stealthily, albeit dramatically, taking the world by surprise. Neither the West nor the Soviet Union was prepared for it.

These developments are not unlike the major shifts that have taken place in the world in the past, such as in Europe in 1815 when the Congress of Vienna was held; or, that at the time of Versailles in 1919 after the First World War; or, that after the Second World War whose post-war dispensations were finalised at Yalta even before the end of the conflict. As we know today, these turning points in history were not a prelude to peace and prosperity. Nineteenth century Europe was largely free from warfare, only at the expense of shifting the scene of conflict to the "new world". The First World War was an unfinished business and its termination through an inequitous treaty then resulted in the next war. The end of the Second World War introduced a new kind of war, the cold war.

It has been said : "If war has been the midwife of history, the cold war was its taxidermist". It froze for many decades a condition of hostility between contending forces divided by ideology. It was characterised by status quo and zero-sum game, where open conflict was not permitted in the central areas of their confrontation. What does its end portend?

The idea of a new world order was spelt out by President George Bush on September 11, 1990, in a speech for the build-up to the Gulf War. In defining the purpose of the war, apart from its four broad strategic aspects, he mentioned a fifth overarching objective, as "A New World order... a new era... free from the threat of terror, stronger in the pursuit of justice, and more secure in the quest for peace, an era in which the nations of the world can prosper and live in harmony."

Subsequently, the new world order has been described in different ways. With reference to Voltaire, who described the Holy Roman Empire as "neither holy, nor Roman and not an empire", it has been characterised as "not new, not orderly and not even addressed to the world". Yet, it has grasped global attention. Lawrence Freedman outlines two extreme parameters. He says that if it were to be interpreted as the "triumph of liberalism and free markets, the rule of international law and an era of peace and prosperity", it would surely be found wanting. On the other hand, if it is considered as "merely descriptive, requiring no more than an acceptance that the current situation is unique and clearly different in critical respects," then it might serve a purpose. In the latter case then the new world order will hardly make any substantial contribution to stability. This was the underlying theme considered by James Schlesinger when he said : "The world order of the future will revert to that which existed before 1939 and most notably after World War I. It will be marked by power politics, national rivalry and ethnic tensions".

Another consequence of the end of the cold war is that regional conflicts are now decoupled from the earlier superpower confrontation. It is as if the lid has been suddenly removed from the cauldron allowing the witches' brew to boil over. This is what seemed to have happened in Yugoslavia and may well be replicated elsewhere.

The East-West confrontation of the cold war has ended. Nothing has replaced it yet. But, with the shaping of the new global agenda, a North-South conflictual environment may well be on the cards. The industrialised developed countries of the North are going to find themselves on the same side of the divide, in spite of their differences, and confront the underdeveloped South. The issues around which these differences are likely to be focussed are some of the following :

(a) *Global Wanning Ozone Layer Depletion, and Other Environmental Issues.* Increasingly, these will emerge as major political questions. The profligacy of the North has brought about the current deteriorated conditions, yet it will attempt to restrict not its own expanding consumption but those of the South.

(b) *Population Movement.* The population of the North will remain static and may even decline marginally, but in the South it is expected to double every 25 years. This will accentuate pressures for population transfers, which will be resisted sharply in the North and give rise to fascist tendencies as already apparent.

(c) *Arms Transfers.* Surplus arms production in the developed countries will impel its transfer to the

South, accentuating existing conflicts and raising their destructive thresholds.

(*d*) Arbitrary imposition of Western concepts of democracy and human rights, often at the expense of national sovereignty.

(*e*) Propagation of unequal non-proliferation clauses in national and international treaties and linking these with issues such as technology transfers and aid disbursements.

A distinct shift is the growing importance of economic over political questions. Global competition now is centered more on economic issues, and questions of trade, tariff, market access and investment are dominating political discourse. This, in turn, is linked to domestic economic advancement. The continuing recession in Europe and North America are exacerbating the problem. National power is being measured more in terms of per capita growth in GNP than military strength. While this is giving rise at one level to what is termed as competitive co-operation, at the same time the world is getting increasingly interdependent, and is in the process of unification in Europe, Asia-pacific and North America.

The end of the cold war has also seen the birth of a new era of nationalism. Actually, it is difficult to say whether it was the cause or the consequence of the end of the cold war. In the past, whether in Europe, Africa or Asia, national and political maps had not always coincided. With the end of the cold war and the resurgence of nationalism, we are witnessing a new kind of fragmentation, often without sufficient cause or acrimony, as in the case of Czechoslovakia, but, on other and more frequent occasions, through great violence. The growth of nationalism is splintering the world into a body of many new nation-states. In 1776, the world had around 35 empires, kingdoms, countries and states. By the end of the Second World War, the number was about 70. In the late 1960s it was around 130. Today there are some

200 nation-states in the world which are all sovereign in their own rights. An immediate consequence of this new nationalism is the emergence of ethnic separatism, with its new terms such as "ethnic cleansing".

Another dimension of a search for identity is the emergence of religious fundamentalism. Although its recent reappearance goes back to well over a decade, the consequence of this for the international political environment is being heightened by recent developments. The emergence of Central Asia as a new political entity, with five Islamic states adjacent to other Muslim nations further south, is significant. It is hardly to be expected that these states will be united even though only recently they have formed a joint economic organisation. They may not also entirely be cohesive, but the very fact of its formation will need to be noted and its implications considered. What consequence will this have on the emerging political scenario in the neighbourhood, especially in the Gulf region? How will this affect the periphery of the Islamic world, which now must encompass Eastern Europe, Israel, Russia, China and India?

It is in this perspective that new military strategic scenarios are begin discussed in the West. One particular case was that by the *Economist* of London, which reflects the general tenor of arguments being considered there. It concedes the emergence of pluralism in the world. But this in itself will not necessarily be of the democratic variety, hence there may be "explosions". While all such explosions need not be responded to, those that directly affect the accession of necessary raw materials by the North will need "some pretty rapid action". Such conflicts are termed as "wars of interest". Continuing on the same theme, it is assessed that outside this pole, may be other horror stories not related to economic interests, but those that shock the conscience of the world in a substantial manner. There may be a need to stop this horror through military actions which are being termed as "wars of conscience."

Such ideas of global participation in the resolution of conflicts is likely to remain remote, unless they threaten vital interests of a state or coalition of states. The Gulf War was an exception due to a large number of rather special circumstances, the details of which we do not need to go into at this stage. But a repetition of those conditions is remote. There are many alternative scenarios of regional aggression rather than a cross-border blitzkrieg. Subtler versions ranging from subversion, infiltration, insurgency and/or externally sponsored terrorism may well be the future norm. These are sufficiently ambiguous to make it difficult to rally international support in countering them. It is safe to assume then that in the foreseeable future, instability in the international system will continue as it has always done in the past. Instead the ebbing of the cold war may witness and upsurge of regional political turbulence with ethnic and religious overtones.

At the international level, dramatic developments have promised a major reduction in the strategic nuclear arsenals of both the USA and Russia. By the year 2003 AD, approximately two-thirds of the existing weapons are likely to be destroyed. Positive though this may be, the middle level nuclear powers, France, Britain and China, are yet to join the process. There is some uncertainty regarding the nuclear weapons in Ukraine as well. This development again addresses security questions at the core level, but leaves the periphery much as before.

Of immediate concern to us are developments in Asia and their impact on security. One view that has been expressed is that as the cold war was essentially a Eurocentric affair, the effects of its demise are to be felt on-line that environment. That is only partially true. As we have discussed earlier, it was in East-West conflict of global dimension and its end has seen fundamental changes and reorientation of policies all over the world. Only its military confrontation was directly and most intensely in Europe. With its termination, the security scenario there has turned considerably benign and is resulting in a rapid degradation of military capabilities that is only natural and to be welcomed.

On the other hand, in Asia, the security concerns were essentially regional, with external powers involved to the extent that it was a part of the overall bipolar situation. With their decoupling from the earlier superpower linkage there is now a higher local and ethnic content in these tensions. Hence they may be globally less critical, but regionally they are likely to be more free to rise to higher levels of violence. These will then also prove more difficult to resolve.

An area of immediate relevant to India are the emerging developments in Central and West Asia. A region that had long historical, strategic and cultural ties with the subcontinent has suddenly emerged on the international scene as a fractured, yet cohesive identity. The five Central Asian States are now grappling with major economic problems in the wake of their break-up from the erstwhile Soviet Union and, at the same time, attempting to shape their own national identities. In this they are encountering challenges from Islamic revivalism with strong support from Iran, Pakistan and Saudi Arabia. While there are strong influences within these countries towards religious tolerance, the possibility of a resurgence of Islamic identity cannot be discounted, especially if economic recovery is sluggish and prolonged. Currently, there is a desire to move towards Turkey and through it to Europe. Yet they are now also a part of the Economic Co-operation Organisation, along with Afghanistan, Pakistan, Iran and Turkey.

To our west, Afghanistan is no near a solution and with a level of violence, especially in its southern areas, that is about the same as in earlier years. In South-east

Asia, the Cambodian question continues to elude a solution. The largest and most ambitious United Nation operations in history is not able to make any headway against the intransigence of the Khmer Rouge. The failure of high level talks at Beijing has highlighted two things : The continued strategic role of China in Southeast Asia; the other, a fairly successful attempt by the Khmer Rouge to stir up latent anti-Vietnam feelings of the Khmer people and thus legitimise for itself a role much larger than what can be justified rationally. Till as long as these trends prevail a solution does not seem likely. The region may move ahead on other issues and frame its post-cold war policies, but incipient instability is likely to persist.

For a change, Russia may be considered first, primarily to eliminate it from serious discussion, even though only for the present. Its internal problems presently are of a massive dimension and there appears very little likelihood of a quick turn around. In fact, both economically and politically things are likely to get worse. Therefore, notwithstanding recent rhetorics, Russia is likely to withdraw from serious international engagements in the near future. Not much may be expected from it except perhaps in a negative way. But equally, Russia will have a major role in the future. Writing it off for long in a strategic sense will be an even greater mistake.

The USA is likely to maintain a continuity in its foreign policy under the new administration. But there will be some change particularly in nuances and emphasis as was brought out clearly in the run up to the election. Concerns of the USA are overwhelmingly domestic and essentially economic. Dimensions of the problem are gigantic. With a $ 400 billion annual deficit, $4 trillion accumulated national debt going towards $5 trillion, the nation is in serious economic trouble.

For the present the US remains committed to Asia. Admiral David E. Jeremiah, Vice-Chairman of the JCS, in a speech at Canberra on September 27, 1991, said : "The bottom line is this : the US itself is a Pacific nation, and we intend to remain so." This was elaborated in the East Asia Strategic Initiative in end of August 1992, the key elements in which were :

- US regional role will shift from secondary to primary.
- Aim at preventing the rise of a hegemonic power, which is the key US objective in the post-cold war world.
- Continuing its security relations with Japan.

The USA has been a major beneficiary of the dynamism that has characterised East Asia. US trans-Pacific trade now exceeds trade with Europe by a half. Asia's capital invested in the United States has helped cover essential US investment needs. No doubt, Japan and the East Asian States less China find US strategic pressure beneficial.

The question is how long can this continue? President Clinton is committed to cut defence spending by $ 100 billion by 1997. US forces in Asia were planned to be cut back from 135,000 (including 25,000 afloat) in 1989 by 15,520 (or 11 per cent), plus an additional 8,100 from the based in the Philippines by 1992. This will bring down its forces to 111,650. But public and Congressional pressures can bring this down further. Around 10 per cent additional cuts are expected by 1994. In this scenario of diminishing US capabilities, what are the regional responses?

Prime Minister Toshiki Kaifu described Japan's goals in the new international order in the Diet in March 1990 as follows :

- To ensure peace and security.
- To respect freedom and democracy.
- To generate world prosperity through open market economies.

- To preserve an environment where all people can live rewarding lives.
- To create a stable international order founded upon dialogue and co-operation.

In more concrete terms, even as Tokyo attempts to break out of its self-imposed exile from independent strategic thinking, it will find itself relying more and more on the USA. This new relationship will be one of strategic interdependence, based on their enormous economic interaction as well as Japanese security dependence. US-Japan trade exceeded $ 142 billion in 1990. This was twice Japan's trade with the European Community (EC) and 80 per cent of all US trade with the entire EC. Cumulative Japanese investment in the US was $ 130.5 billion by March 1991. There are enormous financial flows between the countries. Therefore, even though there are strains in their relationship due to public resentment in both countries over different issues, Japan can go on paying $ 70,000 (likely to go up to about $ 100,000) for every US serviceman or servicewoman in Japan to maintain this relationship.

In all these happenings in the post-cold war world China remains an enigma. Not because enough is not known about China to form a clear opinion, for it has been quite open to the world in recent years, but because the post-cold war developments have largely passed it by. Its economy opened up since 1978, even though market mechanisms emerged later and are not yet fully in place. Its own road of "socialist market economy" is a new path altogether. Whether it can liberalise economically without political pluralism is a question that will only be answered when the new generation leaders assume power in the future. The time is surely not too far off. Tensions, if any, seem to be managed very successfully so far, yet doubts remain. What is not in doubt, however, is the rapid growth of Chinese economic, political and military power.

This condition is considered by Brzezinski. According to his line of argument, with the present rate of economic development, China will join the US, EC and Japan as one of the world's four leading powers by the year 2010. This will then transform the security environment in Asia as dramatically as has happened in Europe in 1990. It may even happen earlier. The question is in what way the change will take place and in which dimension?

A powerful united China has historically always been assertive and dominant, effects of which have been felt all over Asia. On the other hand, in the changed international environment and the need for greater interdependence, conditions may well be different. Thus an approach of greater interaction and dialogue with China may well be warranted.

The disintegration of the Soviet empire has left behind a world that is warily awakening after an intense cold war. No coalition or nation can justly claim victory and all have to pay a price, some perhaps more than others. Yet, the 45 years of the cold war have changed the world in fundamental ways. It will, thus, not be right to assume that the world order will revert to that, which existed between the two World Wars and be marked by power politics, national rivalry and attempts at balance of power.

6

INDIA AND NUCLEAR MISSILE DEFENCE

Interview with M. Dubey

Ques: This month marks the third anniversary of the Pokhran-II and Chagai nuclear tests that enabled India and Pakistan to cross the Rubicon and emerge as *de facto* nuclear weapon states on the world scene. On this occasion many people in both the countries are organising protests against what they describe as nuclearisation of South-Asia. You, sir were among those who had welcomed the nuclear tests conducted at Pokhran on May 11 and 13, 1998 on the ground that they helped India to acquire the much needed credible nuclear deterrence that was imperative in the prevailing security environment in our region. After three years how would you look back and evaluate that development from the standpoint of national security?

Ans: I had no doubt welcomed the nuclear tests carried out by India in May 1998 but I had also said that the tests did not indicate that India had already acquired a credible nuclear deterrence. The purpose of the tests lay in the fact that they publicly announced India's intention to acquire such a deterrence. And, I think, having once done that it would be very difficult for this government or for that matter any government to go back on it.

I certainly have been very much in favour of India having a credible nuclear deterrence. But looking back at the event after three years of the Pokhran-II tests I am not quite sure whether we still have a credible nuclear deterrence. I do not fully know what is going on but my general impression is that we are still quite a distance from becoming a nuclear weapon power in the real sense of the term. We have tested only one thermonuclear device at the time of Pokhran-II. Since it is generally agreed among experts that thermonuclear devices are more economical and easier to handle, one would have thought that we should have gone about developing these devices in a more purposeful and meaningful manner. But there is no indication that we have really done so.

The same is true of the delivery vehicles. Whereas in order to operationalise a delivery vehicle, one has to test it several times over—in the case of a Russian system, they carried out 12 to 13 such tests before deploying it—we in our case kept on postponing the Agni-II test and at long last it was carried out; but that was done only once and since then no further tests have been conducted. Thus, there is no indication that we have at least developed a medium range delivery vehicle which is reliable, can be produced in numbers, and can be deployed.

I think the same can be said with regard to the miniaturisation of nuclear devices. After we carried out the nuclear tests we unilaterally declared a moratorium on further testing which is good. But this was done on the assumption that whatever needs to be achieved by testing we will do that by laboratory tests through computer simulation and, if necessary, even by subcritical testing. And again, there is no indication as to how far we have progressed in the direction of miniaturisation. In any case, there have not been any subcritical tests.

It is really surprising that whereas we want to keep our option of testing open by not signing the CTBT we are not willing to carry out even those tests which are permissible under the CTBT, subcritical tests being one of them. Our scientists have gone on record stating that they are capable of carrying out such tests. The officially declared nuclear weapon powers like the United States have been carrying out such tests, and I do not understand what is coming in the way of our doing so.

So, on balance my guess and inference—I can only guess since I have no access to information—is that we have not made much progress since Pokhran-II towards developing an autonomous nuclear deterrence of our own, that we have not even developed a deployable credible medium range delivery vehicle, that because of lack of progress in miniaturisation we have not been able to couple warheads with the delivery vehicles, let alone really deploying them, and having a command and control system. Thus three years after the Pokhran-II tests we seem to be very very far from the position of having a credible nuclear deterrence.

In retrospect, therefore, one starts wondering whether the nuclear tests that were carried out in May 1998 were not because of the desire to gain political mileage out of a one-time affair. One also starts wondering to what extent pressures by military powers, with whom we are trying to develop important strategic relations, have come in the way of our not doing what is required to be done for actually becoming a nuclear weapon power.

I would like to add one more point. We also got a draft prepared on the nuclear doctrine that India should follow. The government went to the extent of getting this draft made public even at the cost of antagonising some of the friendly countries and frightening others. I was a member of the National Security Advisory Board at that time. But I was not present in the Board meeting when a decision was taken to publicise it. I would certainly not have been in favour of doing so. Because the doctrine basically enunciates what we should have without taking into account our capability of getting it and without going into the time dimension, that is, the time to be taken for acquiring it.

In my view tactically it was very undesirable to have made a public announcement of intentions which are based on plans and projects some of which are still on the drawing board and some of them only in the form of conceptions. For example, I thought there was no need for us to tell the world that our nuclear doctrine would include the acquisition of ICBMs, that we would have all the three tiers of a nuclear war-fighting machine, that is, airborne, land-based and sea-based, and about our having enough weapons to survive a first strike and be able to deliver a crippling second strike. The latter made nonsense of our declaration to have only a minimum nuclear deterrence. I am, therefore, not surprised that for a long time now the government has left the draft nuclear doctrine languishing, there has been no further discussion on it, no attempt to evolve a consensus on it, let alone finalising it and putting some of its operational elements into effect.

Ques: How do you analyse the US President's latest statement on the national missile defence system? How would it affect the Indian quest for a credible nuclear deterrence on its now, that presumably prompted the Government of India to exercise the nuclear option in May 1998? And in this context how do you view the Government of India's apparently unreserved welcome of the US head of state's statement (due to the promise of unilateral reduction of nuclear arsenals, the decision to move away from the hair-trigger alerts associated with the prevailing nuclear order, and the call for consultations with several countries including India in the matter)?

Ans: I must say that I was little surprised by the unreserved welcome that was given to the announcement of the intention of the US Government to develop and deploy a defensive system. I was particularly surprised by the endorsement that the statement of the Government of India implied of the defensive weapon system itself and the belief that the Government of India expressed in the technological inevitability of such a defensive system.

There are, of course, some positive elements in the statement made by President Bush and you have yourself noted three of them, that is, his intention to unilaterally reduce the US nuclear force, his intention to take measures for de-alerting, and his approach to consult friends and allies at this stage of the development of the defensive system which has been described as a cooperative approach to the development of the system.

Now, I think it is very difficult to take such positive aspects on their face value. I would not like to question the US intention; but at the same time I would not go overboard and shower lavish praise by using such terms as 'welcome', 'laud', etc. For, the unilateral cut in the US nuclear force is something which would have been expected in any case. The entire US nuclear force was built to counter a possible attack from the then Soviet Union, and after the end of the Cold War it is very difficult for the United States of justify—in the eyes of its own people and its own Congress—the retention of such a large force even after the reductions according to START-I and START-II. Besides, any cut by the United States is now bound to be unilateral since Russia is no longer in a position to negotiate. Because of its financial problems Russia is finding it very difficult to even maintain anything but a very modest nuclear arsenal. And, therefore, it doesn't have much to offer in lieu of getting the US to reduce its force. So in future unilateral nuclear cut was something which everybody was expecting.

I would say the same thing about de-alerting, started right from the end of the Cold War. The intelligence that was sought to be gathered from very close to the boundary of the then Soviet Union stopped, the targetting of the missiles towards each other was stopped by common agreement, the Western powers voluntarily gave up tactical weapons which were weapons of first strike and one would expect that now the adversarial relationship between the two countries is no longer there, this kind of de-alerting would move further apace.

I would say the same thing about this cooperative approach of the United States. All that President Bush said in the statement is that the NMD will be deployed with the approval of the US Congress. So the consultation is basically to give an impression to the world that the whole thing is being developed in cooperation with a group of countries. But most of these countries being consulted are hardly in a position to technologically contribute to the development of the system. As a matter of fact the individual pieces of the system have already been developed in a preliminary form and all that is needed to be done is to agree on an optimum package—and further refining those pieces—and put that package in operation. And this would be entirely the US work and initiative.

So this cooperative or multilateral approach with regard to the system is, to my mind, just for the sake of giving it a nice appearance in the public mind.

So far as the Indian deterrence is concerned, I think our deterrence is not directed against the United States. Therefore, it would not be a direct target of the US defensive system. But our deterrence, definitely gets degraded with the development of more offensive weapons by China in response to the likely degradation of its own deterrence, as it would then go in for more ICBMs of qualitatively higher types with multiple warheads. And with the induction of these weapons in the Chinese armory, our deterrence will become less effective unless we also get into the race of developing our nuclear arms further, something that would carry a huge economic cost. So this definitely poses a problem for our nuclear deterrence.

Ques: While exercising the nuclear option three years ago the government had assured that it would work tirelessly for security global nuclear disarmament. What has been the record of the government on that front? We know that you were the architect of the Rajiv Gandhi Action Plan for Nuclear Disarmament unveiled at the UN more than ten years ago. That, if I am not mistaken, was the first comprehensive and practical blueprint for realising a nuclear weapons-free world. Has the present Government of India done enough for materialising this goal? What concrete steps, in your opinion, can even now be taken in this regard?

Ans: I do not think that over the last three years we have done very much by way of promoting our idea of elimination of nuclear weapons or establishing a nuclear weapons-free world. It was a part of the nuclear policy enunciated by the Prime Minister after Pokhran-II—and it was also mentioned in the draft nuclear doctrine prepared by the NSA Board—but by way of further elaboration, by way of building a platform for it, by way of putting forward proposals in international fora I do not think that we have done very much.

This is partly because of our lack of initiative, our problems in the disarmament field today and partly because of the general international climate. I think traditionally the non-aligned forum has been the main platform through which we advanced this idea. And in recent years and non-aligned forum has not been particularly active in this area. This is mainly because of its general decline and erosion of its effectiveness as an international platform. There have been other groups (that were established immediately after Pokhran-II) which adopted elimination of nuclear weapons as a definite objective. There was a Latin American group, and there was also group of 12 (including Sweden, Ireland, South Africa). However, after their initial pronouncements, they have not done much on this front. I think India's constraint in playing an active role in this regard is due to the loss of its credibility with the international community because of the nuclear tests it carried out in Pokhran in May 1998 and therefore, if India wants to join these groups of countries or take an initiative in the NAM on the issue, I fear there would not be much of an enthusiasm to collaborate with India.

The signing of the CTBT would have restored this credibility to some extent and brought India into the disarmament dialogue but apparently there have been considerations of wider nature that have come in the way of our signing the CTBT.

Finally there is also the question: how seriously is the government committed to the public stance it has taken or is it only part of a tactic? It is very difficult to pronounce a judgement on this question one way or the other, but surely the question itself cannot be ignored.

Ques: Has all this happened because the present government is not keen to highlight the Rajiv Gandhi Action Plan?

Ans: Yes, that can be one factor.

Ques: Why couldn't they spell out a follow-up of that Action Plan?

Ans: That should have been done. But I also think there could be the international factor in the sense that there are not many takers for this idea today in the world partly because of the way in which we have lost our credibility with so many developing countries in the NAM.

Ques: But don't you think for that very reason the Government of India should have lent more vigour to this campaign?

Ans: Yes, I agree with you. That should have been done and we have not done so.

Ques: But then what needs to be done now?

Ans: Now we are in a very different ball game. With this unqualified support for a defensive system I think we are in a very different kind of situation.

The present situation in the world would have warranted our working for a transition to a nuclear-free world. But what we have now announced is that we regard a transition to a defensive system as being inevitable. It must be remembered that a defensive system is a weapon system, it is not a system of elimination of weapons.

So we are in a different paradigm—the paradigm of a new weapon system. This is not the route to ensure elimination of nuclear weapons—as a matter of fact it is getting on to a new arms race because of this new weapon system.

Ques: So you think the Government of India's present course should be altered?

Ans: Absolutely. That alone will be consistent with our avowed policy of seeking an elimination of nuclear weapons. We should not join the major power in the world—or for that matter any power—in the development of a new weapon system.

I don't know how we can restore our credibility with the non-aligned countries unless and until we get out of the US bandwagon we have jumped into, and retain autonomy of thinking on this subject.

Ques: That autonomy has been considerably eroded of late?

Ans: Yes, of course, you see, if you have joined hands with the United States and other like-minded countries in developing a new weapon system you get really far removed from your objective of seeking your security through the elimination of nuclear weapons. Instead of that you are trying to ensure your security through the protection that can be provided by the defensive system of the United States. Since you have been invited for consultations you have taken it that you are in the category of friends who are entitled for protection.

But it is very unlikely that the US would have a very strong incentive to provide that protection to us from the powers against which we need to be protected. The perception of such a protection is bound to lead to a great deal of loss of momentum to the process of developing our capability for protection which we are engaged in.

Ques: This is akin to seeking the US umbrella....

Ans: yes absolutely.

Ques: ....as we sought in 1963 after the Chinese aggression.

Ans: At that time we sought the umbrella and they said 'no'. This time what is happening is that we think that what they have said amounts to saying 'yes' and agreeing to provide the umbrella. And therefore, we have lowered our guard, thrown caution to four winds and jumped into the bandwagon.

Ques: And this call for consultations, this is just a rhetorical statement?

Ans: Yes. As I said, they have been at it for years and, individual components have already been developed. As far as the 'evolution' of the system is concerned, it is 'evolution' within the American polity. They need no one's help for evolving it. So consultations with other countries is just a device to win international support for the new system.

Ques: There is this argument which has been voiced by some experts that there is no alternative to living with the new system as the US will go ahead with it in any case. How would you react to this argument?

Ans: For that matter so many other wrong and dangerous trends may appear inevitable both in domestic politics and internationally. Is it not the duty of a right-thinking individual or nation, whose attitude and vision are guided by basic human values, to stand up to such trends and schemes and resist them? Nobody can predict success but waging a battle against something evil and pernicious itself should be regarded as an individual of national virtue.

In this particular case, however, the chances of success of a movement to avert the possibility of a new weapon system cannot be underestimated. After all, in the teeth of heavy opposition inside the United States and the international community President Reagan had to fold back his Star Wars project. President Clinton put the idea of the modified system, as is now being proposed by President Bush, to the backburner. How has then this project suddenly become a technological inevitability simply because the new US Administration has decided to push it in pursuance of the promise given in its election platform? Even today there is a great deal of opposition to it from different sections of public and intellectual opinion in the United States and the feasibility of the project is yet to be demonstrated.

Ques: Does the United States need such a sophisticated and expensive system to protect itself and its friends from the threats emanating from the so-called rogue countries?

Ans: I do not think so. Firstly, there is no protection from nuclear devices that can be smuggled in a suitcase by terrorists into the territory of the United States or that of its friends and allies.

Secondly, the United States has already demonstrated its awesome capacity to put down the so-called rogue states by its highly sophisticated conventional arms, particularly its missiles and air power. It has been using this power effectively against Iraq and used it against Yugoslavia to destroy much of the latter's infrastructure. So far as major nuclear powers like China and Russia are concerned, they would try to counter and most probably succeed in countering the defensive system by developing such systems of their own or by multiplying their offensive systems to saturate the US defensive system.

Ques: Will our joining the US in missile defence give us the bargaining power to extract other concessions?

Ans: I have seen some of our experts suggesting that we should use our collaboration with the United States on the NMD to extract such concessions as getting removed the sanctions against the supply of defence equipment and technology; being treated as a member-state in the exclusive groupings like the Australia Club, London Club and the Missile Technology Control Regime (MTCR) so as to be able to qualify for the transfer of dual-purpose technology, substances and equipment under these regimes; and for even getting admitted as a nuclear weapon power in the NPT regime. I do not think that this is going to work. I believe that endorsement of the US NMD hardly gives us any leverage in this regard. For, the US does not expect any substantive contribution from India or most of the other countries being consulted, nor does it need such a contribution. As I have already stated, the call for consultation and cooperation is intended mainly as a selling-device for the NMD. In the ultimate analysis India's leverage can be built only on the basis of its economic strength, and after it succeeds in developing a credible nuclear deterrence and thus becoming a full-fledged nuclear power.

Ques: Do you share the enthusiasm in some Indian circles that President Bush's statement amounts to India being treated as a friend and ally and Pakistan being included in the "states for whom terror and blackmail are a way of life"?

Ans: This is not at all correct. India will have to prove its loyalty at every step to remain a friend of the United States in this sense of the term, and this will mean continuous, unending and open-ended adjustments in its domestic and foreign policies to suit the US' interests. Can India, with its more than fifty years' policy of non-alignment, with its legacy of applying moral values while making a judgement on international issues, afford to do so? The nation must squarely address this issue and come to a conclusion.

So far as Pakistan is concerned, it is still too important a country for the United States to be dumped. That it is so is demonstrated by the fact that the US has helped enabling out Pakistan from economic crises repeatedly during the last couple of years, refused to declare it as a terrorist state, and continued its high-level and multipronged dealings with Pakistan even after the military takeover in the country. In this connection we must take careful note of recent news reports that Foreign Minister Sattar would be visiting Washington for high-level talks and soon thereafter General Pervez Musharraf might be invited to Washington for talks.

Indian Support to NMD

Not since the 1969 Rebuff at Rabat—where we had rushed in to participate in the inaugural Islamic Summit, only to be ejected almost instantly—has there been a foreign policy *faux pas* comparable to statement by the Ministry of External Affairs (MEA) virtually applauding the U.S. President, Mr. George Bush's announcement of his plans for the highly controversial national missile defence (NMD).

Its objectionable features included the inexplicable haste with which it was issued, its fawning tone and its blatant reversal of established policy on crucial aspects of the nuclear issue, such as the deployment of weapons in space and the trashing of the 1972 Anti-Ballistic Missile (ABM) Treaty. Altogether the regretable statement has made this country the lone drum-beater in the wide world for the new Bush doctrine. Ironically, all the traditional allies of the U.S., including Britain that has tended to endorse every initiative emanating from Washington, have refrained from committing themselves.

They have confined themselves to welcoming the assurance of consultations with "all concerned" and promised to give their considered response only after these have been held. Japan and South Korea have, in fact, expressed concern over what NMD—and its inevitable offshoot, theatre missile defence (TMD)—is bound to do the chronic frictions in East Asia. Only India, like the new convert, seems to have gone out on a limb. No wonder that the U.S. diplomats in New Delhi were taken by pleasant surprise because the Indian reaction to Mr. Bush's speech "exceeded their wildest expectations."

To say all this is not to suggest by any means that this country should not do all that it can to promote friendly and cooperative relations with the U.S., especially in the context of America's own willingness to embark on a "qualitatively new relationship" with it. But to achieve this objective it is not at all necessary to issue statements that are crass. These, as Pakistan's long experience in an earlier era underscores, may yield short-term dividends but is likely to be self-defeating in the long run.

Faced with mounting criticism of its statement that ought to have been predictable, the MEA has reverted to its typical, aggressively defensive mould. Its official spokespersons and unofficial apologists say, with an air of injured innocence. "But we haven't endorsed NMD as such". In that case, pray, what exactly has the Ministry endorsed, indeed applauded and hailed? Surely, it is quixotic to steer clear of the core and substance of Mr. Bush's pronouncement and jump with joy over some peripheral point.

As it happens, this incidental point is the U.S. president's promise of unilateral "deep cuts" in his nuclear arsenals. But, sadly, it is clear even to the meanest intelligence that this vague vow is wholly conditional on a workable missile defence being in place first. In *The Economist's* words, the Republican right's concept of deep cuts is such as to "make a disarmer's hair stand on end." Since the MEA cannot be accused of lacking in intelligence, its song and dance about the "deep cuts" must have had some other driving force behind it. It is equally significant that ABM, not even alluded to in the Ministry's statement, suddenly reappeared on its agenda only after the meeting between the External Affairs and Defence Minister, Mr. Jaswant Singh, and his Russian opposite number, Mr. Igor Ivanov.

In one respect the MEA statement touched the extremes of fatuity. No one yet knows whether NMD can be made to work and, if so, at what cost. Of the four tests held during the Clinton years, three and a half had failed. There are profound doubts about the technical feasibility of NMD even among its supporters in the U.S. But the Indian statement, long on flowery rhetoric and short on realism, glibly talks of "strategic and technological inevitability" of a move in the direction desired by Mr. Bush!

Two other elements in the disturbing situation are particularly worrisome. The first is the lack of adequate consultations within the Government on the content and implications of the statement of this grave import, It is inconceivable that in Mr. P.V. Narasimha Rao's days, or even those of Indira Gandhi, a statement of this kind would have been issued without the Cabinet Committee on Political Affairs—now called the Cabinet Committee on Security—approving it line by line. Nothing of the kind was done, or even contemplated, in the present case. According to some reports even consultations between the MEA and the Prime Minister's Office (PMO) were perfunctory: if true, this is startling reversal of roles.

Secondly, and more importantly, the meaning of the NMD is totally transparent. By deploring highly versatile missile defence systems on land, under sea and in air and space, together with its "reduced but still superior offensive missile forces", the U.S. would be well on the way to 'establishing a domineering, deeply threatening, global military posture,' according to *The Guardian*, Mr. John Local, one of the bright backroom boys, who has worked on Mr. Bush's grandiose scheme, is even more explicit. Deployment of NMD, he says gleefully, "will give the U.S., a credible first strike capability that Russia (or anyone else) cannot resist". Is this the brave, new nuclear world order the authors of effusive statement want India joyously to accept?

Indian Enthusiasm

The elements of the Bush administration's new nuclear doctrine, hailed of exuberantly by New Delhi, are simple enough: A move away from the offensive 'deterrence' doctrine that maintains that any attempt to attack the US would be met by a devastating counterattack. A shift towards a defensive ballistic missile-based system that would enable the US block attacks, and in the process make it more discriminate in suing its retaliatory capacity.

Separated by two oceans and without a missile power to its north and south, one can see the logic of those in the US who think that a ballistic missile defence scheme would add to their national security. Whether or not this will promote stability in a world is quite another thing. There is the question of whether the technology will work. Related to this is the issue as to whether it will destabilise the prevailing deterrence-based security framework..

States that are deterred by the US nuclear capability may feel that the new shield could devalue their capacity to scare the US. During crisis periods, they could be encouraged to launch a preemptive attack. There is also another script that mist be considered. Given America's past record, would not its enormous dominance of both defensive and offensive technologies encourage irresponsible behaviour?

These and a host of other issues compel attention, but here in India, which has hailed the move, the first question that needs tb be asked is: What's in it for us?

Certainly, there would be little benefit from the NMD as a shield. India's potential and real adversaries are on its borders. The missile delivery time is one-fifth of what would obtain in the US scenario and there are many other ways of delivering nuclear warheads. For this reason, apologists of the government have dressed up the Indian shift in the garb of geopolitics. The step, it is argued, is part of a grand architecture of the post-cold war world, where India will reap great benefits by aligning itself with the world's hyperpower—the US. To those who may think this is too far-fetched, there are also whispered suggestions that the US may lift all the sanctions imposed on India since Pokhran I, and, possible realign its Kashmir policy towards recognising the LoC as the international border.

There is a somewhat more implausible argument being retailed by otherwise hard-headed analysts. This is that India is not going along with this for any gain, but from the belief that US aims, as expounded by Mr. Bush, were identical to New Delhi's theology featuring an opposition to MAD and the 'discriminatory' world nuclear order. That this was sought to be done by a selective reading of the Bush speech is quite another thing. Actually there is little the US can offer to India that ought to make it throw caution to the winds and take positions that are likely to undermine its national security and erode its autonomy. India's size, location and demography give it a geopolitical character distinct from that of any other country in the world. This is the reason why India gravitated towards a feisty non-alignment in the aftermath of Partition. This is also the justification provided by the Vajpayee government for crossing the nuclear threshold. Jaswant Singh toured, world capitals justifying the Indian nuclear tests on the ground that India had to safeguard its strategic autonomy. In now proposing that Indian align itself closer to the US, the BJP-led coalition is not serving India's national interest.

When the US anti-proliferation pressure was at its peak in the early 1990, it was suggested that India would get unspecified goodies from the US in exchange for participating in the five-nation conference mooted by the US. Since the US government provides little bilateral aid to India and does not block direct or institutional investment, the only leverage it has is with dual-use technologies that it has prohibited. Many of these are available from Europe or Russia. A quick audit of the US technology denial regime would suggest that it has at best been an irritant, but not a major obstacle for India.

US recognition of the LoC as the international border would be a major gain for India, but it will hardly settle the Kashmir problem. Indeed, the chances are that it would exacerbate the situation, at least in the short-to-medium term. Such an outcome is better obtained through patient negotiation rather than a diplomatic coup.

Perhaps the most dangerous subtext of New Delhi's thinking has been in relation to China. Officially, New Delhi claims that it does not view China as an adversary. But Prime Minister Vajpayee's letters to World leaders in the wake of the nuclear tests offered the potential Chinese threat as a substantial justification. The Chinese opposition to the NMD and the consequences of this are bound to singe India. Did the government consider this at all?

Bush-Putin Summit

The first ever summit near the Slovenian capital Ljubuana between the U.S. President, Mr. George Bush and his Russian counterpart, Mr. Vladimir Putin opens a new chapter in the America-Russia relations. While President Bush urged to move away from the cold war mentality and see the world as 'it is' and not as 'it used to be'. He also mentioned that when Russia and America work together it is good for the world peace and prosperity. President Putin reciprocated the new warmth and said their dialogue exceeded his expectations. He was frank in saying that differences in their approaches do exist, but the differences are not of fundamental nature. These differences can be resolved with a constructive dialogue. Mr. Putin was clear about the points of differences and at the same time he was emphatic about the positive prospects of their new relationship.

During Mr. Bush's first European tour, the divisions in trans-Atlantic relations appeared in his NATO meeting at Brussels, the European leaders expressed their unhappiness about American rejection of the Kyoto Treaty on climate change by saying that they are going ahead to ratify it in any case. What marks out the Bush-Putin summit is a clear message that any unilateral approach will not be good in today's interdependent world. President Bush did his best to remove misgivings about his isolationist approach and expressed his desire to work together.

Bush-Putin talks were wide ranging and touched upon areas of concern for both sides. President Bush raised sensitive subjects for Russia like Chechnya, media relations, the Balkans and relations with neighbours especially the support needed by Georgia. After the disintegration of the former Soviet Union, America is helping these new republics in the name of democracy and freedom. President Putin in his quiet style is trying to consolidate the Russian sphere of influence. His visit to Yugoslavia, the first in a decade by any Russian president is very significant. Yugoslavia's fragile economy needs financial support and America is putting pressure to handover the former President Slomadom Milosovich to the vague tribunal for trial for war crimes. Yugoslavia wanted to try Mr. Milosovich according to the domestic laws, but now laws are being changed because of growing pressure to enable his extradition to the Hague tribunal. Russia still has its influence over Yugoslavia. So here a great tension is building up. Macedonia is another flash point in the Balkans.

President Bush highlighted sound investment climate in Russia with simple flat tax rate which he is not able to do in his country. He mentioned about Russia's rich resources especially in the field of energy. The Caspian Sea Gas pipeline project, a very important project on the energy scene, is a joint American-Russian project. President Putin was quick to point out that their economic ties do not correspond to the potential of the two countries. He said there is a need for an additional impulse. Therefore, both leaders agreed that a high level business delegation will soon visit Russia to take advantage of the favourable business climate created in Russia recently.

Keen to have a pragmatic approach and build on cooperation, President Putin however made it clear that the 1972 Anti-Ballistic Missile Treaty, (ABM Treaty) remains a cornerstone of modern architecture of security. The treaty has been described as a relic of the past by President Bush. Mr. Putin warned America that any unilateral approach will complicate the issues. He said both Russia and America have amassed largest number of weapons of mass destruction. Therefore, they have a special responsibility. After listening to how and what of the U.S. missile defence system directly from President Bush, he wants the experts to go into the specifics rather than just keep talking about the vague, general concept of deterrence. It was clear that Russia was not ready to take the new U.S. proposal on faith, details of which will be suppled later. Here Mr. Putin was unyielding as he insisted that the new threats have to be defined and also the ways to counter them, which can of course be done together by Russia and America. Mr. Putin said the question of proliferation was closely linked to the ABM Treaty and threshold states will be happy if the treaty is destroyed. Indeed he suggested a thorough review of the whole rang of strategic non-strategic ABM agreements to evolve a common approach.

Many experts fell that the ABM Treaty could serve as a bridge to a new era in which further reductions in offensive missiles could be accompanied by the testing and building of limited systems to blunt emerging threats from unpredictable countries like North Korea, Iran and Iraq. Therefore, the answer is not in rejecting the ABM Treaty, but in building on it. The answer is to seek a new strategic equation that encourages the United States, Russia and China to field a minimal number of offensive weapons with reasonable defensive systems.

On NATO, the second most contentious issue between America and Russia, Mr. Putin expressed his doubts and suspicions. He said Russia is cooperating with NATO, even expressed its desire to join it which was rejected by the western military alliance. Mr. Putin read out in the press Conference from a top secret U.S. document recently much to Mr. Bush's discomfort that NATO did not want to consider the Russia request and Mr. Putin concluded that when Russia is cooperating with NATO there is no need to fire up the whole situation. There is no need for NATO to move towards Russian borders.

The fact remains that America needs Russian help to evolve its missile defence system and Russia needs American investment. So it is in the common interest to carry on the dialogue.

Mr. Bush and Mr. Putin both have been keen students of history, having done their history major. They have emerged as negotiators for peace and prosperity. There is no doubt if both America and Russia seize the opportunity to work together, the world will be safer. One hopes, gradually they will be able to iron out their deferences and evolve a joint strategy for a better tomorrow.

Whether or not the NMD succeeds is something that will be decided by the American people. The government's ill-considered support for the US will not buy the ticket needed to sup at the high table of world powers. The genuine ticket will come, as it came to China, because on its economic engagement with the US and its national interest-oriented policy.

India, too, would be wise to engage the US in the economic, rather than the more hazardous military-political, field. But the essential condition for this is in an infrastructure upon which India agriculture and industry can flourish and a legal and administrative foundation that promotes Indian commerce. This is no longer an academic issue, and one does it brook any more waste of time. Poor human and physical infrastructure has created near-crisis situations in several important sectors of Indian industry and agriculture. The opening of world trade requires urgent steps other than tariff barriers to promote Indian competitiveness. The challenge now is not what the US can do for India, but what the Vajpayee government can do for the country.

Uzbekistan was admitted to the "Shanghai Five" and will now join the six-member Shanghai Cooperation Organisation (SCO) to be launched in the Chinese city of Shanghai during the two-day summit which opened on June 14. On the sidelines of the "Shanghai Five" Plus One (Uzbekistan) meeting, the Russian President, Mr. Vladimir Putin, and his Chinese counterpart, Mr. Jiang Zemin, reiterated their opposition to American plans to deploy a National Missile Defence (NMD) shield and pledged to keep "close contact" in the issue. Uzbekistan will be considered a "founding member" of the SCO which will now compromise six countries—China, Russia, Kazakhastan, Kyrgyzstan, Tajikistan and Uzbekistan.

The Chinese news agency, Xinhua, reported that the Presidents of the six countries met in an "informal summit" in Shanghai today, Xinhua said the Heads of State "endorsed Uzbekistan's application as a co-founder of SCO and a signatory of the SCO inaugural declaration and treaty on crackdown of terrorism, separatism and extremism". On its part Uzbekistan, endorsed the spirit and principle of the "Shanghai Five" mechanism and said it was willing to join the process in the basis of "complete equality."

Uzbekistan also said it was committed to the treaty on deepening military trust in border regions the treaty on reduction of troops in these regions and the "principles" behind other agreements signed by the "Shanghai Five" nations. The Shanghai Five Plus Uzbekistan process (which began in 1996 in Shanghai) is an indicator of how seriously Russia, China and the Central Asian nations take the problem of religious extremism. These countries are aware of the Taliban-led extremist links in their countries and are determined that the problem of religious extremism and terrorism is effectively controlled. Greater cooperation between these countries can be expected as they deal with a common problem. A formal agreement on the issue is to be concluded at the current summit which will set out the leaders' opposition to terrorism, separatism and extremism. "The document will explicitly express the position of all the countries to crack down on separatist forces", a Chinese Foreign Ministry spokesman was quoted as saying.

Giving an account of the meeting between Mr. Putin and Mr. Jiang, Xinhua quoted the Chinese President said about the SCO: "This will have great importance to the development of our bilateral relations, the maintenance of regional security and stability and the promotion of (the) multi-polarisation of the world". The Chinese President said he is looking forward to the state visit to Russia next month when the two leaders will sign aspect on Sino-Russian good neighbourly friendship and cooperation, "the agency reported". The pact will function as a legal document guiding the development of Sino-Russian relations in the new century and will have a deep and far-reaching impact on the steady development of the bilateral ties in the long run", Mr. Jiang was reported to have told Mr. Putin. "Mr. Putin reiterated Russia's principle and stance on the missile defence issue, Mr. Jiang expressed the view that China will continue to support Russia's efforts in maintaining global strategic stability. The two sides agreed to keep a close contact on the issue," the Xinhua report added.

7

S&T PLATFORM : INDIA'S STRIDES IN SPACE

I

If one is asked to name the best known and all pervasive technology mission in India, the INSAT easily stands out from the others. In less than ten years of the operation, it has made its presence felt in every corner of the country. It has brought about a kind of revolution in communications and television transmission.

INSAT Series

The lunch of INSAT-2A on July 10, 1992 by Ariane, European Space Agency in French Gunana marks the beginning of the second phase of INSAT programme, with indigenously built satellites and enhanced capability. It is the first INSAT to be designed, assembled and tested by ISRO at different work units in India. Like its predecessors, INSAT-2A is planned to render four types of services. TV relay through INSAT has already made it well-known throughout India. With 520 TV transmiters and over 100,000 direct reception sets, Doordarshan programmes can now be received by over 75 per cent in India's population. INSAT is also being used to provide regional TV services in some states. Nation-wide radio networking through INSAT has not only improved reception quality, it has enabled even remote areas to become part of the national mainstream.

In the area of telecommunications, the commissioning of many new STD routes and the relative ease in getting outstation lines must have been noticed by many in recent years. This has been possible thanks to INSAT. The third service relates to meteorological services. The familiar weather map which is shown in the TV news bulletin every night is received from INSAT. The fourth service provided by INSAT is relay of the data received from specially installed unmanned weather data collection platforms, primarily on the east coast which are used for disaster warning systems. Combining these four services makes INSAT technically a unique satellite.

Components

The INSAT-2A spacecraft can't be split into three components, bulkwise. About 60 per cent of it is the fuel. Rest of it is referred to as dry mass. The part of the satellite which performs the service-related functions such as imaging, data relay etc. is referred to as payload. About one-third of the dry spacecraft mass is made up of payload systems. The rest consists of what are called spacecraft sub-systems. They provide for smooth and efficient functioning of the payload systems by creating the right environment, and giving necessary engineering support.

After launch one board an Ariane rocket, INSAT-2A was put in a transfer orbit (200 km x 36,000 km), which is to be raised to the circular geosynchronous orbit at a height of 35.786 km over the equator. INSAT carries a bit-propellant system and a liquid apogee motor to achieve this. On July 13 firing of the apogee motor raised the satellite into an intermediate orbit and the next day its solar panels and the C/s band antennae were deployed. It is expected to be put in its final orbit by the end of the month.

Once in the right orbit, the next job is to put the satellite in the right spot (station acquisition) and to maintain it in that position (station keeping). The geostationary orbit is a kind of natural resource, and slots on it are limited and already scarce. An international body allots the slot (74 deg E for INSAT-2A) and the satellite has to remain within 0.1 deg of the same. INSAT carries 16 small thrusters to do the job.

Ground Network

The INSAT system functions through a massive ground network, spread throughout India. It consists of a master facility at Hassan in Andhra Pradesh, besides many ground receiving stations, transmitting stations, data reception stations and remote area terminals. It is through extensive network that we are able to get country-wide TV transmission, telephone service, radio networking and the meterological services. This complex network will now have on Indian heart. Considering the complexities involved in designing and fabrication of a multipurpose geostationary satellite, INSAT-2A is indeed an achievement.

Despite the failure of INSAT-1A and INSAT-1C, the INSAT network today provides about 4500 two-way speech circuits over 140 routes through 126 telecommunication terminals. The INSAT system also provides a novel rural telegraphic service in the remote north-eastern part of the country where the hilly terrain makes use of conventional wire telegraphy impracticable. The system also provides nationwide data communication links between district and state capitals through the National Informatics Centre Network (NICNET). Work is also underway for library networking on a large scale.

The 23-metre satellite system (when deployed fully with solar sails) has 12 C-band transponders for telecommunications and another six extended C-band transponders. These could be used for improving teleprinter and computer networks to transfer large volumes of data at high speeds. Television signals too could be broadcast using these transponders. INSAT-1D does not have extended C-band transponders. Currently, it provides 4,514 two-way speech circuits (for telecom) through 11 C-band transponders. INSAT-2A also has two S-band transponders for the use of Doordarshan (to broadcast its regional network) and All India Radio (to further link its far-flung stations), (for differences between INSAT 1 and INSAT 2 series see Table 1).

TABLE 1

INSAT-1	*Differences in the Satellites*	*INSAT-2*
19 Equivalent to 5-Storey building	HEIGHT (metres)	23 Equivalent to 6-Storey building
1,200 Equivalent to the weight of two Maruti Cars	WEIGHT (kg)	1,900 Equivalent to the weight of three Maruti Cars
930 Enough to run one electric iron	POWER OUTPUT (watts)	1,040 Enough to run an immersion heater
12 Can handle 4,300 telephone circuits	C-BAND TRANSPONDERS (numbers)	18 Can handle 6,400 telephone circuits
2.7 km	RADIOMETER RESOLUTION VISIBLE	2.0 km
11.0 km	INFRA-RED	8.0 km Better weather predictions
Asymmetrical	SOLAR ARRAY	Accordian type

Another important payload on INSAT-2AA is the very high resolution radiometer (VHRR) which provides pictures of the cloud cover, every three hours, over the country. These pictures, along with other information such as wind velocity in the upper atmosphere, sea surface temperature and precipitation play a key role in predicting the weather over the country and also help develop better mathematical prediction models.

The experimental transponder for the search and rescue service is a bonus. Presently, the world-wide service used four low-earth orbit satellites which pick up distress signals from stranded ships, aircraft or groups of people held up in remote areas such as mountains and forests and transmit them to the nearest rescue centre. The rescue efforts are then set in motion locally. Using a geostationary satellite will help cut down the time spent in alerting the rescue centres. INSAT-2A will activate the disaster warning systems located on the east coast and provide accurate information on approaching cyclones. Most countries have used such satellites only for telecommunication and television and radio broadcasting facilities. India pioneered adding the weather service and other facilities to make the satellite programme cost-effective. So far, this approach has served the country well.

Satellites such as INSAT are placed in geostationary orbit situated at 36,000 km (35,976 km for INSAT-2A) from the earth's surface. At this height, it will orbit around the earth with an acquired velocity equal to that of the earth's speed of revolution around itself. This means that it will appear to be stationary to a particular place on the earth. So signals could be sent to it from the earth and retransmitted over a wider areas easily.

All the satellites of INSAT-1 series were built by Ford Aerospace of USA as per design specifications provided by ISRO. INSAT-2A is the first in the series of indigenously built second generation INSAT satellites which will in future become the workhorse of the INSAT programme. By the turn of the century India may even have developed the capability to launch its own INSAT with the Geosynchronous Satellite Launch Vehicle (GSLV). (For important dates in India's space programme see Table 2).

TABLE 2
Landmarks in India's Space Programme

Satellite	*Date*	*Launcher*	*Result*
ARYABHATTA	March 19, 1975	USSR	Success
BHASKARA-1	June 7, 1979		Success
ROHINI	Aug 10, 1979	SLV-3	Failure
ROHINI	July 18, 1980	SLV-3	Success
APPLE	June 19, 1981	ARIANE	Success
BHASKARA-2	Nov 20, 1981	USSR	Success
ROHINI	May 31, 1981	SLV-3	Failure
ROHINI	April 17, 1983	SLV-3	Success
SROSS-1	March 24, 1987	ASLV	Failure
IRS-1A	March 19, 1988	USSR	Success
SROSS-2	July 13, 1988	ASLV	Failure
IRS-1B	Aug 29, 1991	USSR	Success
SROSS-3	May 19, 1992	ASLV	Success
INSAT-1A	Sept. 4, 1982	USA	Failure
INSAT-2B	Aug 30, 1982	USA	Success
INSAT-1C	July 22, 1988	ARIANE	Failure
INSAT-1D	June 12, 1990	USA	Success
INSAT-2A	July 10, 1992	ARIANE	Success

IRS-S

India launched its first IRS-A remote sensing satellite on March 1, 1988 and the second, IRS-1B, was lifted into a polar orbit on 29th August 1991 by a Soviet Vostok rocket from the Baikanour cosmodrome. But, like its predecessor IRS-IA, the satellite was designed and built by Indian scientists and engineers at the Indian Space Research Organisation. After launch, the 970-kg satellite has been put in a polar orbit at an altitude of 940 km. When a violet cyclone hit the state of Andhra Pradesh in May 1990, the havoc it wreaked was recorded by IRS-1A. When the swollen, Brahamputra river flooded its banks in 1988, 1989 and 1990, IRS-A imagery was used in real time mapping of floods.

Some of the application areas which have shown encouraging results include ground water potential zone mapping, large area crop acreage, urban sprawl, land use mapping, saline/alkaline soil mapping, flood mapping and geological mapping. Similarly the application of remote sensing for groundwater potential zone mapping has found an important place in the National Mission on Drinking Water Technology being co-ordinated by the Department of Rural Development. Under this programme 57 mini-mission districts have been selected for detailed ground water potential zone mapping through remote sensing methods. It is planned to cover the entire country during the mission period.

The Department of Agriculture of Cooperation and the Department of Space has jointly launched a major project on Remote Sensing Application Mission for agricultural applications as a central sector (Planning) scheme funded by Department of Agriculture and Cooperation. Wasteland mapping of 146 critically affected districts have been successfully completed and the maps have been distributed to the state level authorities. Urban sprawl maps of major cities of Bombay, Hyderabad, Madras, Ahmedabad, Nagpur and Bangalore have been completed. Such maps which show the growth trend of the cities can be an effective tool in planning the expansion of cities consistent with their infrastructure which otherwise could inevitably result in unplanned growth.

IRS-1B was the last of the IRS series launched from foreign soil. The next generation of IRS satellites, IRS-1C and IRS-1D, will be more advanced resolution of as low as 20 metres, IRS-1C will be lunched in 1994 by India's own launch vehicle.

Modest Beginning

ISRO made the modest achievement by launching Rohini, a small rocket, in 1967; which was followed by an advanced version of Rohini in 1973. The most spectacular achievement was the launching of SLV-3 which put a 35 kg. Rohini, a liquid rocket in low earth orbit.

APPLE (Ariane Passenger Payload Experiment) Satellite launched in June 1981 was a successful experiment which helped in enhancing India's capabilities in space and paved the way for use of space technology for communication.

The first Indian satellite Aryabhata was launched on April 19, 1975. This 360 kg. satellite was launched into space into a near circular orbit of 600 km at an inclination of 51° to the equator from a cosmodrome in Soviet Union. Aryabhata had no direct application value but it boosted the morale of the Indian scientists. Four year after Aryabhata was put into space the second Indian satellite, Bhaskara, was put into orbit, again from a Russian cosmodrome. It carried sophisticated instruments for remote sensing experiments over the country using TV cameras and microwave radio meters.

India had her first domestic service satellite INSAT-1A launched in August 1983. But it could not be put to use because of a series of technical snags, INSAT-1B and INSAT-1C followed later of which only INSAT-1B could be made fully operational. With the launch of INSAT-1D, in June 1990, the first phase of the INSAT programme was completed. These satellites were built by the Ford Aerospace of USA as per specifications provided by ISRO. The future generation of INSATs will be all indigenously made.

Institutions

The state of India's space programme is generally traced in November 1963 for the first time, a sounding rocket was fired from Indian soil. The first Indian space body, 'National Committee for Space Research', was set up as part of the Department of Atomic Energy under the Chairmanship of Dr. Sarabhai. In 1972 the Department of Space was born which is now located at Bangalore. If Dr. Homi Bhabha is remembered for the success of Indian nuclear programme, Dr. Vikram Sarabhai, will always be referred to as the father of the space programme.

A number of organisations and institutions have come up in the past 15 years to carry forward the space programme, the Vikram Sarabhai Space Centre at Trivandrum; the Satellite Centre at Bangalore, the Auxiliary Propulsion Centre at Bangalore and Trivandrum, the Sriharikota High Attitude Range Centre in Andhra Pradesh, Space Application Centre Ahmedabad, Physical Research Laboratory Ahmedabad and National Remote Sensing Agency, Hyderabad.

Milestone

Another important milestone in India's space endeavour came after two successive failures when the third development flight of the Augmented Satellite Launch Vehicle (ASLV) lifted off to a perfect launch at dawn on Wednesday, 20 May 1992 from Sriharikota on the east cost. Nine minutes and 18 seconds into the flight, it released a 106-kg. satellite of the Stretched Rohini Series called SROSS-C into orbit.

The ASLV, as the name implies, is an augmented version of the SLV-3 which was used to put two small (45 kg) Rohini satellite into orbit in 1980 and 1983. The greater power of the ASLV comes from two additional solid propellant boosters which are "strapped on" to the main rocket body.

Both the earlier flights of the ASLV, incidentally, had perfect lift-offs, but later went off course and crashed into the sea due to anomalies which have now been identified. First launch on 24 March 1987 failed primarily because the first-stage motor of the main rocket did not ignite in time to take over power from the two strap-on boosters (also called the zero-stage). As a result the rocket veered off course and plummeted into the sea less then three minutes after lift-off. In the second attempt on 13 July

1988, the first stage did ignite as planned, but as a result of a flaw in the on-board automatic control system, the burnt-out boosters failed to separate. This made the rocket break up and splash into the sea.

All the control systems in the present version of the 23.8 m tall five-stage rocket, weighing almost 42 tonnes at launch, were redesigned in the light of the findings of the expert review committees which looked into the causes of the failure of the first two flights. In fact, the ASLV launches are primarily intended to validate new technologies that will be used in the PSLV, and later in the still more powerful Geostationary Satellite Launch Vehicle (GSLV) which is designed to launch 2500-kg. INSATs into the geostationary orbit in future.

PSLV

The more powerful PSLV with a launch weight of 275 tonnes, is designed for putting 1000-kg. satellites of the IRS-type for remote sensing application into a 900-km polar sunsynchronous orbit. The main difference between the ALSV and the PSLV, besides size and power, would be the use of alternate liquid and solid stage.

SROSS-C Satellite put into orbit by the ASLV, carries two payloads—one called Retardation Potential Analyser (RTA) for studying the ionosphere, and the other called Gamma Ray Burst (GRB) detector to analyses solar activity in the atmosphere. The RTA, designed and fabricated at the National Physical Laboratory, New Delhi will be used to study the ionosphere, the region of earth's upper atmosphere in which free electrons and ions occur as a result of ionization of the air by ultraviolet radiation and x-rays from the sun. This region is important for long distance communication on earth as it can reflect radio waves back like a mirror. SROSS will study the variation in the density of electrons and ions from the top in the ionosphere.

The GRB detector is an instrument designed and fabricated by ISRO to story short bursts of high energy gamma radiation that impinges on the earth's atmosphere from the sun and some other astronomical bodies where violent processes occur.

But the greatest challenge for ISRO will come in the shape of the GSLV which will use a cryogenic engine for its upper stages. The powerful launch vehicle, to be used to launch 2500-kg INSAT-type satellites into the geostationary orbit, will be a modified version of the PSLV. The upper two stages of PSLV will be replaced by a single cryogenic stage in the GSLV. In place of the six solid propellant strap-on boosters in the PSLV, the GSLV will have four liquid propellant strap-on engines derived from the second stage of the PSLV. Under the original plan of ISRO, Russia was to provide the cryogenic engine for GSLV, but the recent US action forbidding the sale may means that India will have to go own units. In that case, according to ISRO sources, the GSLV programme may be further delayed.

Involvement of Industries

While about 50 industries were involved in making the SLV-3, nearly 80 private and public sector, small and large will contribute to the ASLV. An even larger number will participate in the making of the PSLV. Systematically, and in a phased manner, the ISRO has been transferring technology to these industrial units. Yet the fundamental character of industrial participation in space activities remains substantially unchanged. All the R&D is still being done by the ISRO, and the industries merely have to produce items with the designs and technology provided to them.

The assembly of components and turning them into functional units is perhaps more difficult than their production, with extremely stringent quality checks at each stage. When complex launch vehicles are involved with hundreds of kilometres of wiring (the PSLV has 160 km) linking several thousand components, even a single badly soldered joint can be catastrophic.

Transfer of Technology

ISRO has plans to set up a company to market technologies developed by it though modalities of setting up the autonomous company are still to be worked out. ISRO's proposal was approved by the Indian Government more than a year ago. Except for the initial capital which will be provided by the Indian Government, the company will generate its own revenue and plough back profit for further business. It will build satellite sub-systems and components and also provide launch services. The company will function under ISRO with a small and compact team.

ISRO made its first international bid for business in 1990, when it attempted to get a multi-million dollar contract from the International Maritime Satellite Organisation (INIMASAT) for building a new class of satellites. Although ISRO lost, it had the pride of being the only developing country to make the bid. ISRO has already executed a consultancy project for establishing a sugar factory in Burundi in central Africa, making use of the remote sensing satellite of IRS-1A. It also conducted a photograpic survey project for a road alignment feasibility study in Nepal. Within India, ISRO has so far sold 189 space technologies to domestic industry in the fields of electronics, chemicals, telecommunications, navigation, mechanics and others.

The company that ISRO plans to set up can reap profits from the sale of space technology, considering that India is almost self-reliant in building satellites. It has successfully built the INSAT series of communication satellites, but needs to improve on its poor launch record.

American Concern

Satellite launching is a good business. Almost every country on the development path wants to put its own communication weather observation and other satellites on each synchronous orbits which are getting crowded. But very few countries can launch the satellites. The USA, Russia and the European Space Agency can lift huge satellites while Indian, Chinese and Japanese launchers are light-weight carriers. But they are developing better rockets that can carry heavier satellites. India, had depended on the U.S. Delta rockets, the Russian Vostok and European Ariane to launch its heavy satellites. These agencies thus earn millions of dollars to launch the satellites for other countries. India's GSLV is reporting to be coming at heavier payloads than what many big launchers can carry. It might be able to lift 5000 kg and if plans fructify by 1995 would be one of the most sought after launchers in the world.

India would be in a position to launch the 1.9 tonnes of INSAT-2A as well as INSAT-3 satellites from its own launcher after 1995. Currently these services are being done by the French Ariane-4, launch vehicle. If the Indian capacity to launch communication satellite is demonstrated, it would also offer launch vehicle services to other countries, a market which is currently shared between U.S., France, Russia and China. These charge anything between 25 to 30 million dollars for launching communication satellite. According to Prof. U.R. Rao, Secretary, Department of Space, intensive efforts in the near future could enable India to export space products and services, a fair share of the 20 billion dollar a year international market.

But Western observers feel that Indian remote sensing satellites could also be used for high resolution image applications. IRS class satellites are reported to be of the same class as the French remote sensing satellite system SPOT. If they are launched as planned in 1994, it would be another commercial competitor in providing space-based high resolution images in the global market. Besides, Indian remote sensing would also offer alternative perspective of verification of arms control or security related information. Both prospects would not be quite welcomed by the members of the information oligarchy.

Primarily due to commercial concern, the Russians who were the primary suppliers of rocket technology to India were requested by U.S.A. to cancel the contract which was finalised in January 1991. On May 11, 1992, American government announced the imposition of sanctions suspending supplies of U.S. technology to the Indian Space Research Organisation and Russian Space Agency Glavkosmos. In fact Indo-Russian technology deal has given the U.S.A. just an execuse to come down on India's satellite fabrication plan itself. The sanctions on Indian Space Research Organisation (ISRO) have cut out the supply of many critical electronic components and devices which are used not only in satellite launch vehicles, but also in the fabrication of satellites.

II

The successful launch of the Polar Satellite Launch Vehicle (PSLV-D2) on October 15, 1994, marks yet another milestone in India's space programme. The launch has come as a morale booster for the scientists of the Indian Space Research Organisation after the failure of the last launch in September 1993 because of a software error.

The PSLV-D2 placed an 870 kg Indian Remote Sensing (IRS) satellite in low earth orbit 817 km above the earth. This marked a giant stride in India's quest for self-reliance in the area of space applications. India has joined the exclusive six-nation club of countries that have the capability to place satellites in low earth orbit and the launch will considerably reduce its dependence on others for launching satellites. Indian space scientists indigenously developed the technology, and only 30 per cent of the components for the satellites and 25 per cent for the launch vehicles were imported.

The immediate task is to upgrade PSLV's payload capability and to send up the more ambitious next generation Geostationary Satellite Launch Vehicle (GSLV). By joining the global satellite launch market, which includes the United States, Russia, France, Japan and China, India has given a fitting rebuff to those powers opposed to it acquiring the expertise in the field. The US, viewing India as a potential challenge to its monopoly, had pressured Russia to cancel the cryogenic engine deal with this country on the ostensible ground that it violated the provisions of the Missile Technology Control Regime (MTCR). The West can at best only delay India's mastery of the cryogenic engine, but Indian scientists are capable of developing it indigenously. India has come a step closer to claiming a share in the satellite launch market. It is upto ISRO scientists to demonstrate not just India's technology, but its managerial and marketing abilities as well, to all the programme to potential buyers.

GSLV

According to ISRO Chairman K. Kasturirangan, work on the GSLV project was progressing at a brisk rate and the first experimental launch would be during 1997-98.

The first launch of the three-state GSLV would be made with the Russian cryogenic stage, replacing the third and fourth stages of the successfully launched four-stage PSLV. The PSLV's giant first stage (solid motors) and the second stage with the Vikas liquid engine would be retained on the GSLV. The cryogenic stage would constitute the third stage of the GSLV. Instead of six strap-ones in the PSLV, there would be four strap-ones in the GSLV. Dr. Kasturirangan said the indigenous cryogenic stage would be ready for flight by the end of the century.

Dr. A.E. Muthunayagam, Director of the Liquid Propulsion Systems Centres, said the major parameters of the indigenous cryogenic stage would be identical to the imported Russian ones being used for the first GSLV. While identical to the Russian cryogenic stage in the matter of performance and sophistication, the material and design would be changed.

Dr. Kasturirangan said another PSLV development flight was slated for 12 to 18 months from now. This would be followed by three successive operational flights. The liquid stage of the PSLV would be upgraded to 40 tonnes from 37.5 tonnes for use in the GSLV.

The ISRO Chairman said the country would achieve self-reliance in satellites and launch vehicles by the turn of the century. The existing gap between satellite technology and launch vehicle technology would also be filled by that time.

PSLV

By slinging quite perfectly the remote sensing satellite, IRS-P2, into orbit 820 km above the earth, ISRO emphatically announced its entry into the big league. The PSLV has now proven itself capable of injecting setellites into low earth orbit.

While the triumph marks another milestone for ISRO, its larger significance ought not to be missed: it provides the nation yet another reason for reposing more faith in itself and in the quality of skills available indigenously, the PSLV development has been achieved despite the US turning the screws of the Missile Technology control Regime and denying ISRO access to vital components from abroad.

Over the past few years, ISRO has put together remote sensing satellites (the IRS series) and geostationary communication satellites (the Insat 2 series), and, with latest trial, demonstrated that it can launch the former kind. In another three or four years, it will acquire the capability of sending satellites into geostationary orbit as well. So India stands today on the threshold of the global aerospace arena, which the US, Europes and the Russians had to themselves until China's rocket technology flowered. China's Long March rocket, aided by an aggressive pricing strategy, has picked up a piece of the market despite some spectacular launch failures.

According to Dr. Kasturirangan, ISRO too can join the game, and even call the play. ISRO can offer low earth orbit satellite launches for with a price tag of less than $25 million, a good deal lower than the charges prevalent today.

Indian competence could well have matured at just the right time since the demand for launch services could witness an exponential growth in the next five years. Several competing organisations have announced plans to set up global networks for handheld mobile telephones services by a chain of satellites in low earth orbit, 800-1,000 km above the earth. By one estimate, there could be as many as 1,000 satellites in this slot in the next few years; such is the pace of activity in this emerging telecommunications segment. The PSLV, when fine tuned, will be capable of hoisting two such satellites at one go. It will then stand a good chance of getting a piece of the action.

INSAT satellites are the only geostationary ones in this part of the globe with a meteorological package, yet its weather pictures have not been marketed overseas in any significant way, nor have the imageries from the remove sensing satellites. Despite having mastered the technology and built two telecommunication satellites of the Insat 2 series, ISRO is far from winning orders from anyone other than the Government of India. It is another matter that the government has effectively bared the lease of transponders on the INSATs to private parties. Although more than a dozen requests for transponders were received from television broadcasters, some well-known such as CNN, no action was taken on them. It is ironic that private Indian television channels such as Zee, Sun and Jain use foreign satellites to beam their programmes into India, paying lease charges of about $ 15 million (Rs. 45 crore) a year when slots are available on the INSAT cluster of satellites.

Antrix Corporation, the corporate marketing avatar of ISRO set up recently to correct the deficiency, has its job cut out given such restrictions at home and the fact that marketing space products and services abroad is not just a matter of dangling lower price tags. Geopolitical considerations play overwhelming roles and the Indian government will need to lend its weight if Antrix is to make any headway, whether at home or abroad. The government must unambiguously pronounce that it is in favour of the Indian space programme going commercial and seriously an immediately go about pulling out all the stops. Much money has been invested into the country's space efforts; the dividends can be enlarged only if the government can see a market beyond itself.

PSLV Launch

India's most challenging space venture so far, the PSLV achieved a grand success with the launching of its second, development flight, the PSLV-D2, from Sriharikota on October 15.

The 44 metre-tall 283 tonne, four-stage rocket completed its 17-minutes flight flawlessly and put in orbit the 804 kg TRS-P2 at an altitude of 820 km.

ISRO described the launch of the PSLV-D2 as 'a very significant milestone' in the country's space programme, saying it successfully demonstrated the use of liquid propellant for the second and fourth stages. The PSLV also has a massive first stage, rated as third largest solid booster in the world.

The PSLV-D2 took off in clear weather with the ignition of its core first stage and tow strap on motors.

Thereafter, it was a systematic sequence of four additional strap-on motors igniting at 30.6 seconds, separation of the strap-ons, separation of the first stage and ignition of the second stage, takeover by the third stage, and finally a long coasting phase before ignition of the fourth stage at 591.4 seconds.

The unerring passage of the PSLV was in part aided by the closed loop guidance system which came into effect at 157 seconds and continued until the ejection of the satellite.

"It is a great day for us, ISRO and the country", said a jubilant Dr. Kasturirangan, at the mission control centre when it was clear that the PSLV had met its objective. He said ISRO had realised the full capability of guided injection of a spacecraft into orbit with the success of the launch.

At a press conference after the launch, the ISRO Chairman said it was possible to upgrade the capability of the PSLV to deploy a one-tonne satellite in a 900 km orbit. Scientists were looking into eight items which would help reduce the weight of the vehicle, and enable the addition of 30 to 40 kg to the payload.

A project had been formulated for the third developmental flight of the PSLV. A sequence of PSLV flights every 12 or 18 months was envisaged at present, without any strain on the facilities already created.

The entire PSLV project cost Rs. 415 crore which covered, among other things, the cost of facilities for design, fabrication, production and testing of various vehicle systems, and the infrastructure built at Thiruvananthapuram, Mahendragiri, and Sriharikota. The two PSLVs launched cost Rs. 45 crore each and the next one is estimated to cost in the region of Rs. 70 crore (the launch vehicle and part of the satellite).

During its first developmental flight in September 1993, the PSLV had encountered a problem of 'overflow' resulting in a compounding of errors and ending in a sub-orbital flight. Even in the first flight, all the motors worked to specification.

The Linear Imaging Self-Scanner (LISS-II) camera on board the IRS-P2 launched by PSLV-D2 was successfully switched on from the Spacecraft Control Centre of the ISRO Telemetry, Tracking and Command Network (ISTRAC).

Satellite

According to ISRO, the satellite path covered north-eastern India during the 15th orbit and the north-western part during the 16th orbit. The imagery data was received at the Data Reception Centre of the National Remote Sensing Agency at Shadnagar near Hyderabad. A quick look analysis indicated good data quality. All systems on board the satellite were functioning well.

The LISS-II was operating in a scanning mode using a charged couple devices (CCD) array. The camera gave a field of view of plus or minus 2.5 degrees and a focal length of 324.4 mm. It operated in four spectral bands in the visible and infra-red bands between 0.45 and 0.86 micrometers. Placed at 825 km altitude, the LISS-II had an orbital period of 101 minutes and repetitive cycle of 24 days.

The solar panels, which power the satellite by generating 510 watts and by charging the nicklecadmium batteries, were deployed immediately after the satellite was injected into orbit. The life of the satellite would, however, depend on the life of the solar and batteries.

Welcomed

President Shanker Dayal Sharma and Prime Minister P.V. Narasimha Rao hailed the successful launch, describing it as "Yet another milestone" in India's journey to complete self-sufficiency in the area of space applications.

In a congratulatory message to ISRO scientists and other personnel involved in the launch, Dr. Sharma said "the PSLV's launch success is a step towards our quest for self-reliance".

In a message, Mr. Rao said the successful launch was a matter of great pride and satisfaction for the entire nation. Not only had the PSLV been developed by indigenous technology and manpower, even the remote sensing satellite put into orbit by the launch vehicle had been manufactured indigenously.

The Bharatiya Janata Party congratulated the scientists saying India had attained a "significant position" among both developing and developed countries.

Former ISRO Chairman U.R. Rao who witnessed the launch at the ISRO Telemetry, Tracking and Command Network (ISTRAC), said that the "perfect launch proved beyond doubt India's maturity in rocket technology. Probably after two or three developmental flights of the PSLV, India would not only be launching its own remote sensing satellites, but the satellites of other countries too".

Possibilities

The successful flight of the PSLV has raised the exciting possibility of India entering the global satellite launch market and turning Sriharikota into an international launch pad.

India has now emerged as the sixth country in the world and the second in the developing world after China to have the capability to launch satellites in low earth orbit. The Sriharikota success is a step forward in ending India's dependence on foreign countries to launch its remote sensing satellites. The last launch of IRS-1B in August, 1991, from the former Soviet Union had cost India Rs. 20 crore.

A successful PSLV launch, which represented India's first attempt to acquire indigenous capabilities to put remote sensing satellites into orbit, was crucial to the country's efforts to save foreign exchange and to earn more cash in the space sector in the long run.

ISRO has estimated that it could corner a $ 60 million market through launching small communications satellites in low earth orbits, using Augmented Satellite Launch Vehicle (ASLV) and PSLV, between 1996 and 2000.

ISRO says it could compete with the French space agency, Arianespace, in offering PSLV services to launch 400 kg to 450 kg communications satellites at a cost of $10 million to $15 million. Arianespace had announced charges of $10 million to $20 million for launching 400 kg to 800 kg satellites for communications.

The world market for launch services, dominated by a few large companies, is currently estimated at $1.3 billion. This is 19 per cent of the total market for space products and services, which is expected to grow at a rate of 5 per cent to 10 per cent every year.

While three PSLV launches of 400 kg satellites can rope in $45 million, three ASLV launches of 15 kg satellites in low earth orbit can bring in $45 million, and another $15 million can be earned through PSLV launches of small satellites, according to ISRO's calculations.

There is considerable international demand for launching of such satellites carrying 6 to 12 transponders. Worldwide, about 50 launches of such satellites are expected between 1996 and 2000.

The successful PSLV launch also paves the way for Indian space scientists to go full steam ahead with the GSLV project to put 2000 kg INSAT-type satellites into orbit, the final stamp required for India to be a leading space power. A successful GSLV launch, which ISRO hopes will materialise by 1997, is necessary for India to offer launches of geostationary communications satellites weighing over 1,000 kg.

Although India still has a long way to go to achieve this capacity, ISRO scientists calculate that offering ASLVs and PSLVs to launch small satellites, and renting out

SHAR facilities for other international agencies can bring in considerable revenue.

A launch from Sriharikota, which is close to the equator and can offer an 18 degree inclination orbit, will work out to be cheaper compared to launches from China or Japan. Satellites launched from Sriharikota can carry heavier payloads compared to those from these two countries.

ISRO estimates that in price of $4 million to $5 million for launching a 1,400 kg satellite from SHAR is a reasonable fee to charge.

The gains from a SHAR launch are likely to outweigh the extra cost of setting up a launch pad and facilities and of transporting the rocket and satellite to the site, provided a minimum of three or four launches are involved.

Market

After the successful launch of the PSLV, India is set to enter the lucrative commercial satellite market now controlled by a handful of nations.

Several international firms are already examining the possible use of the Indian-built launch vehicle to slot in communication satellites, according to Dr. Kasturirangan.

The PSLV can place three communication satellites weighing 300 kg each in the 400-km Low Earth Orbit (LEO), meeting the possible requirement of leading global communication firms.

The US high technology giant, Motorola, plans sending a constellation of 66 satellites in LEO. The London-based Inmarsat is on the lookout for a suitable vehicle to eject a configuaration of around 40 satellites. Other global competitors are making similar bids.

"The PSLV can also help replace snag-ridden satellites quickly, preventing major communication breakdowns. The turnaround time to replace satellites is crucial because these companies propose to provide continuous communication", Dr. Kasturirangan said.

US Opposition

The success of the PSLV comes in the teeth of US-led opposition. US laws deny any transfer of technology destined for the PSLV. The project-centered guidelines of the 1991 Extended Proliferation Control Initiative (EPCI) ban transfer of US know-how to the PSLV fearing that its success could help India build long-range nuclear missiles.

The US Export Administration Act, inspired by the EPCI guidelines, also target ISRO's solid fueled SLV-3 and ASLV rocket projects. The GSLV, capable of carrying a 2.5-tonne payload, and one in the making, is also targeted.

The Defence Research and Development Organisation's (DRDO) Agni and Prithvi missile programmes also feature on the US ban list. "Not even a pin or pencil can be sold by the US for these projects," sources here said.

India has already objected to the Western curbs on the Indian civilian rocketry programme and this was conveyed to representatives of the Missile Technology Control Regime (MTCR) who visited the capital recently.

Low Cost Launches

Charging an estimated $20-25 million per launch by the PSLV can help India enter the international satellite launching league. Until a few years ago, the US was charging $6,000 for each pound of satellite weight, propelling launching costs to anywhere between $30-35 million.

The French Arianespace, charged around $40 million and the Russians demanded $30 million.

Indian could create a niche for itself, as the record of Western launching firms is far from spotless. In 1984, the US placed a Western Union-owned satellite and another owned by Indonesia into wrong orbits. The satellite-bearing space shuttle exploded soon after launch, tarnishing the US image further.

Confidence in French satellite launch capabilities has also taken a beating. Four of the first 18 launches by Ariane exploded or ditched in the sea.

China charging 20 to 30 per cent less than its Western counterparts, could emerge as the biggest competitor to India. Being as specialised in sending satellites to the higher geostationary orbit and has successfully sent up several satellites, including the Asiasat-1.

Washington, fearing the possible hold by China, has signed a MoU with Bejing disallowing the latter to outbid it out of the launch market. "China will take steps to ensure that its providers do not materially impair the smooth and effective functioning of the international market for commercial launch services. Among these steps, China will ensure that any support to its providers is in line with the practices of market economies", the MoU said.

According to the agreement, Beijing will also maintain insurance charges at par with the Western companies, thereby eroding its competitive edge.

The PSLV's success has also allowed India to become self-sufficient in placing earth imaging, remote sensing satellites in a 1000 km high sun-synchronous orbit. The imaging satellites, besides their several civilian uses, can help in military surveillance.

India buys the 10 metre resolution pictures taken by the French-built SPOT satellite. But the PSLV is expected to carry the IRS-IC reportedly of the same class as SPOT next year, opening more options for India planners.

Background

The India space programme is a three-pronged effort encompassing development of applications, satellites to enable applications and vehicle capabilities to launch these satellites. Since Aryabhatta in 1975, 11 Indian satellites now circle the earth. Of these, only five have been launched by Indian vehicles. The thrust of the launch vehicle programme is to operationalise the GSLV and put into orbit commercial class satellites of 2.5 tonnes. The ASLV series of launchers with payload capacities of 100 kg and the PSLV series of launchers with payload capacities of one tonne each are stepping stones to that goal.

The successful launch of the ASLV validated a clutch of subsystems used in the PSLV launched in October. Significant among these are the closed loop guidance system and separation stage control that were thought to have been responsible for the failure of the PSLV in September 1993.

India space officials hope to achieve one launch per year capability with PSLV and market it internationally for launching low earth orbit satellites.

The ASLV success also demonstrates the non-productiveness of coercive sanctions beyond a point. The report by an autonomous business group in the US makes the point that the two-year US embargo on ISRO has far from crippled the Indian programme. Parallels are drawn between the space embargo on ISRO and the one on supply of supercomputers to India and China. While the indigenously developed Chinese supercomputer is competing with Western machines in the Chinese market, the Indian supercomputer class of parallel computer is a modest success in Western markets.

Check-list

- The launch of INSAT-2A on July 10, 1992 by Ariane, European Space Agency in French Guryana marks the beginning of the second phase of INSAT programme, with indigenously built satellites and enhanced capability.
- It is the first INSAT to be designed, assembled and tested by ISRO at different work units in India.

TABLE 3
Milestones in Indian Space Programme

The following are the landmarks in the Indian space research programme:

1969:	Formation of the Indian Space Research Organisation (ISRO).
1975:	First Indian satellite, Aryabhatta, launched from the Soviet Union.
1979:	Second satellite, Bhaskara-1, for earth observation, launched from the Soviet Union.
1980:	SLV-3, India's first satellite launch vehicle launched from Sriharikota with Rohini satellite.
1981:	First experimental geo-stationary communication satellite, Apple, launched from Kourou, France.
1981:	Bhaskara-2 launched from the Soviet Union.
1983:	SLV-3 with Rohini-2 launched from Sriharikota.
1983:	INSAT-1B, multipurpose satellite launched from USA.
1984:	First Indo-Soviet space mission began.
1988:	IRS-1A, first Indian remote sensing satellite, launched from the Soviet Union.
1990:	INSAT-1D launched from Kourou, France.
1991:	IRS-1B launched from the Soviet Union.
1992:	ASLV-D3 launched from Sriharikota with SROSS-C satellite.
1992:	INSAT-2A, first indigenously built second generation satellite in INSAT series, launched from Kourou.
1993:	INSAT-2B launched from Sriharikota with SROSS-C2 satellite.
May 4, 1994:	ASLV-D4 launched from Sriharikota with SROSS-C2 satellite.
Oct. 15, 1994:	PSLV-D2 launched from Sriharikota with IRS-P2 satellite.

- After launch on board an Ariane rocket, INSAT-2A was put in a transfer orbit (200 km. 36000 km), which is to be raised to the circular geosynchronous orbit at a height of 35,786 km. over the equator.
- The INSAT system functions through a massive ground network, spread throughout India.
- Despite the failure of INSAT-1A and INSAT-1C, the INSAT network today provides about 4500-two-

TABLE 4
India's Rocket Launches

The following is the history of India's rocket launching programmes at a glance

SLV-3		
1. First experimental launch	(10.8.79)	(partial success)
2. Second experimental launch (Rohini satellite on board)	(18.7.80)	(success)
3. First developmental launch (RS-D1 on board)	(31.5.81)	(success)
4. Second developmental launch (RS-D2 on board)	(17.4.83)	(success)
ASLV		
5. First developmental launch	(24.3.87)	(failure)
6. Second developmental launch	(13.7.88)	(failure)
7. Third developmental launch	(20.5.92)	(success)
8. Fourth developmental launch	(04.5.94)	(success)
PSLV		
9. First developmental launch	(20.9.93)	(failure)
10. Second developmental launch	(15.10.94)	(success)

ISRO Launch Vehicles

	SLV-3	*ASLV*	*PSLV*	*GSLV*
Lift-off Weight (tonnes)	17	40	275	400
Height (m)	23	23	42	51
Payload Weight (kg)	45	150	1000	2500

way speech circuits over 140 routes through 126 tele-communication terminals.

- The system also provides nationwide data communication links between district and state capitals through the National Informatics Centre Network (NICNET).
- Another important payload on INSAT-2A is the very high resolution radiometer (VHRR) which provides pictures of the cloud cover, every three hours, over the country.

- The successful launch of the Polar Satellite Launch Vehicle (PSLV-D2) on October 15, 1994, marks yet another milestone in India's space programme.
- The PSLV-D2 placed an 870 kg Indian Remote Sensing (IRS) satellite in low earth orbit 817 km above the earth. This marked a giant stride in India's quest for self-reliance in the area of space applications.
- The immediate task is to upgrade PSLV's payload capability and send up the more ambitious next generation Geostationary Satellite Launch Vehicle (GSLV).
- According to ISRO Chairman K. Kasturirangan, work on the GSLV project was progressing at a brisk rate and the first experimental launch would be during 1997-98.
- The successful flight of the PSLV has raised the exciting possibility of India entering the global satellite launch market and burning Sriharikota into an international launch pad.
- The success of the PSLV comes in the teeth of US-led opposition. US laws deny any transfer of technology destined for the PSLV.
- The PSLV's success has also allowed India to become self-sufficient in placing earth imaging remote sensing satellites in a 1000 km high sun-synchronous orbit. The imaging satellites, besides their several civilian uses, can help in military surveillance.

8

NUCLEAR POLITICS : THE NATO CONNECTION

NATO was established to deter a perceived Soviet threat to Western Europe. At the time when it was established the threat was mostly a conventional one and NATO had a superiority in nuclear capability. Some people had argued even at that stage that the Soviet conventional superiority itself was meant as a deterrent against the nuclear superiority of the West. At this stage it is not necessary to go into the question as to which factor was causal and which the reaction. Subsequently, the NATO nuclear strategy underwent a number of changes. It started with the threat of massive retaliation. It was also advocated that tactical nuclear weapons could halt massive Soviet armour thrusts. Following the Soviet testing of intercontinental rockets and achieving the capability to threaten the continental United States, the strategy of flexible response was advocated by the US and reluctantly adopted by the other members of the NATO. Then came concepts of assured destruction, soon to be followed by counter-force deterrence. In the late seventies, the prevalent philosophy, embodied in Presidential Directive-59, was that NATO should have the capability to destroy the war-sustaining infrastructure of the Soviet Union embodied in the Communist Party organisation. All through, it was a case of tactical and strategic doctrines adjusting themselves to fast developing technology and the continuous accumulation of warheads.

Meanwhile, from the late seventies, the very basis of nuclear war doctrines began to be challenged. The controllability of the rate of fire in a nuclear war, the feasibility of effective command and control over rapid escalation and the nuclear winter hypothesis, were factors which raised serious doubts about the use of nuclear weapons in wars, where the avowed purpose is to apply force economically and purposefully to gain preferred objectives. Then came the Reagan-Gorbachev declaration in Geneva, in November 1985, that a nuclear war could not be won and, therefore, should not be initiated.

Starting with this declaration, a number of arms control and arms reduction steps followed. First was the Intermediate Nuclear Forces Treaty, which eliminated a whole category of weapons. Then came START-I in July 1971. This was followed by the unilateral elimination of most of tactical nuclear weapons by the US in September 1991, reciprocated by the Soviet Union in October 1991. Britain and France also announced cutbacks of their tactical nuclear arsenals. Though START-I has not yet been implemented, pending the accession of Ukraine to the Non-proliferation Treaty, the US and Russia are committed, under START-II, to bring down their strategic nuclear arsenals to 3,500 and 3,000 respectively, by the year 2003 A.D. The British, however, are modernising their submarine-based nuclear deterrent with Trident class submarines and increasing their warheads. The French too are following the British and modernising their nuclear arsenals.

Meanwhile, Russia and other former Soviet republics have joined the Conference on Security and Cooperation in Europe (CSCE). They have also joined the Partnership for Peace offered by NATO. Russia is drastically cutting down its conventional arms and defence budget. The cold war is over. Russia, US and UK have declared that they have de-targeted the erstwhile adversaries for their nuclear missiles.

Germany and Russia are holding military exercises in one anothers' territories. In these circumstances, it is a legitimate question as to what role nuclear weapons have in the NATO alliance?

The NATO powers continue to justify their possession of nuclear weapons for the following reasons: (*i*) So long as other countries in the world have nuclear weapons they would also need them. These are weapons of defence of last report. (*ii*) There are strategic uncertainties, to cover which they will continue to retain their weapons. (*iii*) It is not possible to assume that the direction of democratisation and marketisation in Russia will be irreversible. These processes might reverse themselves and in that event Russia could again pose a threat. (*iv*) They need nuclear weapons as deterrence against 'rogue' nations, such as Saddam Hussein's Iraq, which might develop nuclear capabilities.

These arguments, put forward in the official publications of NATO, lack credibility. If the NATO powers need nuclear weapons for the above reasons then many other nations, such as India, which are not as fortunate as the NATO countries which have no adversaries after the end of the cold war, will have more valid reasons to acquires a nuclear arsenal. Strategic uncertainties affect them as much as NATO nations. They are nearer to Russia and possible future 'rogue' nations than the US and, therefore, their need for nuclear weapons, on the basis of the above reasoning, are even more compelling. The NATO nations' logic collapses when they oppose other nations which, on the basis of the NATO reasoning, need nuclear weapons more urgently. It is, therefore, obvious that NATO's need for nuclear weapons is no longer based on military necessity. The real basis for the continued possession of nuclear weapons by three NATO powers is political and they want to use the nuclear weapons as currency of power in international relations.

There is today a correlation between the possession of nuclear weapons and permanent membership of the Security Council. Permanent membership in the Security Council was determined by the victorious powers of the Second World War and understandably the defeated Axis powers, Japan, Germany and Italy, were excluded from permanent membership. The Non-proliferation Treaty was formulated by US, USSR and UK with the main purpose of preventing Japan and Germany from acquiring nuclear weapons.

Now the cold war is over. Japan and Germany have became the second and third most powerful countries in the international power hierarchy. Both countries have staked their claims for permanent seats in the Security Council. UK and France are not anxious to enlarge the number of permanent seats in the Security Council and accommodate Germany and Japan. They fear that the European Union, in which they are members along with Germany, is already German dominant, in view of Germany being more populous, having a higher GNP and a larger conventional force and being more advanced technologically. The only way they can countervail German dominance in the European Union is for Britain and France to continue to be nuclear powers and to keep Germany non-nuclear and deny it a permanent seat in the Security Council. From this perspective nuclear weapons have become a currency of power in the hand of UK and France and unavailable to Germany.

The US, which has a self-image of being the sole superpower, does not want to give up the nuclear weapons since they are not only the most potent currency of power, as projected in all strategic literature of the last four decades, but also provides a ready reckoner of such an index of power in terms of strategic arsenals. Russia is today counted as a global power only on account of its nuclear arsenal and hence does not want to part with it. In these circumstances, the US aims to keep its nuclear arsenal at a level equal to all other strategic arsenals of the world put together. Therefore, it sensitiveness on keeping 3,500 strategic warheads by 2003 A.D. For NATO, nuclear weapons have no meaning in military terms. It is absurd for NATO to talk of the need for nuclear weapons as a defence of last resort. The NATO nations today have the most powerful and numerically the strongest conventional armed force in the world. They also have the most powerful and numerically superior nuclear arsenal. Therefore, it does not make any sense to talk of defence last resort.

The purpose of NATO, it used to be said, was to keep the Russians out, keep the Americans in and the Germans down. That continues to be the NATO philosophy, and the role of nuclear weapons in NATO is mainly to keep the Germans, if not down, at least contained in terms of their dominance.

NATO does no longer need nuclear weapons for deterrence and it is widely recognised that nuclear weapons cannot be used against other nuclear weapon powers to win a war. Therefore, NATO weapons will not have a role to play in future. Surely, NATO does not need thousands of weapons to retaliate against a 'rogue' state, if at all a 'rogue' state acquires nuclear weapons. It is also highly doubtful, whether a 'rogue' state can acquire nuclear weapons unless it is extended the kind of permissiveness Saddam Hussein enjoyed at the hands of western powers in the eighties, or it gets in from the ex-Soviet arsenal. In either case the arsenals of hundreds and thousands of nuclear weapons make no sense.

What is the future of nuclear weapons in NATO? The probability of NATO having to engage in high intensity conflicts with other industrial nations is almost negligible. The future NATO operations are likely to be more in the nature of intervention operations in the developing world. Such operations are not likely to call for the use, or even threat of use, of nuclear weapons. No 'rogue' nation is likely to use, or threaten to use, nuclear weapons in circumstances which will invite justified strike against its nuclear capability and its elimination. Therefore, the probability of nuclear weapons being used, or threatened to be used, appears to be virtually non-existent. Over a period of time, the concept of deterrence is bound to decay slowly and steadily. Nuclear weapons cannot deter ethno-nationalist or tribal conflicts in the developing world. As the years roll by, and no use can be found for nuclear weapons, the legislatures in the nuclear weapon countries are bound to raise questions on the need to incur expenditure on maintaining unusable nuclear arsenals.

At the same time, the risks of leakage of nuclear weapons, nuclear fissile materials and technical expertise to put together nuclear weapons, are bound to increase and so also the probability of their falling into the hands of international terrorist organisations. Such terrorist organisations cannot be deterred with the large arsenals of nuclear weapon nations. On the other hand, the insistence of the nuclear weapon powers to legitimise their possession of nuclear weapons also lends legitimacy to their use in the eyes of terrorists and supporters of their causes. Only a non-discriminatory convention, on the lines of the chemical weapons convention, will give the international community adequate legitimacy to have intrusive search and verification operations and to count on societal verification to monitor clandestine nuclear transactions. NATO does not appear to have given adequate thought to the implications of its continuing to keep nuclear weapons and vest in them legitimacy. The NATO attitude towards nuclear weapons is a continuation of the cold war nuclear theological approach and does not serve any meaningful strategic or military purpose.

Increasingly, opinion in gaining ground in Europe that European security should be the primary responsibility of the Western European Union (WEU), which excludes six NATO nations (US, Canada, Iceland, Norway, Denmark and Turkey). The French are the strongest proponents of this concept. By excluding the US, the French, with their versatile nuclear arsenal and large intervention capability, expect to play a significant role in any operation determined by WEU to be in its interest. France aims at WEU replacing NATO in Europe, which in turn would mean the US having no role in European affairs. The US maintains, and such countries as Britain support, the view that US leadership is absolutely essential to being Europe together in security terms. In this silent struggle, nuclear weapons have a crucial role to play in political terms. Without an independent nuclear capability, the WEU would not have much credibility as a military entity. By providing that capability, France hopes to carve for itself a leading role in WEU and to countervail German dominance in the European Union. On the other hand, the emergence of such an independent and assertive Western European Union would means the fading away of NATO. Presumably, in anticipation of this, NATO is building the Partnership for Peace with Russia and the Eastern European countries to have an overarching structure over and about WEU, which would justify the continuance of NATO and the US leadership over Europe.

Given this political struggle in the industrialised world, the nuclear weapon powers are keen to retain the primacy of nuclear weapons as a currency of power and hence, their reluctance to accept the widespead demand for no first use doctrine as a negative security guarantee. Given the extraordinary significance the NATO powers attach to nuclear weapons as a currency of power and their reluctance to accept no first use doctrine, the Russians have also revised their earlier acceptance of no first use and now adopted the same doctrine as NATO. For Russia nuclear weapons play a more vital role, than for UK and France, in vesting it with the great power prestige, because without them the Russians would be totally ignored in international relations.

NATO's nuclear doctrines were always the engine of nuclear proliferation and they continue to be so even after the end of the cold war. They are not likely to serve any useful military purpose, except to legitimise nuclear weapons and hamper the advance towards ending nuclear proliferation and a nuclear-weapon free world.

Nuclear Arms Control

Four interrealated developments disintegration of the Soviet Union, unification of Germany, relative economic decline of the United States, and rise of Japan as an economic superpower—have ushered in an era of turbulence in the international system of states as well as in the global economy. Each of these developments by itself would have led to major changes in the balance of power; the four combined amount to a profound transformation of the world scene. The global diffusion of science and technology has further accelerated the reshuffling of power hierarchies.

A recent Harvard study entitled *Cooperative Denuclearisation* has succinctly summarised the present nuclear predicament: about 50,000 nuclear warheads are scattered at hundreds of locations throughout Eurasia and North America; approximately 3,000 strategic nuclear weapons of the former Soviet Union are located in Ukraine, Belarus, and Kazakhstan; hundreds of tons of plutonium and highly enriched uranium with half-lives of hundreds of thousands of years have been stockpiled; more than a million individuals, who have spent their entire careers and earned their livelihood in nuclear weapon complexes, now face an uncertain future; and many facilities in these nuclear weapon complexes are contaminated with radioactive and toxic waste. While the spectre of a global nuclear war has mercifully faded there is an increased probability of accidental detonation of nuclear weapons as a result of the crisis in the former Soviet Union.

The era of substantive reductions in the nuclear stockpiles of the United States and the former Soviet Union began with the INF Treaty of 1987. This was followed by START I, Bush-Gorbachev-Yeltsin initiatives and START II agreement. A substantial portion of tactical nuclear weapons have been withdrawn from forward locations and dramatic cuts made in the strategic nuclear arsenals of the two countries. By the year 2003 the United States and Russia, the legal heir to the Soviet stockpile, will have between 3,000 and 3,500 strategic warheads each. It must, however, be pointed out that when the reductions are completed, the American and Russian arsenals would be roughly equal to the 1960s and 1970s level respectively. Warren Christopher has recently assured the US Senate that American stockpiles even after START II will "have a capacity to destroy civilisation as we know it several times over". Moreover, the stockpiles of Britain, France and China are being augmented. Research and development continues in the secrecy of weapons laboratories. There are reports that the US Strategic Command has begun work on computer models to aim nuclear weapons at potentially hostile developing countries. Addressing senior commanders in Moscow in November 1992, President Yeltsin observed that Russia's prestige as a great power "largely depends on the fact that its forces have nuclear weapons".

Sergei Kortunov, Director of the Department of Non-Proliferation, Arms Transfers Controls and Conversion in the Ministry of Foreign Affairs of the Russian Federation, wrote in 1992: "Nuclear deference is a *modus vivendi* of the world we live in, and will continue to be until nations devise a fundamentally new system of maintaining international security".

When the nuclear age began, non-proliferation was almost synonymous with the total elimination of nuclear weapons. Gradually, it came to be viewed in two different contexts: as a dangerous element in the international security arena which necessitated its removal, and as an interest of nuclear weapon powers which wanted geopolitical control and political stability in the central strategic balance. It was assumed that the two nuclear superpowers were invulnerable to internal or external pressures with the exception of each others' nuclear forces and that it was not only irrational but even mischievous for any country to doubt it. History, however, is a record of the failure of events to conform to projections made even by the best funded think tanks.

The elaborate non-proliferation regime, with the Non-Proliferation Treaty (NPT) as its main pillar, consists of nuclear safeguards and an expanding web of technology controls. The early history of the nuclear age represents an overt nuclear culture which accorded great significance to the visibility of nuclear weapons. The NPT was evolved when this was the predominant culture. The five declared nuclear weapon powers followed the path of development, testing and proclamation of their nuclear status. The bulging nuclear armouries provided opportunities for deterrence, competence and even swaggering. The NPT does not sit well in a milieu informed by covert nuclear culture.

The NPT safeguards, drafted to proved the commercial and proprietary interests of the industrialised states, apply to the flow of nuclear material measured by instruments located at strategic points in the fuel cycle. The objective is timely detection of diversion of significant quantities of nuclear material from peaceful to military activities and its deterrence through risk of early detection. The IAEA is not authorised to search for clandestine facilities. The safeguards system is basically a system of nuclear material accountancy designed to detect diversion for military purposes. A significant quantity of nuclear material is defined as 8 kg of plutonium and 25 kg of highly enriched uranium, enough to make at least one bomb. The safeguards system makes provisions for material unaccounted for (MUF); in a sophisticated nuclear fuel cycle the amount of MUF would obviously be considerable. As a Japanese expert. Ryukichi Imai, has pointed out: "Put cynically, the amount of material unaccounted for could total 10 to 15 bombs every six months".

The NPT allows non-explosive military research: nuclear propulsion which generally needs highly enriched uranium is permitted. This is not a loophole in the treaty as some non-proliferation enthusiasts are now suggesting; this provision was deliberately inserted at the instance of the industrially advanced nations.

West Germany, Japan, Italy, Australia and many other countries, which are now main pillars of the non-proliferation regime, were initially reluctant to join the NPT. West Germany insisted upon safeguards being applied to the flow of nuclear materials, made several reservations, and asked for US assurances on unrestricted access to materials and technologies for peaceful uses of nuclear energy. There was a hard core of resistance to the NPT in the Bundestag of which 90 deputies voted against ratification of the treaty. The United States accepted the West Germany reservation that the dissolution of NATO would lead to West Germany withdrawal from the treaty. West Germany also proposed a duration of five and later 10 years. Italy was instrumental in getting Article IV, regarding the inalienable right of the parties to use nuclear energy for peaceful purposes, inserted into the treaty. Permission to pursue non-explosive military application of nuclear energy was also due to Italian efforts. It was at the Italian suggestion that the duration of the treaty was fixed for 25 years, to be followed by a conference which would decide about its further extension.

Japan acceded to the treaty in February 1970, being one of the last countries to do so before it went into force on March 5, 1970. Japan wanted to participate in the negotiations for model NPT safeguards agreement. Another important consideration was uninterrupted supply of enriched uranium fuel from the USA for its reactors. The Japanese Defence White Paper of 1970 had maintained that "Defensive" nuclear weapons were not inconsistent with the pacifist provisions of its constitution. The treaty was not popular in Japan and the government issued a long list of reservations about the adverse impact of safeguards as well as the long duration of the treaty. There should be no restriction on peaceful nuclear activities and no discrimination in the application of safeguards between Japan and the West European countries. A safeguards agreement with the IAEA was concluded only in February 1975, and the treaty was ratified a year later. The Japanese Government also pointedly took note of the withdrawal clause in the treaty.

During the 1970s, a series of developments drastically transformed the implementation of the treaty provisions. A nuclear suppliers cartel was formed which created a new division between suppliers and recipients of nuclear materials and technologies; this was in addition to the distinction between nuclear weapon powers and non-nuclear weapon states. The new division was artificial because most of the countries were importers as well as exporters. Another layer of demarcation was added when a distinction was made between safe and dangerous technologies. Certain technologies, such as reprocessing and breeders were now considered dangerous even under IAEA safeguards. All this created a political storm in which West European countries and Japan found themselves being coerced by the United States. A truce was finally achieved which allowed the industrially advanced countries to have complete nuclear fuel cycles while the others were left with fragmented nuclear industries. The United States thereby forged a collective nuclear hegemony of the industrialised world.

France and China had not acceded to the Partial Test Ban Treaty (PTBT) of 1963, because it would have hindered their incipient nuclear weapon programmes. French hesitation in acceding to the NPT was tinged with satisfaction because West Germany nuclear ambitions were effectively frustrated by it. French policy was gradually modified in the late 1970s, partly as a result of covert nuclear co-operation between France and the United States. France has now become party to the NPT as a nuclear weapon state. Its joining the fold hardly makes any substantive change in the non proliferation regime.

China must have been relieved when Japan finally ratified the treaty in 1976. It, however, regarded the treaty as another attempt to consolidate the monopoly of certain nuclear weapon states and to perpetuate inequality on the basis of economic and military power. Its objections were of a substantive kind. As Wu Xiu Quan, Chairman of the Beijing Institute for International Strategic Studies, put it in 1985: "The obligations imposed on the non-nuclear weapon states parties are specific and strict, whereas the obligation on the nuclear weapon states... is devoid of any binding force and therefore of little meaning". The treaty attempted to freeze inequality and did not give assurances to non-nuclear weapon states against attack by the nuclear weapon powers. China assisted Pakistan in its nuclear weapon programme and is also reported to have supplied enriched uranium to South Africa, Argentina and Brazil. Having indulged in considerable amount of proliferation activity, China joined the NPT as a nuclear weapon power.

Argentina and Brazil have refused to accede to the treaty because of its discriminatory provisions. Both countries have devoted a large portion of research to develop their nuclear propulsion programmes and, therefore, established uranium enrichment facilities, as highly enriched uranium is needed for such a programme. They moved from rivalry to cooperation in the nuclear field in a general atmosphere of a comprehensive detente, which included the Act for Argentina-Brazilian Integration of 1986 together with 12 protocols for co-operation in diverse areas. In December 1990, they signed a bilateral inspection agreement and established an agency for this purpose in July 1991. This agency entered into an agreement with the IAEA in December 1991. The IAEA Safeguards on the Argentina-Brazilian installations will cost $ 2,100,000 in 1993 alone.

In response to growing pressure within the IAEA General Conference to suspend South Africa Government expressed willingness to accede to the NPT. The prospect of a Black African government being installed at some future date also contributed to this willingness. South Africa has been engaged in producing highly enriched uranium and Foreign Minister Pik Botha had declared in August 1988 that his country had the capacity to make nuclear weapons. After accession to the treaty in July 1991 the IAEA inspected 77 locations including a visit to the Kalahari desert. Reporting the complexities of inspecting installations of a *de facto* nuclear weapon state, the Director General of the IAEA declared that the inspection team had found no evidence of undeclared facilities. President de Klerk then made the disclosure of a weapons programme started in 1974 and said that six nuclear devices had been manufactured by the time he came to power in 1989. The devices were dismantled in 1990 on his orders and the programme was abandoned. Representatives of the African national Congress have expressed reservations about these disclosures. The fact that the South African weapons programme could not be detected by the IAEA inspectors is a sad commentary on the effectiveness of Agency inspections. Moreover, the world community cannot accept the government assurance that the weapons were dismantled and the programme abandoned without some concrete evidence in support of it. It has been reported that the United States is trying to purchase all highly enriched uranium produced in South Africa.

After considerable hesitation, North Korea acceded to the NPT in 1985 and a Safeguards agreement with the IAEA was concluded in January 1992. Since then six *ad hoc* inspections of the 12 nuclear facilities mentioned in the agreement have been conducted and the Director General of the IAEA had a fruitful visit in May 1992. Reports suggest that a reprocessing plant is under construction at the Nyongbyon complex. The IAEA demanded challenge inspections, a new procedure recently, approved by the Board of Governors of the IAEA, of two sites at the complex. Pyongyang rejected the demand maintaining that the two sides had nothing to do with its nuclear programme. Japan, which has an extensive reprocessing programme under IAEA Safeguards, has insisted that of North Korea built a reprocessing facility and even if it operated under similar Safeguards, it would not provide financial compensation for its occupation of Korea in the recent past. The North Koreans have accused Japan of double standards. Japan, observed a West European diplomat, "needed IAEA Safeguards to legitimise its plutonium recycling programme, but clearly had no faith that Safeguards would work to prevent North Korea from using its plutonium to make bombs". The North Korean announcement of March 12, 1993, giving notice of its intention to withdraw from the NPT is an unprecedented development. As it is the first country to make use of the withdrawal clause requiring advance notice of three months, the manner in which this crisis is resolved would set a precedent. China has publicly opposed sanctions; as it has a veto in the Security Council, no coercive action can be taken without Chinese approval. Moreover, sanctions cannot succeed without Chinese co-operation because most of North Korean trade is with China. Diplomatic persuasion is favoured by a large number of countries. The withdrawal clause had facilitated accession to the treaty when it was opened for signature; without such a clause, it may be conjectured, several industrialised countries would have been reluctant to join it. The international pressure on North Korea to revoke its decision seems to indicate that this clause is being nullified.

The disintegration of a nuclear superpower has raised totally unexpected and complex problems for the non-proliferation regime. Belarus, Ukraine and Kazakhstan have promised to join the NPT as non-nuclear weapon states but none of them has done it so far. Ukraine and Kazakhstan are using the nuclear weapons located within their borders as bargaining chips to get financial and technical assistance and to obtain security assurances. Nursultan Nazarbayev has pointed out that Kazakhstan is sandwiched between two nuclear weapon powers—Russia and China—both of which have territorial claims on it. Ukraine has a number of contentious issues with Russia and seems most reluctant to part with its nuclear assets. If Ukraine and Kazakhstan somehow manage to retain control over the nuclear weapons, they will become the third and fourth largest nuclear weapon powers respectively. Ukraine has 16 nuclear power plants and the nuclear test site Semiplantisk is located in Kazakhstan. Accession to the NPT would necessitate preparation of an authentic inventory of nuclear material within Ukraine so that IAEA Safeguards become operational. As nuclear installations in Ukraine were part of the Soviet nuclear weapons complex, some of the nuclear material may have been used for weapons purposes. This will further complicate the time-consuming task of preparing the inventory of material in installations which have been in operation for a considerable period of time. The IAEA has so far not taken a nuclear test site within its inspection arrangements.

The additional safeguards responsibilities in Argentina and Brazil, South Africa, North Korea, Israel and in the three non-Russian republics of the CIS would entail considerable investment in financial and human resources. The recently concluded Chemical Weapons Convention has elaborate inspection arrangements. Who will pay for all these sareguards and inspections? The United States, the European Community and Japan offered financial and technical assistance to deal with the problems resulting from the fragmentation of the Soviet stockpile. These include assistance in establishing an International Science and Technology Centre in Moscow and a Science and Technology Centre in Keiv to provide fruitful employment to the thousands of scientists and engineers who operated the Soviet nuclear weapons complex.

The prospective dismantling of warheads in Russia and the United States will release large amounts of weapons-grade plutonium and enriched uranium. The United States has entered into an agreement with Russia for the purchase of 500 metric tonnes of highly enriched uranium, over the next two decades. It has been estimated that this material is enough to produce about ten thousand nuclear weapons. The United States intends to dilute it for use as low-enriched uranium fuel in its power plants. This transaction, involving transport of explosive material, raises questions about safety and security. It is a purely bilateral transaction without international verification.

Fissile material from dismantled warheads will be released at a time when there is already a surfeit of such material released from the civilian nuclear programmes within the industrialised world. It is estimated that 310 tonnes of plutonium will be available by the end of the century and 545 tonnes by the year 2010. Highly enriched uranium can be used for naval propulsion and can be diluted for use in power plants. Surplus plutonium raises difficult problems. It can be used in breeder reactors, but they produce more plutonium. It can also be fabricated into mixed-oxide (MOX) fuel for reactors but this is a costly enterprise. Theodore B. Taylor, a former American weapons designer, has proposed the novel solution of incineration in the sun; huge rockets will have to be designed for this purpose, but it can hardly be a cheap method of getting rid of this dangerous stuff. The real danger with the growing stockpiles of weapons-grade plutonium and uranium is not so much diversion as the denunciation of the NPT obligations. The industrialised countries which have accumulated this material can, at least theoretically, withdraw from the NPT and quickly fabricate large stocks of nuclear weapons.

The NPT provides for periodic review conferences and an extension conference in 1995. Four review conferences have been held in 1975, 1980, 1985, and 1990. Only 58 states party to the treaty attended the first conference; 75 states in 1980, 83 states in 1985, and 84 states in 1990 participated in such conferences. Only the first conference achieved a reluctant consensus. There was no consensus at the second and fourth conferences, while efforts were made to pretend that there was a consensus at the third when in reality there was none. A comprehensive test ban treaty has been the persistent demand of the non-nuclear weapon states at these conferences. They have also pleaded for substantial nuclear disarmament and complained about restrictions on technology transfers.

It is generally assumed that the conference of 1995 will extend the treaty either for a fixed period or indefinitely. The decision of the conference will be not by the majority of those attending the conference but by a majority of states party to the treaty. There are various possibilities; the treaty may be extended for a fixed period during which a comprehensive review could be conducted or extension could be made conditional on the conclusion of a comprehensive test ban treaty. Dramatic changes in power relationships, decline in American ability to orchestrate the nonproliferation regimes, delays in the accession to the treaty by Ukraine or Kazakhastan, failure to resolve the North Korean crisis, or inability to conclude a comprehensive test ban treaty—all these would certainly impinge on the deliberations at the extension conference.

It would be an act of extraordinary renunciation on the part of Germany and Japan to reconcile themselves to the status of non-nuclear weapon states forever while Britain, France and China retain their nuclear status in a post-cold war world. Germany and Japan do have a stake in the non-proliferation regime and they would not like it to be terminated without something better taking its place. They might support extension of the treaty but might also insist on a review leading to substantive changes. Many other states party to the treaty have expressed reservations at successive review conferences. There is a general awareness regarding the shortcomings of the non-proliferation regime, but this is coupled with a fear that any tinkering with the treaty in its present form could have cascading consequences. One argument originally advanced in favour of establishing an international system of safeguards was that this would provide a "working model" for the distantly envisioned inspection system needed for nuclear disarmament. Now is the time for nuclear *glasnost* in the installations of nuclear weapon powers. Such a transparency would provide opportunities to hammer out a more realistic, balanced and equitable non-proliferation regime.

BIBLIOGRAPHY

1. Bengi Broms, "The Role of United Nations in Peaceful Settlement of Disputes" in the United Nations and the Maintenance of International Peace and Security, UNITAR, 1987.
2. F.S. Northledge and M.D. Donelan, "International Disputes: The Political Aspect", London, 1971.
3. L.N. Rangarajan, "The Limitation of Conflict : A Theory of Bargaining the Negotiation, London, 1985.
4. David Wainhouse, International Peacekeeping at the Cross-roads, Baltimore, 1973.
5. K.S. Nagar and Gautam Sharma, ed. "India's Security : Super Power Threat", Reliance, Delhi, 1989.
6. Leela Yadav, "US Policy in South Asia", Harman, Delhi, 1989.
7. M.D. Nalapat, "The Red Herring : Pakistan Role in Dividing Asia", The Times of India, 12 March 1996.
8. Morganthan H., "Politics Among Nations : The Struggle for Power and Peace", Kalyani Publishers, New Delhi, 1985.
9. Russell Bertran, "Common Sense and Nuclear Warfare", London : Allen and Unwin, 1959.
10. Clarke, Robin, "The Science of War and Peace", New York MacGraw Hills, 1972.
11. Bowett, D.W., "The Search for Peace", London, 1972.
12. Fishes, David, "Stopping the Spread of Nuclear Weapons : The Past and the Prospects", London-Routledge, 1992.
13. Falk, Richard, Merowitz, L. and Jack Anderson, "Nucelar Weapons and International Law", Indian Journal of International Law, Vol. 20, 1980.
14. Brown, Michael E., *et al.* (ed) "The Perils of Anarchy : Contemporary Realism and International Security", Cambridge, Massachusetts : The MIT Press, 1955.
15. Sengupta, Bhabani, "Nuclear Weapons? Policy Options for India", Sage, New Delhi, 1983.
16. Young, Elizabeth, "A Farewell to Arms Control", London : Pelican, 1972.
17. Sagan, Scolt D., "Why Do States Build Nuclear Weapons?" International Security, Vol. 21, No. 3, Winter, 1996-97.

18. Crevald, Martin Van, "Nuclear Proliferation and the Future of Conflict", The Free Press, New York, 1993.
19. Subramanyam, K., "India Keeping the Option Open" in Lawrence, Robert M. and Joel Larus (ed.) 'Nuclear Proliferation : Phase II' University of Kansas Press, Kansas, 1974.
20. Fisher, David, "Towards 1995 : The Prospects for Ending the Proliferation of Nuclear Weapons", Aldershat, England, Dartmouth, 1993.
21. Ghosh, Sekhar, "Superpower Cooperation and Transit Passage though Straits" EPW Vol. XX, No. 18 May 9, 1985.
22. Dhanapala J., "Fulfilling the Promise of the NPI : The CTBT and Beyond", Arms Control Today, May, 1996.
23. Specter Leonard, "The Undeclared Bomb : The Spread of Nuclear Weapons, 1987-88", Cambridge, Massachussets: Ballinger, 1988.
24. Cohen, Stephen P., "Nuclear Proliferation in South Asia : Prospects for Arms Control", Boulder, Lacorads : Westview Press, 1991.
25. Bose T.C., "Twenty Five Years of NPT : What Next?" Journal of International Relations, Jadavpur, Vol. I, 1998.
26. Bagchi, K.N., "Double Standard Issues : Security Assurances of the NPT and the Comprehensive Test Ban Treaty", Asian Studies (Calcutta), Vol. 15, No. 6, 1996.
27. Noorani, A.G., "Nuclear Weapons : India's Duty As Compaigner". The Statesman, Calcutta, April 7, 1997.
28. Ghosh, Sekhar, 'UN Peace-keeping During the Post-Cold War Period : Implications for the third world.' The 1995 conference souvenir of the West Bengal Political Science Association.
29. Perry, Willian, "Defense in an Age of Hope", Foreign Affairs, Vol. 75, No. 6 1996.
30. Patil, R.L.M., "India-Nuclear Weapons and International Politics", National, New Delhi, 1969.
31. Johnson, Rebecca, "The CTBT : Hanging in the Balance Arms Control Today, July 1996.
32. Vanaik, Achin, "India in a Changing World", Orient Longman, New Delhi, 1995.
33. Blackwill, Robert and Albert Carnesale (ed.) "New Nuclear Nations: Consequences for US Policy" Council for Foreign Relations Press, New York, 1993.
34. Travis Tom A., "The Emerging World System : Grounds for optimism and Pessimissm," Strategic Analysis Vol. XVII, No. 4, July 1994.
35. Banerjee D., "Emerging International Order : Conflict or Cooperation?" Strategic Analysis, Vol. XVI, No. 9, December 1993.
36. Bhandari, Romesh "The Relevance of NAM", Indian Express, August 31, 1992.

INDEX

A

Action plan aimed at total elimination of nuclear weapons, 10
Afghanistan, 24-25, 145-148
Afghanistan-Pakistan control, 151
Africa, 147-48
Agni, 56, 59-60, 239
Agni II, 193
AK-47, 148
Akash, 56, 58
Albeit, 168
Alpine resort, 19
American licensed exports, 38
American non-proliferation policy, 26
American soviet relations, 28
American strategic establishment, 158-59
American thinking about nuclear weapons, 160
Angola, 148
Ante-Ballistic Missile Treaty, 18-19, 176, 204, 206, 211-12
Anti-personal Mines, 127-28
Antrix corporation, 233
Appadoral, 36
Argentina, 26, 257-58, 261
Ariane Passenger Payload Experiment Satellite, 223
Ariane rocket, 216-17, 242
Arms Export Control Act for military items, 42
Arms transfer, 183-84
Aryabhata, 223, 240
ASEAN, 13
Asian security, 31, 187
Atlantic block, 32, 75
Atomic Energy Commission, 10, 69-73, 75-76, 118, 171
Atomic energy-peaceful uses of, 167
Attitude and orbit control system, 50
Attlee, C.R., 69-70
Augumented Satellite Launch Vehicle, 224-25, 241
Australia, 23, 40, 255
Austria, 40
Auxiliary Propulsion Centre, 224
Axelord, Robert, 23
Axiy powers, 248
Azores, 155

B

Bacterial warfare, 103-05
Baikonoor, 55
Balkans, 210-11
Ballistic missile systems, 41
Bangladesh, 10
Barlow, Richard, 25
Barrer, Said, 148
Beg, Aslam, 29
Beijing Institute for International Strategic Studies, 257
Belarus, 252, 260

Belgium, 40
Bhabha Atomic Research Centre, 167-68, 171
Bhabha, Homi, 167, 170-72, 223
Bhakti, 36
Bharat Electronics Ltd., 53
Botha, Pik, 258
Brazil, 26, 257-58, 261
Britain, 170, 246
Britain deployed submarine missiles, 164
Broadcasting Satellite Service, 52
Brood Castle, 18
Brezinski, 191
Buddha, 36
Bureau of Disarmament Commission, 17
Bush, George, 18-20, 55, 182, 196-97, 202-03

C

Cambodia, 148, 188
Canada, 39, 251
C-band antenna, 51
Central Electronics Ltd., 53
Central Europe, 152
Central Intelligence Agency, 28
Centre of Advanced Technology, Indore, 171
Centrifuge technology, 172
CFE Treaty, 149
Chagai nuclear test, 192
Chechnya, 146, 177, 210
Chemical and biological weapons, 102
China, 16, 24, 26, 29, 32-34, 54, 148, 153, 170, 185, 190-91, 257-60
China exports, 32
China MII missiles to Pakistan, 25, 45
China rocket technology, 232
Chou en-lai, 32
Christ, 34
Christopher, Warren, 253
CIA, 25, 149
Cirus Research ractor, 169
Clinton, Bill, 146, 174, 189, 202
Cohen, Stephen, 24-25
Cold war, 28, 196, 246
Commission for Conventional Armaments, 73, 75-76
Committee on disarmament, 106
Committee on Natal Defence and Armed Services of France, 165
Committee of Twelve, 75-81
  Appointment and report of sub-committee of four powers, 76
  Area of agreement and possible agreement, 76-78
  Area of disagreement, 78-80
Communist Party of Burma, 153
Comprehensive Nuclear Test Ban Treaty, 1-20, 30, 91-92, 99-101, 162-63, 176, 193, 199
  Additional provisions, 9
  Amendments and review, 7-8
  Arrangements until entry into force, 3
  Disbute settlement, 7
  Duration and withdrawal, 8
  Entry into force, 8-9
  History of, 2
  Implementing organization, 4-5
  India's position on, 9-12
  Negotiation, adoption and signature, 2-3
  Non-accession to, 162
  Other provisions, 8
  Preparatory commission, 3
  Protocol, 9
  Reservation, 9
  Scope, 4
  Significance, 1
  Stalled dialogue, 18
  State's rights, 7
  Summary of Treaty, 3-4

Verification and compliance, 5-7
Conference of Committee on disarmament, 99
Conference of Eighteen Nation Committee on disarmament, 85-86
Conference on disarmament of Geneva, 2, 100
Conference on Security and Cooperation in Europe, 246
Confidence building measures, 6
Consultation and clarification, 6
Conventional Arms Register, 16
Conventional weapons, 109-11
Convention on Bacteriological weapons, 106-08
Convention on Chemical weapons, 108-09
Convention on Prohibition of Development, Production and Stockpiling of Bacteriological and Toxin weapons, 68
Coordination Committee of Multilateral Export Controls, 46, 51
Cross-border blitzkrieg, 186
Cruise missiles, 41
Cryogenic rocket engines, 38, 41-42, 65-66
Cuba, 55
Czechoslovakia, 184

D

Dayton accords, 145
Defence Research and Development Laboratory, 56
Defence Research and Development Organisation, 59, 239
Delivery vehicles, 193
De Mitra Shein, Martha Batriz Lepez, 17
Denmark, 40, 251
Depositary govts., 95
Dept. of Atomic Energy, 223
Dept. of space, 223
Deva Gowda, 24
Dhanapala, Jayanta, 14-15
Dhruva, 168-69
Disarmament commission, 12, 80-84, 104-05
Consideration by General Assembly in Plenary Session, 80-84
Disarmament Commission Review Nuclear Disarmament, 12-17
Disarmament decade, 132-38
Dispute settlement, 7
Doordarshan Broadcasting, 219
Dubey, M., 192

E

East Asia, 32
East Asia Strategic Initiative, 189
East West Confrontation, 183
Economic Cooperation Organisation, 19, 87
Egypt, 23
Electronic items for launch vehicals, 51, 53
Elimination of nuclear weapons, 254
Entry into force, 8-9
Equality idea, 36
Equator, 38
Eurasia, 29, 252
Euro centric affairs, 186
Europe, 29
European Ariane launcher, 49
European Community, 40, 190, 261
European Space Agency, 40, 216, 228, 241
European Union, 16, 22, 248
Evans, Don, 20
Export Administration Act, 42

Extended Proliferation Control Initiative, 239

F

Fast breeder test reactor, 168
Fernandes, George, 29, 31
Finland, 17, 40
Ford Aerospace, 49
France, 39, 76-77, 164-65
France nuclear concept, 165
French ariane, 4, 228, 239
French remote sensing satellite system, 229
Fuel Air Explosive bombs, 62
Fuel reprocessing technology, 167-68

G

G7, 146
Gamma Ray Burst, 225-26
Gandhian, 21, 23
Gandhi, Indira, 24
Gandhi, Mahatma, 23
Gandhi, Rajiv, 10, 24, 158, 161, 163, 199
  Action Plan of, 10, 199
General dynamics, 39, 41
Generalised system of preference, 55
Geneva conference on disarmaments, 173
Geneva Protocol for Prohibition of use in war of Asphyxiating Poisonous or other gasses, 102, 163
Georgia, 210
Geostationary Satellite Launch Vehicle, 225-26, 228, 230-31, 241, 244
Geosynchronous launch vehicle, 38, 55, 220
Germany, 39, 152, 247-48, 263
Geostationary orbit, 220
Giat Metrewave Radio Telescope, Pune, 111
Gita, 21
Glavkosmos, 38-39, 41, 43, 47, 54, 62, 229
Global Wanning Ozone Layer depletion, 183
Good paster, Andrew, 157
Greenpeace, 165-66
Guatemala, 149
Gujral, I.K., 24
Gulf war, 163, 182, 186

H

Haiti, 149
Hasan, 218
Hekmatyar, Gulbuddin, 152
Hoffmann, Wolfgang, 3
Holy Grait, 175
Horner, Charles, 157
Human Rights Arms Watch Report, 150, 152
Hydrogen bomb, 167

I

ICBM, 195, 197
Iceland, 251
IGCR, 171
Imai, Ryukichi, 255
India and nuclear missile defence, 192-215
  Agni II test, 193
  Autonomy eroded, 200
  Bush-Putin summit, 209-15
  Disarmament problems, 198
  Elimination of nuclear weapons, 198, 200
  India and Pakistan to, 203-04
  Indian deterrence, 197
  Indian enthuseias, 207-09
  Indian support to NMD, 204-07
  Interview with M. Dubey, 192

National missile defence system, 195-97, 199
Not signing CTBT, 193
Nuclear doctrine draft, 194-95
Nuclear free world, 200
Nuclear option for security global nuclear disarmament, 197-98
Pokhran test, 192-94
Protection from nuclear devices, 202
Rajiv Gandhi action plan, 199
Seeking VS Umbrella, 201
Star wars project, 202
To gain political milage, 194
US on missile defence, 202-03
India free nuclear, 10-11
Indian atomic power programme, 168
Indian bomb, 29
Indian Integrated Guided Missile Development Programme, 56-57
Indian nuclear weapons programme, 24
Indian Ocean, 165
Indian Remote Sensing Satellite, 52, 229, 243
Indian Space Research Organisation, 38-39, 43, 47, 49, 51-52, 55, 62, 221, 226-27, 229, 231-32, 235
Indian Telephone Industries Ltd. 53
India on CTBT, 9-12
India pursuing security logic, 30
India's no first use doctrine, 174
India's nuclear status, 29
India's pluralism, 35
India support to NMD, 204-07
India's weapon opinion, 166-75
India tested peaceful bomb, 26
Indo-Pakistan relations, 29
Indo-US relations, 55
INMARSAT Satellite, 49, 238
INSAT, 3, 51, 232
INSAT-1, 49, 219-20
INSAT 1A, 223
INSAT 1B, 223
INSAT 1C, 223, 242
INSAT 1D, 219, 223
INSAT 2, 49, 51-53, 216, 219
INSAT 2A, 49, 52, 219-20, 241
INSAT 2A components, 217-18
Institute for Himalayan Ecology, 22
Institute of Plasma Research, Ahmedabad, 171
Intercultural rivalry, 32
Intelligence sharing, 45-46
Interim Test Range, Chancipur, 60
Intermediate Nuclear Force Treaty, 206
International arms transfer, 128-30
International Atomic Energy Agency, 8, 94, 96, 254, 256, 258-60
International Conference on Relationship between Disarmament and Development, 143-44
International Court of Justice, 7
International Data Centre, 4-6
International Decade for Culture of Peaceful non-violence for children, 180
International Maritime Satellite Organisation, 227
International Monitoring System, 4-6, 9
International Science and Technology Centre, Moscow, 261
International Year of Culture of Peace, 180
Interstate rivalry, 32
IRS -A remote sensing satellite, 221

IRS 1A, 49, 227
IRS 1B, 49, 221
IRS 1C, 53
ISI activities in Pakistan, 153
Islamic states, 185
Israel, 30, 40, 185, 261
ISRO Telemetry, Tracking and command network, 236
Italy, 39, 248, 255

J

Jamaica, 17
Japan, 21, 29, 32, 34, 39, 170, 189, 249, 155-56, 261
Japanese Defence White Paper, 256
Jaswant Singh, 206, 208
Jeremich, David E., 188
Jungk, Robert, 23

K

Kaifu, Toshiki, 189
Kaiga, 170
Kakodkar, Anil, 168-69
Kele Pramod, 52-54
Kalpakkan, 168, 171
Kargil Campaign, 31
Kashmir, 24-25, 35, 163, 208
Kasturirangan, K, 230-32, 238
Karakhstan, 55, 252, 260
Khan, A.Q., 25
Khmer Rouge, 188
Khun Sa of Burma, 153
Khushab plutonium production reactor, 25
Korea, 34, 75
Kortunov, Sergei, 253
Kouroy, 38, 49
Kwa Zulu, 151

L

Land sat, 52-53
Launch vehicle programme, 4, 9, 54
Legitimisation of nuclear weapons, 160
Lindquist, Niklas, 17
Linear Imaging Self-Scanner Camera, 235
Local, John, 206
Low earth orbit, 238
LTTT, 146
Luxemburg, 40

M

Macedonia, 211
Mackenize, W.L., 69
Mahavira, 36
Malakand, 151
Martinic, Gabriela, 13
Master Control Facility at Hasan, 52
McNamara, Robat, 157
Medium range delivery vehicle, 193
Milosovich, Slomadom, 210
Miniaturisation, 193
Missile programmers, 26, 56
Missile Research Centre Imrat, 56-57
Missile technology, 38-67
- Advantages, 46-47
- Commission, 54-55
- Fact shet, 62-63
- Guidelines, 40-42
- Indian responses, 47-48
- Intelligence sharing, 45-46
- Missile programme, 56-60
- Missile Technology Control Regime, 39-40, 64
- National Defence Authorization Act, 42-44
- Options, 61-62
- Sebotage, 50-54
- Satellites, 48-50
- Softline, 55-56
- US expectations, 44-45
- US percepions over Indian development, 60-61

Missile Technology Control Regime, 38-46, 59, 62, 203, 239
Missile Technology Proliferation Control Regime, 54
Mizoram, 35
Mobutu, Sese Seko, 150
Morocco, 148
Moratirium on testing, 101-02
Motorola, 238
Mozambique, 148
Mubarakmund, Samar, 25
Musharraf, Pervez, 204
Muthunayagam, A.E., 231
Myanmar, 16, 17

N

Nag, 56-57
Nagasaki, 167, 177
NAM, 199
Narasimha Rao, P.V., 24, 206, 235-36
National Commi:tee for Space Research, 223
National Defence Authorization Act, 42-44, 48
National Informatics Centre Network, 218, 243
National Missile Defence System, 195-96, 203-05, 213
National Mission on Drinking Water of Rural Development, 222
National Remote Sensing Agency, 224, 235
National Security Advisory Board, 194, 198
NATO, 18, 40, 146, 177-78, 212, 240-52
Nayyar, Kuldip, 25
Nazarbayer, Nussurtan, 260
Nazi, holocust, 162
Nehru, Jawaharlal, 2
Nehruesque, 21
Netherlands, 40
New Zealand, 40
Nickel-cadmium batteries, 51
Nitze, Robert, 159
NOAA Satellite imagery, Hyderabad, 52
Non-nuclear weapon country, 17, 163
Non-proliferation, 85
Non-proliferation Treaty, 10-11, 85-88, 160-62, 173, 246, 248, 254-56
  Annex, 88
  Consideration by General Assembly, 86, 88
  Implimentation of provisions, 256
  Review and extension conference, 11, 175, 262-63
North America, 29
North Korea, 212, 259-61
North South conflict, 183
Norway, 40, 251
Nuclear arms control, 252
Nuclear arsenals, 33
Nuclear bomb, 22
Nuclear China, 29
Nuclear deterrance, 192, 253-54
Nuclear disarmament, 12
Nuclear disarmament and western real politik, 157-64
Nuclear expansion, 16
Nuclear issue a human rights issue, 161
Nucelar politics—NATO connection, 245-63
  Britain and France cut backs, 246
  Cold war over, 248
  Correlation between possession of nuclear weapons and permanent membership, 248
  Disintegration of nuclear superpower, 260-61
  Dismantling of warheads in Russia and US, 261-62

- Elimination of nuclear weapons, 254
- Era of reductions, 253
- European security issue, 150-51
- Future of nuclear weapons in NATO, 241-42
- IAEA suspended South Africa, 258-60
- NATO no longer need nuclear weapons, 249
- NATO nuclear Strategy, 245
- NATO powers justify possession of nuclear weapons, 247
- Non-proliferation Treaty, 254-59
- NIP Periodic Review Conferences, 262-63
- Nuclear arms control, 252
- Nuclear war doctrine challenged, 246, 252
- Nuclear weapons powers keen to retain, 251-52
- Partnership for peace offered by NATO, 246-47
- Present nuclear predicament, 252
- Purpose of NATO to keep out Russians, 249
- Renunciation of Germany, 263
- Risks of leakage of nuclear weapons, 250
- Safeguards responsibilities, 261
- Soviet threats to Western Europe, 245
- US self-image of sole superpowers, 248-49
- Western European Union replacing NATO, 251

Nuclear power philosophy, 21
Nuclear power programme and weapon capability, 170
Nuclear prolification, 165
Nuclear Research Reactors, 8
Nuclear Test Ban Treaty, 97-98
Nuclear weapons debat-Indian perspectives, 21-37
- Nuclear balance, 28-31
- Nuclear power philosophy, 21-23
- Post-cold war politics, 31-37
- Weapons programme, 24-28

Nuclear weapons tree zones, 17
Nuclear weapons-proposals, 69
Nuclear weapon test, 2
Nuclear weapon use, 28

O

O'Neill, Paul, 20
Onishchenko, Yurii, 17
On-site inspection, 6
Orbit control system, 50
Osei, Yaw Odei, 12

P

Pacific Rim, 32
Pakistan, 10, 22, 24, 29, 150, 152, 192
- Addicts in, 152

Pakistan-China axis, 26, 28
Pakistan nuclear programme, 24-25
Pakistani support for Mujahideen, 25
Pant, K.C., 40
Partial Test Ban Treaty of 1963, 1, 10, 68, 173, 257
Pay lands for INSAT 2, 52
Physical Research Laboratory, Ahmedabad, 224
Plutonium technology, 167-69, 262
Pokhran II, 21, 192-94
Pokhran test, 10, 24, 169-70, 298
Poland, 72
Polar Satellite Launch Vehicle, 51, 225-26, 229, 231-33, 236, 239, 244
- Launch, 233-35

Population movement, 183
Post-cold wars politics, 31-37
Powell, Colin, 20
Preparatory Commission, 3
Pressler amendment, 25
Pressured Heary Water Reactor, 169-70
Prithvi, 56, 58-59, 239
Propellants, 65-66
Protocol for the Prohibition of use of war of Asphxiating, Poisonous and other goals, 107
Protocol on non-detectable fragments, 125-27
Provisional Technical Secretariat, 3
PSLV-D2, 233, 244
Putin, Vladimir, 18-20, 209-11, 213, 215'
Pyongyang, 259

Q

Quan, Wu Xiu, 257
Quarless, Diane, 12, 14, 17

R

Raul D., 170
Radio telescope, 171
Rana Partap, 22
Rao, U.R., 38, 41, 229, 231
Rawal batta, 170
Reaction control system, 51
reactor grade plutonium, 172
Reagon, 202
Reagon-Gorbachev declaration in Geneva, 246
Real politic, 35
Reduction of arms, 109-11
Register of conventional arms, 130-32
  Armoured combat vehicles, 130
  Attack helicopters, 131
  Battle tanks, 130
  Combat aircraft, 131
  Large calibre artillery systems, 130-31
  Missiles, 131-32
  Warships, 131
Remote Sensing Application Mission for Agricultural Applications, 222
Retardation Potential Analyser, 225
Rifkind, Malcolm, 164-65
Rohini, 222
Rubicon, 192
Rumsfeld, Donald, 20
Russia, 18, 29; 32, 34, 46, 54, 170, 185, 187-88, 211, 246-47
Russian space launch vehicles, 54
Russian space organisation, 39, 229
Russian space technology, 39

S

SAARC, 21
Sabotage, 50-54
Sai Baba, 23
Salander, Diane, 17
Sankaracharya, 23
Sarabhi, Vikram, 223-24
Satellite, 48-50, 235
Satellite Centre, Bangalore, 224
Satellite launching station, 38
Sattar, Abdul, 25
Savinibhi, Jonas, 147
S band Transponders, 219
Schlesinger, James, 183
Schnarkopof, Gen, 148
Science and Technological Centre, Review, 261
Science of Technology Plateform-India's Studies in space, 216-44
  American concern, 228-29
  Augmented Satellite Launch Vehicles, 224-25
  Background, 240
  GSLV, 230-31

INSAT components, 217-18
INSAT ground network, 218-21
INSAT series, 216-17
Institutions, 223-24
Involvement of industries, 226-27
IRS-S, 221-22
Low cost launches, 239-40
Market, 238
Modest beginning, 222-23
Possibilities, 236-38
PSLV, 225-26, 231-33
PSLV launch, 233-35
Rohini, 222
Satellite, 235
Transfer of technology, 227
US opposition, 239
Sea-bed Treaty, 96-97
Semi conductor complex, 50, 53
Semiplantisk, 260
Sen, Amartya, 22
Sethna, Homi, 167
Shahi, Agha, 25
Shanghai Five, 213-14
SHAR, 238
Sharma, Shanker Dayal, 235-36
SIPRI, 40
SLV-3, 222, 226
Socioeconomic development, 179-80
Somalia, 147
Sounding rockets, 41
South Africa, 16, 26, 151, 258-59, 261
South Asia, 34, 192
Soviet move into Afghanistan, 24
Soviet Union, 26-28, 35, 164, 196, 245
Space Application Centre, Ahmedabad, 224
Spain, 40
Sriharikota Propulsion Attitude Range Centre, 38, 224
Sriharikota Test Range, 60
Sri Lanka, 22, 23
SROSS-C satellite, 225
START I, 196, 246, 253
START II, 196, 246, 253
STD, 217
Stengers, 146
Sufism, 36
Suitcase bombs-Menance of nuclear politics, 145-91
Arms dealers operate in black market, 154-55
Conflict factors, 145-46
Covert aid in Africa, 147
Crime levels in Soviet Union, 151-52
Culprits of weapon proliferations and diffusion, 156
Culture of peace, 180-81
Freelance arms dealers, 152
Glut of weapons, 153-54
Gun culture, 146
India's weapon option, 166-75
Intelligences services activities, 153
ISI on Pakistan activities, 153
Israelis accused Ukraine of bartering weapons for oil from Iran, 155
New balance of power, 181-91
New world order, 177-79
Neclear disarmament and western real-politic, 157-64
Socio economic development, 179-80
Source of weapons, 146-47
Soviet and American weapon aid, 148-49
Stocks of weapons supplied to unstable regimes, 147
Terrorism and militancy, 156-57
Threats to third world, 164-66
Transfer of weapons, 155-56
Weapon aid cut-off, 152

Weapon caravans, 150-51
Weapons releasing in tons, 149
Weapons moved into criminal articles, 151
Where these weapon going, 148-49
World peace conference, 175-77
Suspension of nuclear and thermo nuclear test, 98-102
Swadhyaya, 23
Sweden, 16-17, 40
Switzerland, 94

T

Taiwan, 34
Talbot, 22
Tata Institute of Fundamental Research, 171
Technological Challenges, 66-67
Technical Secretariat, Viena, 6-7
Telecommunications, 217
Telemetry Station on Car Nicobar Islands, 60
Telephone, 210
Thailand, 149
Theatre Missile defence, 205
Thermonuclear device, 193
Thorium reserves, 170
Treats to Third World, 164-66
Tito, Josip Broz, 19
TNI equivalent blasting materials, 6
TOPAZ miniature nuclear reactor, 39
TOPAZ technology, 47
Transfer of technology, 227
Travelling wave tribe, 53
Treaty banning nuclear weapons tests, 68
Treaty for Prohibition of Nuclear Weapons in Latin America, 68
Treaty of Non-proliferation of nuclear weapons, 88-96
Treaty on Prohibition of Emplacement of weapons of Mass destruction on Sea bed, 96
Trident, 246
Trilateral commission, 29
Trisul, 56-58
Truman, Harry S., 69
Turkey, 251
TV news, 217
TV transmission, 218

U

UK, 39, 76-77, 164, 246, 248
Ukraine, 17 158, 246, 252, 260
UN, 2-3, 78-79
AS, depository, 8
UN and nuclear weapons, 68-144
Anti-personnal mines, 127-28
Bacterial warfare, 103-05
Chemical and biological weapons, 102-03
Committee of Twelve, 75-80
Conventional weapons, 109-11
Convention on bacteriological weapons, 106-08
Convention on chemical weapons, 108-09
Convention on conventional weapons, 120-21
Disarmament, 68-69
Disarmament and development, 142-43
Disarmament Commission, 80-84
Disarmament decade, 132-38
Follow-up, 143-44
General Assambly Special Session on, 139-40
International arms transfers, 128-30
Non-proliferation Treaty, 85, 88
Nuclear Test Ban Treaty, 97-98

Nuclear weapons, 69-73
Principles governing regulation and reduction of armaments, 111-20
General Assembly adopted, 114-18
Regulation and reduction of armaments, 118-20
US draft resolution, 113-14
Protocol on Non Detectable fragments, 225-27
Register of conventional arms, 130-32
Regulation, limitation and balanced reduction of all armed formes and armaments, 73-75
Sea-bed Treaty, 96-97
Snaping the issue, 73
Suspension of nuclear and thermo nuclear tests, 98-102
Treaty of non-proliferation of nuclear weapons, 88-96
UN conference on prohibiting to restrictive use of certain conventional weapons, 281-85
World disarmament campaign, 140-42
World disarmament conference, 138-39
UN charter, 178
UN conference on disarmament, 11
UN conference on prohibition or restrictions of use of certain conventional weapons, 121-25
Underground exploisions, 1
Under Secretary General for Disarmament Affairs, 14-15
UN Development Decade, 134
UN Disarmament Decade, 68
UN General Assembly, 10, 71, 79-81, 175
UN General Assembly special session in Disarmament, 139-40
UNITA, 152
Unmanned Air Vehicle System, 41
UN Millennium Summit, 174, 180
UN Security Council, 30, 70-73, 79
Uranium enrichment programming, 24, 172, 256, 262
USA, 2, 16, 26-27, 30-31, 39, 42, 75-76, 79, 164, 188-89, 195-97, 246-48, 251
US controls exports of missile related equipment, 42-43
US betta Rocket, 228
US Expectations, 44-45
US-Japan Military Cooperation, 178
US Japan Trade, 190
US nuclear weapons, 29-30
US-Russian relation of serap, 19
US sanctions on Indian space research organisation, 38
US sanctions on Pakistan, 24
US State Dept's Missile Technology Analysis Group, 47
USSR, 2, 72, 76-80, 111-12, 248
Uzbekistan, 213-14

V

Vajpayee, 12, 22, 24, 174, 208, 213
Validated export licences, 50
Van Couver Summit, 173
Variable Every Cyclotron, Calcutta, 171
Very High Resolution Radiometer, 50, 52, 219, 243
Vienna International Conference, 3
Vietnam War, 163
Vikram Sarabhai Space Centre, Trivandrum, 47, 224
Vostok rocket, 221

W

Warheads, 62
Weapons programme, 24-28
Western European Union, 251
Western nuclear technology, 159
West Germany, 255
Woolsey, James, 28
World Bank, 32
World Court's Advisory opinion, 30, 162
World Disarmament campaign, 68, 75, 140-42
World Disarmament Conference, 138-39
World Peace Conference, Athens, 175-76
World War I, 181-83
World War II, 44, 158, 163, 181-82, 184
World Wide Proliferation, 163

X

Xinhua, 213-15

Y

Yeltsin, Boris, 173, 253
Yugoslavia, 149, 151, 183, 210

Z

Zaire, 148, 150
Zemin, Jiang, 213-15
Zia, 150
Zoellnik, Robert, 29
Zulfikar Ali Khan, 25